The Rural State?

Limits to Planning in Rural Society

PAUL CLOKE AND JO LITTLE

CLARENDON PRESS · OXFORD
1990

Oxford University Press, Walton Street, Oxford OX2 6DP

Oxford New York Toronto
Delhi Bombay Calcutta Madras Karachi
Petaling Jaya Singapore Hong Kong Tokyo
Nairobi Dar es Salaam Cape Town
Melbourne Auckland
and associated companies in
Berlin Ibadan

Oxford is a trade mark of Oxford University Press

Published in the United States
by Oxford University Press, New York

British Library Cataloguing in Publication Data
Cloke, Paul J.
The rural state?: limits to planning in rural society.
1. Rural regions. Environment planning. Social aspects
I. Title II. Little, Jo 1958
307'.12'091734
ISBN 0–19–823287–X

Library of Congress Cataloging in Publication Data
Cloke, Paul J.
The rural state?: limits to planning in rural society/Paul
Cloke and Jo Little.
p. cm.
Includes bibliographical references.
1. Rural development. 2. Regional planning. I. Little, Jo,
1958– . II. Title.
HN49.C6C574 1990 307.1'412—dc20 89–49347
ISBN 0–19–823287–X

Typeset by Cambrian Typesetters, Frimley, Surrey
Printed and bound in
Great Britain by Courier International Ltd,
Tiptree, Essex

Acknowledgements

For their friendship and encouragement during various stages of research and writing *Rural State* I would like to thank the following: Rob Page, Rob Young, Mick Griffiths, Phil Bell and Lyn Davies at Lampeter, and Richard Woolley and Joe Watson at Essex Institute. I am particularly grateful to Richard Munton, Terry Marsden, and Sarah Whatmore at UCL for coping so well with my diversification of research involvement and for their genuine concern and interest in the book's progress. Thanks are also due to Peter Fidler at Bristol Polytechnic for his trust and support.

In addition to these individuals I am indebted to colleagues in the Rural Economy and Society Study Group for providing an encouraging and friendly academic context for the discussion of research ideas. I also wish to thank members of the Women and Geography Study Group for their continuing friendship and support, without which all this would have been a lot harder.

Finally, thank you to Paul for carrying more than his fair share of the administrative burden involved in producing this book and for making co-authorship a valuable and pleasurable experience.

J.L.

The editorial staff at Oxford University Press are to be thanked for their help with this project, and the technical staff in the Geography Department at Lampeter—Maureen Hunwicks, Caron Thomas, Connie Gdula, Trevor Harris, and Ian Clewes—who have all contributed to the production of the final manuscript. Thanks also to Jo, for restoring my faith in genuine co-operative effort as a colleague, and for enhancing our lives as a friend.

Special thanks go to Viv, not only for the sensitivity, care, and quality of supportive partnership, but also for the continued efforts of a professional planner to get this particular academic to be 'practical'.

P.C.

Contents

List of Figures

List of Tables

Introduction

Over recent years there has been a rapid increase in the attention paid to rural problems, and to the attempts by 'planners' to respond to these problems. In particular there has been an upsurge of interest in rural planning both on the part of the general public and within the planning and education professions. Uncertainties surrounding the future of agricultural production and the use of rural land, together with a growing concern for the protection of the environment, have, moreover, brought rural issues firmly into the arena of national political debate.

While a heightened interest in rural planning and policy-making has led to a marked growth in research output, current literature on the topic appears rapidly to be reaching a position of saturation by orthodoxy. With some important exceptions (e.g. Newby *et al.*, 1978; Phillips and Williams, 1984; Hoggart and Buller, 1987), the treatment of rural 'planning' and rural 'society' within the burgeoning literature has become a kind of traditional wisdom, in terms both of problem analysis and of prescription of solutions within the planning system.

It is not our intention here to present a detailed review of the way in which issues of rural change, rural planning, and rural policy have been presented using these orthodox perspectives. The merits and otherwise of logical positivism, of rational planning theory, and of attempts to apoliticize and atheorize rural studies have received plenty of attention elsewhere (e.g. Cloke, 1980; Hoggart and Buller, 1987; Gilg, 1985). Neither do we deliberately set out to denigrate such approaches. We realize that some researchers will continue to see rural change in these terms, and indeed that they will wish to interpret some of the material presented in this book very differently from the way we have chosen to do so. We do not see it as our task to introduce research evidence and then to offer several different viewpoints on what it means, although we appreciate that some readers will be drawn into such comparisons. Our intention is to move away from this orthodoxy, and to present an alternative framework for understanding these issues. We believe that new perspectives and insights are long overdue as catalysts for a more detailed and realistic understanding of the scope of planning and policy-making in rural areas, and for an assessment of the limits of power and influence under which planners operate within a societal context.

This book, therefore, seeks to respond to the need for new insight by presenting an analysis of rural planning from a political-economy perspective. In the process, it brings together the contemporary concepts relating to policy studies (predominantly those with an urban basis) so as to test their validity in the area of rural policy, in particular assessing how appropriate the ideas of the 'rural state' and of 'rural policy and planning' are in the context of contemporary government and public policy. The development of a conceptual framework based on political economy recognizes that planning is a function of state activity, and consequently that the theory of the state is crucial in the analysis of planning and policy. The authors argue that the study of rural planning must be founded on state theory, and on an understanding of the role of the state in both a national and local context.

Concentrating as it does on the study of the economy and society of *rural* areas, this book clearly invites the question of whether 'rural' represents an appropriate analytical category. Structuralist explanations of change are essentially aspatial in nature, and do not recognize any rural–urban difference. The reasons why we propose a rural focus are partly pragmatic and partly bound up in contemporary concepts of locality. Pragmatically, there is a need both to update conventional studies of *rural* planning and to counterbalance the urban and regional dominance of political economic study. So far as localities are concerned it is clear that aspatial changes associated with capital restructuring will affect, and will be affected by, the localized configurations of class, politics, economic history, and culture. Although we do not argue that localities should be defined by characteristics of rurality (there are not, therefore, *rural* localities *per se*), we find there is a strong case for subjecting localities which include areas previously considered as rural (by virtue of their economic base, land-use characteristics, population density, etc.) to political economic analysis, in the same way that other locality configurations have been analysed.

While these justifications are important, it is not our intention here to become embroiled in debates surrounding the theoretical justification for the categorization of urban and rural. The arguments have been well rehearsed elsewhere (see Cloke, 1989*a*; Hoggart, 1988) and would, if included in this book, simply detract from its main purpose.

Another area of contention in the use of political-economy perspectives is the relationship between empirical research and theoretical debate. Some authors maintain that the application of empirical 'data' is incompatible with the development of political-economy theory, the latter being based on broad social processes— the manifestation of which is so much a function of specific local characteristics as to make its study *on the ground* counter-productive to the understanding of these processes. This is not, however, our view here. We believe that the development of theoretical perspectives can be enhanced by the application of empirically informed material from the local level, and that the role of such perspectives in helping to understand the rural economy and society is consequently reinforced. The book includes original material from a case study of Gloucestershire. This information reflects many aspects of state theory and policy-making at both local and central level, and also allows the analysis of the relationship between planning and social need by examining the detailed outcome of policy within the rural context.

The Gloucestershire study is supplemented by international perspectives on the role of the state and the operation of the policy process in rural areas. While these perspectives are not as detailed as the British case, they are nevertheless useful in broadening the scope of the debate, and in illustrating cross-national differences and similarities in planning and the allocation of resources.

The material presented in this book has been subdivided as follows. Chapter 1 establishes a political economic framework for the study of the rural economy and society. We discuss in detail what exactly is meant by this approach, and argue its value as a conceptual tool for the understanding of rural social relations. In presenting these arguments, alternative approaches to the study of rural social change are briefly reviewed. The contribution of, for example, positivist approaches to our understanding of rural decision-making is touched upon, although more as means of establishing the context for the development of the main theoretical direction of the book than as a full-blown systematic discussion of these perspectives in their own right. The second part of this chapter is devoted to an examination of the historical evolution of social change in rural communities, and focuses in particular on the importance of social class as a facet of that change. The final section argues the need to look closely at social inequality amongst rural people, and to understand the basis of that inequality in relation to changing local social relations in rural areas.

In Chapter 2 we examine the role and power of the state in rural areas. Different perspectives on the nature of power at the central state level are explored in an examination of theoretical concepts such as structuralism, managerialism, and élitism. Those constraints which influence state activity are also identified, in particular the relationship between different levels of state activity together with the interaction of public and private spheres. In the final part of this chapter we focus on the organization and operation of the local state, by which we mean the institutions and power relations involved in local government, administration, and judiciary (Cockburn, 1977). Here we discuss different aspects of the state's financial and political control, with direct reference to the particular experiences of rural communities.

This discussion of the role and operation of the state is followed, in Chapter 3, by an examination of planning as an expression of the power of the state. In this chapter we present an overview of the various conceptualizations of planning, decision-making, and implementation, supported by practical examples of policy implementation problems. The specific aims and goals of rural planning are identified in an attempt to link the theoretical arguments to the practical implementation of policy. This link is further strengthened by the presentation of evidence from a case study of implementation as it occurs in the context of structure plans (the current statutory development plans at county level) in Britain.

In Chapter 4 the emphasis on original case studies is continued in a discussion of planning and implementation in rural Gloucestershire. A detailed examination of the formulation of rural policy within the structure plan is included in a discussion of the mechanisms and motives involved in the evolution of decision-making within the local authority. Particular attention is directed towards the relative autonomy of the local state. Policy *outcome* in ten villages in north Gloucestershire is also examined in this chapter, with a discussion of six key issues in planning and resource allocation. This discussion provides an important context in which to consider the relationship between policy, implementation, and outcome.

In Chapter 5, we present four brief studies of rural planning and implementation in an international context. The examples used are drawn from New Zealand, Canada, the Netherlands, and Hungary, and provide different perspectives on the role and power of the state in relation to rural policy. While acknowledging these many differences, we focus on the similarities that exist among the case studies (and the earlier observations from Britain), particularly in terms of the operation of the local state and its relative autonomy from the centre.

Chapter 6 introduces another major area of debate surrounding decision-making and policy implementation: public participation. Here we identify the main opportunities for, and constraints on, public involvement in the planning process, and question the extent to which such involvement can be recognized as contributing to the broader operation of democratic decision-making. The principal characteristics of public participation in a rural context are examined, and related to both the extent and the nature of community power in rural society. Finally in this chapter we consider the public response to the withdrawal of resources in rural areas, and discuss participation in the context of self-help or community action. Again, attention here is also devoted to the way in which the encouragement of voluntary action as part of the contemporary planning context has been differently interpreted both as a positive contribution to rural life and as a derogation of the duties of statutory servicing agencies.

In the final chapter of the book we draw the debate together in a number of brief conclusions, which seek in particular to relate the theoretical issues presented to the discussions of original examples. These conclusions do not provide foolproof answers to the problems of inequality and social need within the countryside and we stress here that their analysis in the context of policy and implementation is just one interpretation, and is not intended as a blueprint for the future study and evolution of decision-making in rural areas.

In the conclusions we do look briefly to the future. Rural areas and rural decision-making are undergoing a period of rapid and profound change—the present Conservative Government demonstrating very strong and, in some cases, radical views on the direction of such change. The implications of change for the balance of power and the distribution of resources at local level have yet to be worked through. Clearly, however, there will be significant effects on the lives of those in rural areas and for the broader operation of socio-economic relations within the rural community.

1

A Political Economy of Contemporary Rural Society

INTRODUCTION

Researchers from a range of academic disciplines have, with some regularity, criticized the lack of theoretical development that has characterized the study of the rural economy and society (see e.g. Cloke, 1980; Newby, 1980; Picou *et al.*, 1978). Our understanding of rural areas, it is argued, has suffered from an unwillingness to explore different theories and concepts, particularly those originating from political economy. With some notable exceptions (e.g. Newby *et al.*, 1978; Phillips and Williams, 1984; Hoggart and Buller, 1987), applied research into rural society and the planning and policies to which it has been subjected has conformed to the tried and tested empirical formula without due regard for the wider state/society setting of the phenomena being investigated.

It is difficult to account for this lack of interest in the application of political-economy approaches, especially given the extent of their development in the urban context. Part of the problem clearly lies in the analytical validity of rural space and in the conceptualization of the categories of urban and rural. Rural researchers have for some time been preoccupied with the need to justify their own existence. They have fought long and hard to differentiate *rural* characteristics, to define rurality, and generally to advance some form of rural separatism which provides them with a professional *raison d'être* (Cloke, 1989a). While it is only in extreme cases that this attitude has proposed 'rural' as a distinct theoretical category, it has more generally obscured the importance of broad political, social, and economic issues. Arguments of most political-economy theorists, however, assert the aspatial nature of economy and social processes in advanced capitalist societies. Spatial variations in the manifestations of these processes between, for example, urban, suburban, and rural areas are accepted, but such variation is not seen in itself as legitimation of rural or urban as categories of analysis. Consequently, rural researchers find some difficulty in attempting to reconcile their separate identity with the principles of a political-economy approach.

Linked to the dilemma surrounding the conceptualization of rural space, another barrier to the use of political-economy perspectives in rural socio-economic research has been an over-reliance on the study of substructural themes (Cloke, 1989*a*). Community and anthropological approaches, together with an over-emphasis on description, have helped to ensure a very narrow focus which has detracted from the identification of structural processes. In particular, research has failed to make the link between substructural processes identified at the local level in rural areas and the wider evolution and development of British capitalism. Some attempts have been made to address this inadequacy, in, for example, the treatment of production relations in contemporary agriculture (see Marsden *et al.*, 1986; Whatmore, 1987), but as yet such attempts have been few and far between.

The assertion that rural researchers have fallen behind their urban colleagues in the use of political-economy approaches is hardly novel. Moseley (1980*b*), for example, insisted that rural studies should shift towards an understanding of the producers rather than the consumers of deprivation, while Proudfoot (1984: 11) has noted that 'there have been few examinations of the extent to which appropriate economic or social theory exists which might help in understanding functional activities in rural areas'. Yet mainstream rural research continues to shy away from the issues which would be raised by a political-economy perspective. Thus Pacione (1984), in the introduction to his textbook on rural geography, stresses that 'it is important to appreciate that rural-based investigations are not simply regional applications of some wider perspective' (p. 1), and Robins (1983) suggests that the most important question in British rural planning in the 1980s is that of developing a coherent planning system out of current embryonic approaches to the integrated management of the countryside. It is our contention that significant changes to planning in rural localities will not be brought about unless the relationship between the state and civil society are fully explored. Despite the strong belief by some (notably Gilg, 1985) that existing positive approaches can offer some form of 'true' or factually superior representation of rural planning—a representation that is un-impaired by misguided theoretical distortion—we believe such approaches are unlikely to secure improvement to the planning process, because they take little account of the constraints within which the planning process has to work, and the centrally derived functions which planning has to fulfil. Thus positivist approaches have allowed us to catalogue the 'problems' occurring within rural areas and perhaps to identify the planning responses to these problems (early reports of rural deprivation by the Association of County Councils and the Association of District Councils are obvious examples). But such approaches have not allowed us to evaluate the differential impact of these problems on specific social groups, nor to set the problems themselves within any broader understanding of the relationship between the structure of decision-making and the unequal impact of policy.

The belief that wider state, society, and class issues are crucial to an understanding of rural localities, and the rejection of rural planning as a simple, independent arbitration for competing demands for resources in the countryside, find support in a small but increasingly important group of rural researchers. Following the work of Newby (1977), in which the fortunes of agricultural workers are analysed in the context of the transformation of capitalist agriculture, the study of rural change has gradually begun to be encased within wider explanatory frameworks. Thus Cherry (1978: 10), for example, put forward an interpretation of rural social change based on various stages of capitalist development:

industrial capitalism created the nineteenth century city and particular kinds of economic and social orders acquired territorial significance; post-industrial capitalism has continued to feed on the city, for example in the exploitation of land values. The economic and social structure is now manifest in distinctive spatial patterns, changing over time with emergent areas of advantage and disadvantage.

Perhaps the next stage in this process has been the attempt to marry political-economy views of rural change with those of the role of the state and its various agencies as regulators of this change. The works of Newby *et al.* (1978), linking agricultural ownership with political power, and Phillips and Williams (1984), providing an excellent overview of rural managerialism, have been key pointers to the progress of the political-economy approach to rural society. The Rural Economy and Society Study Group has also acted as pathfinder in this respect (see Bradley and Lowe, 1984).

This book seeks to build on these encouraging beginnings by providing a contemporary analysis of the limitations of planning and policy-making processes for rural people. In so doing, it attempts to make use of various concepts within the umbrella philosophy of political economy, and to test the relevance of these concepts to rural localities. This background of political-economy concepts is therefore a fundamental parameter which requires further discussion.

THE IMPLICATIONS OF A POLITICAL-ECONOMY APPROACH TO PLANNING IN RURAL AREAS

The use of a political-economy approach offers substantial advances in our analysis of economic progress, restructuring in society, the role of the state, and the connections between economy, civil society, and state (Urry, 1981*a*). As Redclift (1985: 5) asserts, such an approach

locates economic analysis within specific social formations and explains development processes in terms of the benefits and costs they carry for different social classes. Policies for the amelioration of poverty, for example, . . . are regarded as the outcome of a struggle between class interests, negotiated by, and with, the state.

Following the directions taken in an interesting discussion paper by Healey (1984), we might expect political-economy concepts to contribute to an understanding of:

(i) the way the organization of the economy produces particular forms of investment (and disinvestment) in rural areas;
(ii) the variety of social groups, their interests in land, property and the environment, and the interaction between social groups and economic processes;
(iii) the way in which, and the reasons why, the state operates as it does in response to, or as an initiator of, economic reorganization.

These themes are clearly central to a realization of the constraints on planning in rural society. Several focal implications are embraced by this form of analysis.

Class Conflict

A materialist analysis of political economy accepts that society is structured by the imperatives of capitalism, and that an unresolvable conflict between the classes representing labour and capital occurs over the production and distribution of the surplus value created by labour. This has particular implications in the context of planning, the 'notion of irresolvable conflict' undermining, as Healey (1982: 187) writes, 'many concepts dear to planners, such as the "general interest" or a "balanced strategy" except as temporary phenomena'. She continues:

From these general premises, then, we are offered principles for grouping society into segments (structuring 'interests') which look quite different to those typical in commmunity power studies or even land use planners' lists of who to consult in public participation exercises.

Political-economy approaches do not demand the interpretation of all social relations on the basis of class. They acknowledge, for example, the importance of gender relations to the division of labour and thus to the wider organization of capitalist society. Such approaches do inevitably, however, demand a reclassification of society from that currently used in much rural research. In particular they indicate a movement away from somewhat *ad hoc* divisions, based upon ill-defined notions of kinship and local authenticity, which have been adopted, often unquestioningly, by some of those involved in rural research (see e.g. Harper, 1987). This debate is taken up again later in this chapter.

Mobility of Capital and Labour

Another central theme of this approach is the recognition of mobility and immobility amongst capital and labour. Bradley and Lowe (1984) stress that in its current monopoly phase, Western capitalism has become increasingly mobile and therefore relatively detached from the constraints of location. In this way industrial capital has been able to relocate so as to tap into cheaper and more compliant sources of labour. Rural areas are affected not only by relocation of capital but also by restructuring:

Capital restructuring alters and reconstitutes various technical divisions of labour, particularly whereby higher and lower level functions of specific firms and enterprises are spatially split, for example through the location of branch plants in peripheral regions. (Bradley and Lowe, 1984: 11)

Clearly, the implications of restructuring for the class composition of rural society are considerable, and constitute an important focus for political economy approaches. These implications are discussed in depth in the following section.

Uneven Capital Expansion

These processes or relocation, restructuring, and recomposition will be differentially distributed in spatial terms, as capital seeks what are considered to be favourable locations for its activities. There are potential conflicts of approach here between the traditional focus of radical rural sociology on the centrality of land and property ownership in the shaping of rural change, and the wider concerns of uneven capital expansion. It has been argued strongly that rural localities and the social relations within them are reproduced as a logical outcome of the discontinuities of capital activity. Thus Rees (1984: 27) has stressed that:

Changes in rural employment structures are central to any understanding of the reality of rural social life. On the one hand they reflect profound shifts in the nature and organization of capitalist production and, more specifically, the widely differing impacts of these shifts on different types of locality. On the other, employment changes themselves have resulted in radical developments in terms of rural class structures, gender divisions, the forms of political conflict occurring in rural areas and, indeed, of the complex processes by which 'rural cultures' are produced and reproduced.

Thus agriculture is seen to represent the dominant fraction of capital from a bygone era of capital circulation, and should not be permitted to dominate ideas of capital expansion in the contemporary countryside.

Localities

This devaluation of agriculture as the major explanatory focus of capital accumulation and investment in rural areas brings with it the question of whether rural areas constitute a significant unit of study at all. Recomposition of local society by capitalist restructuring has been viewed as leading to a series of unique localities, some of which may be regarded as deprived in terms of the stratification of local society. Urry (1984: 59) has reviewed the evidence concerning the occurrence of specifically rural localities and concludes:

various critical notions—of different, overlapping spatial divisions of labour, of all localities as sites for the reproduction of labour-power, of variations in local social structures etc.—render problematic the notion that there are distinct 'rural' localities.

Essentially, Urry suggests that concepts such as 'rural', 'urban', and 'industrial' are fast becoming anachronistic as theoretical units of study. Phillips and Williams (1984) address this question, and attempt to justify 'rural' social geography on a number of grounds:

(i) to counterbalance the predominance of urban socio-geographical studies;

(ii) as a category of analytical convenience;

(iii) to help counterbalance the romantic myths fostered by an anti-urban bias in British social science;

(iv) because rural areas house particular local features—notably distance/accessibility and political frameworks—which give them a distinctive social character.

It may well be that analytical convenience is chief amongst these reasons, but there is more than a grain of legitimacy in each of them. In one sense the existence of identifiable 'rural' localities is of no particular consequence, as comparative study of all types of locality is necessary (including those enclosing previously recognized rural areas). However, the distinction is far more important if it is to be suggested that the activities of the state in rural areas assume a particular façade because of the rural characteristics of the locality. This suggestion is discussed in detail in Chapter 2.

Resource Allocation: The State and Planning

Planning for rural areas has to be recognized as an integral part of state activity within a particular societal context. The relationship between the state and its host society has traditionally been forgotten in the analysis of rural policies, leading to the role of the state being tacitly assumed to be one of an independent arbitrator of the conflicting demands of different interest groups in society. Most political-economy theorists would instead suggest that the state performs the more conservative function of preserving existing social structures by working for the benefit of capital interests, and by tackling social welfare issues only to the extent that is demanded for its own legitimation. Planning, as part of this state role, may be viewed as seeking to bring about resource allocations in line with these priorities, although some account has to be taken of the significant activities of local authorities in distributing resources seemingly independently of the stratification of dominant class forces, or in favour of some fractions of capital rather than others. These questions of the role of the state, and planning within that role, are pursued in Chapter 2.

These, then, are the major tenets of a political-economy approach as used in this book. Underlying each is the recognition that various facets of rural society and its relations with the state must be studied in the context of the wider operation of contemporary capitalism. In terms of achieving this analysis, attention has frequently been drawn to the problems of combining theoretical and empirical method (see Healey, 1984). The contention here is that original empirical data can be used to inform wider theoretical and conceptual issues, and, as Chapter 4 demonstrates, no contradiction is assumed between the application of political-economy approaches and the use of empirical material.

It is, however, our belief that these data, when used alone without the framework of rigorous theoretical analysis, add little to a real understanding of social and economic relations in rural areas. Consequently, before turning to the integration of original locality-based data, we will seek to develop a number of basic theoretical ideas and explore certain key conceptual themes. Chapters 2 and 3 present an assessment of the workings of the state and of the specific role of planning as part of the overall state function; but first we must review the notions of social polarization and the distribution of social need in rural areas. This task forms the basis of the remaining sections of this chapter.

RURAL SOCIAL CHANGE: A POLITICAL-ECONOMY PERSPECTIVE

Existing Approaches

The failure to develop political-economy approaches has meant that the study of rural social and economic relations has remained seriously limited. In particular, a neglect of class-based analyses and of the application of class theory has impeded the understanding of social stratification and polarization in rural communities. Work has remained largely descriptive, and few attempts have been made to link social change to the evolution of property and labour relations, or to the wider processes of economic restructuring. This, in turn, has had far-reaching implications for the interpretation of allocative policy in the countryside and for the treatment of social deprivation.

Such neglect cannot, however, be attributed to a lack of commitment on behalf of either researchers or policy-makers to the actual study of rural communities. On the contrary, an impressive volume of literature has been produced on the changing nature of the rural economy and society and associated cultural, political, and ideological characterstics. The 1960s and early 1970s, in particular, witnessed a glut of what have become known as 'community studies'—detailed descriptions of individual villages or localities (e.g. Williams's study of Ashworthy (1963), Littlejohn's work on Westrigg (1963), and Ambrose's study of Ringmer (1974) and of the social relations, particularly those of kinship, which operated within them. More recently 'community studies' have given way to more broadly based analyses of social change and of the fortunes of specific groups in relation to issues involving collective or privatized consumption—although many of these have also focused on particular 'case study' communities.

In attempting to articulate and analyse the basis of social stratification in rural areas, such work has concentrated overwhelmingly on divisions surrounding local authenticity. The extent of an individual's or of a group's allegiance to a particular community (measured variably in relation, for example, to kinship ties, length of residence, or local familiarity) has been seen as fundamental to the organization of rural social relations and to the distribution of social need. During an era in which dramatic change has taken place in both the economic/employment base of rural areas and the degree of residential choice exercised by large sections of the population, the migration of ex-urban dwellers into the countryside has, not surprisingly, been seen as a major force for change. To a large extent, however, this force has remained 'untheorized'—the locals/newcomers division with which it has become equated emerging simply as a convenient peg upon which

to hang all manner of contemporary (and occasionally historic)
rural change.

The cultural, historical, and ethnographic detail provided by
geographers, sociologists, and anthropologists has clearly made an
important contribution to the explanation of social processes in
rural areas—work, for example, on kinship (Strathern, 1982;
Cohen, 1982; Wenger, 1988) or social identity (Pahl, 1965;
Davidoff *et al.*, 1976) has led to a greater understanding of
behaviour patterns, especially at the local level. The identification
of the different characteristics, values, and expectations of
different sections of rural society has been central to the
development of this understanding. Although this work is important in its own right, it has been the failure to develop it within the
parameters of the political-economy tradition that has undermined
its wider relevance and value. Many studies have remained
simplistic, and modelled on an interpretation of rural society in
which major divisions are seen to originate predominantly (or
even exclusively) from residential qualifications. Early work, in
particular that by Ray Pahl (1965; 1970), was valuable in drawing
attention to the importance of rural migration to the operation of
social relations in initially very accessible and, later on, remoter
parts of the countryside, but these findings have tended to
dominate our interpretation of rural social change and, indeed,
continue to play a prominent part in some analyses. Although
important in its own right, such work has, however, provided a
framework which has downgraded the role of social class in the
stratification of rural society. Class divisions have thus tended
simply to be superimposed upon residential criteria, so that 'local'
has become synonymous with 'working-class' and 'newcomer' with
'middle-class'.

The application of the locals/newcomers dichotomy to the study
of rural society has been important not only in the interpretation
of social behaviour, but also in the assessment of allocative policy.
Questions of social need have been framed to a large extent in
terms of the competition between the two groups, and of the
tendency for 'newcomers' to deny the 'locals' important resources
such as housing, transport, and other basic services. It is
automatically accepted that newcomers have a greater command
of personal wealth, and can thus compete successfully against the
more needy locals for collective resources in both the public and

the private sectors. While there may be a high degree of truth implicit in such assumptions—the price of housing in many rural areas, especially in lowland England, for example, restricting immigrants to only the most wealthy—the lack of explicit reference to class as a principal of social division seriously hinders the explanation of social need and the implications of allocative policy.

As was noted above, it is our contention, as well as a basic principal of political-economy approaches, that the understanding of rural localities recognizes the importance of broader state, society, and class issues, and that local characteristics are explained, not in isolation, but by reference to the underlying forces within capitalist society. An over-dependence on the relationship between locals and newcomers has distracted the study of social change in rural areas from this task. Explanation has relied to a large extent on the manifestation of state/society relations rather than on their derivation. Consequently, the locals/newcomers dichotomy has been interpreted very often as a force for change in its own right, rather than as a specific localized symptom of more general causative social processes.

Essentially, the relationship between established residents and newcomers does not represent a particularly helpful mechanism for the interpretation of rural society. Used in isolation as an analytical tool, it reduces too many variables to the single dichotomy, making assumptions about the association between fundamentally independent socio-economic characteristics such as wealth, kinship, status, and local identity. The result is that, under the analytical umbrella of locals/newcomers, none of the individual attributes of social stratification is given sufficient individual attention, and their particular role in shaping rural society is subsumed within more general explanations of change.

Reference to social class in the analysis of rural society has been overwhelmingly descriptive, and few attempts have been made to explore the basic formation of class relations in rural communities. The restriction to the urban sphere of theoretical debate concerning aspects of class structure and conflict has meant that, even where rural research has acknowledged the role of class as a principle of social stratification, it has done so with little or no consideration of the structuring mechanisms involved in the evolution of class relations (Barlow, 1984). It is essential, in the development and application of political-economy perspectives, that we do not simple transpose preconceived notions about class to the study of rural society, but that we actually question these notions in relation to the specific geographical and historical qualities of rural localities.

In order to do this, we must first consider a number of basic points concerning the broad conceptualization of class as used here. The starting-point, that defining class is essentially a very complex task, is something of a truism, but nevertheless one worth asserting at this point. This is particularly the case in late twentieth-century Britain, as the classic two-class division based on relations of production, as advanced by Marx, has become less distinct. While, as Thrift and Williams (1987) maintain, capitalist society is still based fundamentally on the exploitation of wage labour by the owners of capital, our understanding of the operation of class relations on the ground must now look beyond localized production cultures, and their uneven development over space, to the social relations between classes and in particular to the relations of consumption.

Definition and analysis of class must now account for the existence of an expanding and highly influential middle class which does not fit in with the straightforward wage-labour relation of traditional class analyses. As Wright (1985) points out, members of this class do not share in the ownership of production (and are therefore not 'capitalists'), yet their work is non-productive; they are, according to Thrift (1987a), in an essentially contradictory position, being both exploiters and exploited. The importance of this growth in the middle classes is taken up later in this chapter, with explicit reference to rural society. Here it is simply mentioned in order to reinforce the complexity of class structures, and to demonstrate the need to look beyond the relations of production for an explanation of social stratification.

This complexity creates enormous problems for definition of class and, as a consequence, for the identification of class interests and allegiances. The boundaries between classes have become less and less distinct, not only with the rise in the middle classes but also with changes over time in various sectors of the economy brought about by the restructuring of capital. Traditionally, divisions between classes have been based on occupation (and categorized in the UK according to the classification devised by the Department of Employment). Although this classification provides a consistent and comprehensive data base, it incorporates a number of problems—not least that it does not take account of the unemployed and is strongly gender-biased (Thrift, 1987*a*).

Problems of defining class in relation to socio-economic categories are particularly acute when it comes to the identification of what has become known as the service class (an element of the middle class either in the public sector, in private economic service, or in social services, and displaying characteristics of high income, high job security, and educational attainment—see Abercrombie and Urry, 1983 and Thrift, 1987*a* for further discussion). As argued below, the service class constitutes an important force in terms of the social structure of contemporary rural Britain, and yet there remains considerable confusion as to what exactly we mean by 'the service class'. The discussion here attempts to clarify the position of the service class *vis-à-vis* rural social change. Our overall purpose is to consider the nature and development of broad social relations in the countryside rather than the detailed characteristics of specific class groups. In later chapters, where the notion of 'class' is applied to particular groups or individuals, more concrete definitions have been adopted, based on socio-economic grouping.

Class-Based Analysis

Some discussion has taken placed as to whether property or occupation constitutes the defining principle of rural society. Urry (1984: 46) argues that 'It is the organisation of property relationships, rather than the division of labour which shapes the rural class structure', while as Barlow (1984) points out, such an assertion pays insufficient attention to the specific importance of land in relation to property ownership. It may be added that this assertion also fails to give adequate recognition to the changing spatial division of labour, and the implications of such change for property relations in rural Britain. This section will outline briefly the main features of existing class analysis in rural society and then move on to raise some alternative considerations.

The evolution of class relations in rural society has been based traditionally on the division between landowners, farmers, and agricultural workers. The broadly capitalist mode of production in agriculture, supporting the creation of a landowning class and a proletariat selling its labour (Newby, 1977), demonstrates how the economic control exerted by the landowners in pre-twentieth-century rural society was reinforced by a social, political, and ideological dominance which penetrated all aspects of rural life. A strong system of paternalism and deference became established in which the power exerted by the landowning class, through control over employment and housing, gave rise to an ideological hegemony in which moral and social values were imposed on the agricultural workers. This system was further strengthened during the mid-nineteenth century with the enclosure of agricultural land, concentrating the ownership of land and forcing greater numbers of farmers into wage-labour (Barlow, 1984).

The growing economic and political power of manufacturing industry together with the increasing internationalization of capital that accompanied the 'industrial revolution' was, however, by the end of the eighteenth century to have an important impact on the power of large landowners and, as a result, on the restructuring of rural class relations. The declining economic role of agricultural production prompted the break-up of the large landed estates, and provided the opportunity for existing tenant farmers to become owner-occupiers. At the same time the political power of the rural aristocracy was declining—at both national and local level—with the rising importance of the business sector and of the 'new urban capitalist' (see Weiner, 1981).

Nationally, the economic value of agricultural production in Britain continued to decline in the twentieth century, while at the same time the role of agriculture in the structure of employment in rural areas became less and less important. Changes in the production process, especially the introduction of new techno-logies, had profound implications for the employment-generating capacity of agriculture, and for the development of the social relations of production. In addition to these structural processes, there came, from the middle of the twentieth century, far-reaching changes in the composition of the rural population. For the first time, parts of rural Britain began to be inhabited by significant numbers of people who had no past or existing connection with agricultural production—who were (or had been) employed, generally, outside the immediate locality, and who had no direct dependence on the agricultural industry or those who controlled it.

It has been argued (Newby *et al.*, 1978) that even in the face of such fundamental changes in the nature of rural social relations and, more specifically, the class composition of rural society, the ownership of agricultural land and capital is still an important factor in the distribution of local political power. Dramatic increases in levels of agricultural production, together with continuing state support for the industry, has meant that, while the economic importance of agriculture *per se* has declined, the position of *individual* farmers, albeit in restricted numbers, has been maintained. Barlow (1986) suggests that the power of agricultural landowners at the local level is based on their role in the provision of land for housing, a role, he argues, which owes much to the historical evolution of the relationship between landowners, house-builders, and the local state.

There is little value to be gained here by presenting a detailed analysis of the development of housing provision in Britain in the nineteenth century. This has been well documented elsewhere (see e.g. the review in Bartlett, 1980). What is important is that we consider the importance of the legacy of this system for the operation of class relations in the countryside today, and that contemporary and profound developments in the balance of power and the class composition of rural areas are not interpreted in isolation but with recognition of the historical context in which they have developed. The task of the following section, therefore, is to outline the major direction of class change in present-day rural society, and to look particularly at the processes underlying such change.

Contemporary Class Change in Rural Britain

Until the middle of this century, rural communities in England were generally relatively stable, self-sustaining social units. Dramatic changes in the size or composition of the population were uncommon—those changes that did occur were primarily in the form of outmigration at times of severe hardship (for example during the enclosure of agricultural land), but such migration was relatively short-lived, and, despite the much-publicized 'drift to the towns' at the beginning of the nineteenth century, the population of rural England remained fairly constant. The only other significant migratory trend to affect rural areas during the eighteenth and nineteenth centuries was the movement of early industrial capitalists from the factory environments of the major industrial cities to new landed estates in accessible parts of the countryside (see e.g. Connell, 1978 on the migration of Londoners into the Surrey countryside; also Weiner, 1981). Despite the changes outlined above in the relative fortunes of agriculture and manufacturing industry, and the implications of these changes for the spatial division of labour, constancy in the size and structure of the nineteenth- and early twentieth-century rural population was reflected in the stability of local social relations.

By contrast, the second half of the twentieth century has witnessed rapid and penetrating changes, not only in the size and structure of the rural population, but also in the dominant focus of political power and social control. The extent and direction of migration trends both into and out of rural areas have been very well documented at the national (see e.g. Champion, 1981; 1987; Walford, 1983) and local (Little, 1984; Herington and Evans, 1980) levels. Particular attention has been drawn both to the geographical variation in patterns of population movement, with the early restriction of inmigration to lowland accessible areas followed by a more recent expansion in the remoter regions, for example, and to the social selectivity of the migration process as it has affected rural areas.

Various reasons have been advanced to account for the strength and direction of migration into rural areas (see Newby, 1979; Phillips and Williams, 1984; Pahl, 1970). During the 1950s and 1960s, movement was not all one way, and depopulation of the remoter rural areas was taking place at the same time as the more accessible villages were increasing in size. At this time immigration was largely restricted to the rural areas within easy commuting distance of major employment centres (see e.g. Pahl's (1965) classic study of rural Hertfordshire). Relatively cheap housing and a desire to pursue a 'rural' life-style were prime motivating factors in the migration to the countryside during this period, while the wider availability and great efficiency of private transport provided added encouragement for certain groups. More recently, particularly during the late 1970s and 1980s, other factors have come into play. These include changes in the spatial division of labour and the growing importance of the service class, improved communications, and the status (both economic and social) associated with owning a house in the countryside. All these factors are of considerable relevance to the scale of migration into rural areas and, quite clearly, to the changing composition of the rural population. Any attempt to understand the evolution of class relations in contemporary rural society must therefore include a detailed analysis of the precise role and influence of such factors.

The Spatial Division of Labour. While, as explained above, some rural sociologists have argued that the ownership of property, and in particular of land, is the defining principle of rural social relations (Newby *et al.*, 1978), other commentators (Barlow, 1984; Urry, 1984; Thrift, 1987*a*) believe that changes in the spatial division of labour perform a much more significant role in the structuring of contemporary rural society. The restructuring of the rural economy in general, and specifically the transformation of agricultural production and the growth of manufacturing employment, has ensured that capital accumulated in rural areas is largely externally owned. At a macro-level, capital is now 'relatively spatially-indifferent as to location' (Urry, 1984: 53—see also Massey, 1984) and can thus seek out different labour markets to take advantage of price, availability, skills, and local organization. Urry argues that this process has encouraged the extension of civil society beyond the urban areas. For rural localities this means not only an expansion in manufacturing employment but also, and just as importantly, a greater freedom of choice for individuals concerning the location of the reproduction of their labour power.

Changes in the location of manufacturing industry (the urban–rural shift, as it is commonly known) have become the focus for quite extensive academic attention. Probably most well known in this respect is the work of Fothergill and Gudgin (1979; 1982), who argue that the shift from urban to rural areas, initiated, as they see it, largely by the availability of 'greenfield sites' in rural areas, is the major trend in contemporary industrial location in Britain. Others, such as Keeble (1980) and Owen *et al.*, (1986), have also sought to examine the extent of changes in the location of industry, some identifying specific characteristics within the more general trends—for example, the particular role of high technology and associated industry (Gould and Keeble, 1984) or spatial variations in the provisions of part time employment (Townsend, 1986).

In general this work has placed a higher priority on description than on explanation. Very few studies have acknowledged the importance of employment shifts to the composition of the rural population, or examined the implications for class relations in rural society. One exception to this is the work of Cloke and Thrift (1987), who focus on the growing influence of the service industry in rural areas as just one facet of the urban–rural manufacturing shift. Thrift (1987a: 207) has argued that changes in the form of the capitalist economy have meant that 'basic manufacturing has become encircled by a vast service economy', parts of which, he suggests are a specifically twentieth-century phenomenon. Thus it is no longer the case that the majority of the population are involved in the production of material goods for exchange, but rather that increasing numbers are engaged in the provision of services. According to Thrift, these changes have led to 'the growth of large and effective middle class or, more accurately perhaps, a set of middle classes' (p. 208).

Three reasons are advanced by Thrift (1987a) and Cloke and Thrift (1987) in order to explain the current prominence of the service class in the British economy: firstly, the tendency of the social and technical division of labour has been to produce well-paid and highly skilled jobs which offer advantageous working conditions in exchange for good educational qualifications; secondly, the superior buying power of the service classes allows them to impose a degree of social and cultural hegemony over consumption choices; and thirdly, the service class command a high degree of political power, both nationally and locally.

This general prominence bestows on the service class important causal powers in terms of the evolution of social and economic relations in rural areas, powers which are not simply the result of a numerical growth. The middle classes in rural areas, especially in southern Britain, have exerted a profound influence over the social and physical characteristics of created space, through which they have imposed various cultural preferences. These preferences include strict controls over levels of development as well as the protection of certain social values and traditions. More practically, the financial resources of the middle classes have allowed them to dominate the housing market, and consequently to occupy powerful positions in local political organization and in the allocation of basic resources.

These various aspects of service class presence and power in rural areas are clearly all interconnected. It is worth considering two specific aspects in more detail: the importance of the rural image or idyll in relation to residential preference, and the middle-class control of consumption issues, in particular housing. Both factors are closely tied to the penetration and sustainability of middle-class influence in rural areas, and are of fundamental importance to wider social relations in the countryside.

The Rural Idyll.   The rural idyll, its evolution, and its maintenance has attracted a high degree of interest from rural geographers, sociologists, and anthropologists (see e.g. Newby, 1979; Pahl, 1965; McLaughlin, 1986; Williams, 1973). The phrase 'village in the mind' was first coined by Pahl (1965) in the context of his work on population change in Hertfordshire, to account for the idealized image of rural life which persuaded urban dwellers to give up their established town life and move to the countryside. The phrase quickly became accepted terminology, used to depict a huge range of values, expectations, and emotions which colour the residential preferences of immigrants and established residents alike. In his classic book *The Country and the City*, Williams (1973) attempts to articulate some of these values in relation to cultural traditions associated with recent history. He uses examples from literature and art to illustrate the dominant images of rural and urban society, and shows how these images have helped to shape not only the composition of the rural community but also the characteristics of rural social change.

Williams, along with other authors (e.g. Daniels, 1982; Weiner, 1981), demonstrates the durability of images which depict the country as peaceful, natural, and healthy—the location of close and caring communities, inhabited by genuine, friendly people. McLaughlin (1986), for example, demonstrates the use of such images in advertising and in the 'selling' of rural locations to manufacturers. Such images are in stark contrast to those of the city, which portray a deeply alien environment, a threatening, soulless place characterized by violence and poverty. While these rural images have been sustained over decades and even centuries, they are not static or unchanging, and indeed their very persistence is an indication of their ability to adapt to suit the particular needs of that time. The continued existence of these images is, however, as Williams (1973) points out, indicative of some permanent or effectively permanent need.

The rural idyll is a concept that has been described extensively by rural researchers and, increasingly, by politicians and media personnel. It has been applied in an atheoretical way to help explain the attraction of rural life to urban dwellers, especially the retired. Close analysis of the concept, however, in particular a questioning of the values it represents, helps demonstrate something of the specific direction of the power behind the rural idyll as a force for contemporary rural social change. Broadly, images of city and country demonstrate a strong anti-urban culture which is regarded by some as traditionally English (see Bouquet and Winter, 1987). Indeed Weiner (1981) argues that such a culture has adversely affected Britain's industrial and economic performance in the past. Even today, it is suggested, the prevailing image of Britain is a rural one, and this is reflected in contemporary social and political values. These values, so Weiner (1981) maintains, are shared by 'both radical and conservative elements within British political culture' (Bouquet and Winter, 1987: 5). This is a view challenged by other authors, however, who stress the conservative nature of present rural values. Bradley (1983), for example, notes the importance of 'the community', patriotism, and the family to rural society, equating such values to those of modern-day Conservatism. Clearly there are serious implications for the role of the state in the fostering of these values—and in particular those of self-help and 'pulling together'. These implications are discussed in greater detail in Chapter 6.

The protection of these values, in terms of the preservation of both landscape and community, has become a very important force in contemporary rural society. Although class allegiance has, more recently, tended to become much more disparate as a result of the complexity of class relations, with conflicts and allegiances between classes tending to evolve in relation to single issues (Thrift, 1987*a*), it is certainly the case that the 'values' of rural conservation and heritage often form a focus for, in particular, middle-class mobilization in rural areas. This is most obvious in the anti-development attitude of many rural dwellers. Much has been written of the NIMBY (Not In My Back Yard) phenomenon in rural areas, whereby, having secured their own 'place in the country', individuals become obsessively protective and opposed to all other forms of development. Indeed the term appears to have become accepted planning and political jargon, such is the prevelance of this type of attitude.

Such attitudes are also sustained through planning policy—a point which is taken up in greater detail elsewhere in this book. Strict controls on development, of both existing and new property, have been applied to the vast majority of rural areas, certainly in lowland England. Policies of individual planning authorities are supported by a range of designations at the national level (Areas of Outstanding Natural Beauty, Special Landscape Areas, Heritage Coasts) designed to safeguard the 'quality' of the rural environment. The rigidity of the protectionist stance of much countryside policy promotes the value of privacy and property (Bouquet and Winter, 1987; Little, 1987), helping, moreover, to shape not only the physical but also the social characteristics of rural areas. It is strongly argued (Punter, 1982), that, through its support of private property, the planning system has encouraged the social polarization of rural communities, reinforcing the notion of the countryside as a positional good to which access is limited and dependent on personal wealth (Hirsch, 1977; Newby, 1979).

Thrift (1987a) suggests that the maintenance of the rural idyll and of the 'rural tradition' is achieved not only through the conservation of existing communities but in the development of created space. He again acknowledges the importance of the service class in this respect, arguing that the economic and political power of this class allows them to mould residential areas in accordance with their own values and expectations, which are, themselves, largely 'rural'. Thrift's arguments are clearly supported by recent urban-fringe development and proposals for 'new villages' which all build on the image of rurality, articulated through architectural styles, 'features' such as village greens and duck ponds, and even place-names.

The rural idyll, then, is evidently an important and long-standing agent of social change (despite being itself based on a presumption *against* change). The prevailing images, as expressed through contemporary culture, have long portrayed the countryside as a desirable place to live, and one which appeals in particular to middle-class, conservative values. The ability to determine (within limits) their own residential location, together with their control over consumption issues, places the middle classes in a strong position to take advantage of the perceived attributes of rural life and, in doing so, to impose quite profound changes on the social and physical environment. It seems ironic that a rural life-style, sought by many as a reaction against the more visible outcomes of the productive forces of contemporary capitalism, is increasingly dependent on the minority ownership of capital which forms part of such a system. As Punter (1982: 8) writes: 'In the form of rural gentrification the conservation of the rose covered cottage, the second house, the village-in-the-mind mentality, the mediations of productive forces are transparently obvious.'

The implications of gentrification and of middle-class influence on rural society are nowhere so obvious as in the property market, in the control over rural housing.

Class Change and the Rural Housing Market.   It was noted above that the powerful position of the service class in rural society, and their consequent influence over the social and economic relations of rural communities, derives partly from their control over consumption issues and in particular housing. It is helpful here to look more closely at the precise nature and implications of this control. Up until the late 1960s, housing in the majority of 'truly rural' areas was cheap in relation to that in towns and suburbs. Much was substandard, and there were large private rented and tied sectors. A house in the country represented an inexpensive option, and prices in most areas were little affected by competition from migrants, second-homers, and the retired.

From the late 1960s, improved communications, together with changes in the spatial distribution of labour as referred to above, have allowed certain social groups far greater freedom of choice in terms of residential location. One of the results of this freedom has been drastically to increase pressure on rural housing, firstly in the more accessible areas but, increasingly, in remoter parts of the countryside. Competition has served to push up prices such that a house in a rural area no longer represents a cheap option. Indeed, studies have demonstrated (Clark, 1980; Little, 1986) that in parts of Britain, especially in the south, rural property may be significantly more expensive than that in urban areas. Competition is enhanced by the relative scarcity of rural housing and by the recent practice of repair and renovation which serves to limit further the stock of smaller, cheaper properties.

The effect of middle-class competition in the rural housing market is to disadvantage and even exclude poorer members of society. Unable to afford the price of private ownership, many are restricted to an ever-declining rented sector (Phillips and Williams, 1982) or forced to move in search of cheaper accommodation. This is the classic scenario of the so-called locals/newcomers conflict. But while the conflict may be largely played out through these groups, it is essentially one based on social class; it is the superior access to financial resources commanded by the middle classes which enables them to outbid the working classes regardless of any residential qualifications. Once established, middle-class competition leads to the gentrification of rural communities, and to a self-perpetuating situation in which different classes become increasingly polarized.

Current trends in the provision of housing in rural areas only serve to reinforce competition between middle- and working-class residents. Restrictions on development, as referred to above, have remained pretty well intact, especially in the most scenic areas, breached only in the building of small numbers of 'executive-style' houses which do nothing to reduce competition or to control prices. Very recently, speculation has surrounded the potential for growth in rural areas. Uncertainties over the future use of agricultural land and an increasing need for housing, especially in the south-east, have prompted a call by politicians and planners for more flexible attitudes towards house building in the countryside (e.g. Ridley, 1987; Housebuilders' Federation, 1988; National Agricultural Centre Rural Trust, 1988). It is unlikely however, that even a relaxation of controls on development would result in the provision of large quantities of low-cost housing in rural areas or ensure a reduction in competition for existing property.

As arguably the ultimate example of conspicuous consumption, and one of finite supply, housing provides a very clear example of the competition for resources that has arisen within rural society. It also demonstrates how, ultimately, this competition can help shape the social composition of rural communities. While conflict between different groups has emerged over other rural resources, class has generally intervened in a much more subtle way to influence resource allocation. It is argued (Newby, 1979; Phillips and Williams, 1984) that the greater independence of middle-class residents in, for example, transport provision, education, and health services acts to the disadvantage of working-class groups since it reduces the take-up and therefore the perceived need for local facilities. This issue is explored in greater depth below in the context of social need. Its inclusion here simply serves to reinforce the point that the control of the middle classes over consumption issues is a powerful instrument in the shaping of rural social change.

This brief review of the contemporary class structure of rural society has attempted to demonstrate both the centrality of class relations and the ways in which this centrality is sustained. It has argued the growing importance of the service class in the changing composition of the rural population, and has noted the powerful influence of this class in the allocation of resources, particularly housing. This theme is taken up again in the following section of the chapter. In stressing the role of class it has not been the intention, however, to reduce all social and economic relations in rural society to those surrounding the ownership of capital and the division of labour. Political-economy approaches recognize the importance of other factors such as gender and race and, as was noted above, pay particular attention to the specific interrelationship of such factors, with class, at the local level.

There is insufficient space here to undertake a detailed discussion of the precise role of, for example, gender relations or age in the development of rural society. Some attention has been devoted to such factors elsewhere (e.g. Little, 1987; Harper, 1987; Wenger, 1988), but there still remains a considerably need for further research. In particular, it is the operation of these mechanisms within different rural localities which must be studied. As with social class, it is possible to talk at a general level about the influences of global processes on the broad configuration of rural social relations. In order fully to understand the impact of such processes on the daily lives of individuals, it is essential that they be studied in the context of particular localities, where they can be set within a specific cultural, historical, and political environment. Chapter 4 goes some way towards addressing this issue by analysing questions of social structure and resource distribution in the context of case study parishes in Gloucestershire. In order to complete our discussion of the wider contemporary rural society, however, we turn now to consider some of the broader implications of social change in rural areas, in particular the extent and characteristics of social need as illustrated in rural Britain.

THE DISTRIBUTION OF NEED IN RURAL COMMUNITIES

The acceptance of rural deprivation as a very real important social phenomenon with, ultimately, a profoundly political message provided fuel for rural research and debate throughout the late 1970s and early 1980s. Within this relatively short time, studies have progressed from highly specific, empirical 'reports' on the occurrence of one or more instances of deprivation (typical of this genre are Moseley, 1978; Shaw, 1979; Walker, 1978) to more holistic and (occasionally) theoretical work (e.g. McLaughlin, 1983; Moseley, 1980*a*) in which rural poverty is set more clearly within the broad allocative climate of mature capitalist society. In many instances, however, studies have done little more than simply describe need, failing to relate examples of inequality to either general and specific aspects of policy or, more importantly, the whole structure and operation of the decision-making process. In general there has been a significant gap between the recognition of need and the formulation of policy. Need has been analysed, moreover, in isolation from issues such as the distribution of power and the formulation and implementation of policy, and consequently little insight has been achieved into how and why inequalities exist or how they may be eliminated. Again, we attribute these limitations at least in part to the inadequacies inherent in the use of positivist approaches, and maintain that key insights into the decision-making process and its relationship with social need are obtainable by means of developing political-economy perspectives.

This section looks briefly at the basic characteristics of need in relation to four policy areas; housing, employment, transport, and other services. The discussion here provides an important context for more specific arguments (see Chapter 4), in which the occurrence of need is linked much more directly to particular local-level decisions and policy environments. The assessment of need itself is, in both quantitative and qualitative terms, problematic. Geographers have periodically become caught up in the difficulty of agreeing on a workable definition, and rural geographers have proved no exception. A fourfold classification by Bradshaw (1972) is commonly referred to (see e.g. Gilder, 1984 and Dunn *et al.*, 1981, in the rural context) in which expressed need, normative need, felt or potential need, and comparative need are identified as important and intrinsically individual constituents. Despite the apparent sophistication of such a classification, there are still inadequacies; is it possible, for example, to identify need where it is unrecognized by the individual concerned? The mentality of 'making do' is still an enduring 'quality' of rural society. It is not our intention in this book to attempt to resolve such problems— they are simply noted to draw attention to the potential inadequacies in the analysis of deprivation in the context of either academic research or policy-making.

Housing Need

The inequalities which surround the issue of rural housing have long provided a focus for study. While earlier work concentrated primarily on the quality and condition of the rural housing stock (see e.g. Penfold, 1974; Rawson and Rogers, 1976; Larkin, 1978), more recent studies have been directed towards problems of access and distribution together with the role of housing policy (Shucksmith, 1981; Phillips and Williams, 1982; Clark, 1982; Flynn, 1986; Richmond, 1985). It is these latter issues which concern us here, for although substandard housing does still exist in some rural areas (in the Department of the Environment's English Housing Condition Survey of 1981, 67 per cent of rural housing was described as unfit), it is actual access to suitable housing which is the root of much current need.

The precise level and distribution of housing need in rural areas is impossible to estimate. Traditional indicators of need amongst the working classes have been local-authority waiting lists. It is widely acknowledged, however, that such lists are far from accurate as a measurement of need, taking no account, for instance, of those people who register in urban areas because the housing stock is larger, or those whose past experience simply dissuades them from applying on the grounds that they will not qualify or be placed high up on the list. Moreover, in the present climate of owner-occupation, the demand for small, cheap housing may be a more efficient indicator of need than the length of local-authority waiting lists. Information of this type will always be inaccurate, since it cannot account for those people who would wish to live in a rural area, but are prevented, owing to lack of supply, from doing so.

The previous section of this chapter has noted the increased competition that has arisen within the rural housing market as a result of changes in the class composition of rural society. This competition has been accentuated by three major factors: the decline in rural council house stocks; the superior purchasing power of the middle classes; and the strict controls enforced by planning policy on the building of new housing outside existing built-up areas. The combination of these factors has encouraged a significant rise in rural house prices, together with a growth in housing need. The influence of the middle class and of planning controls have already been discussed in some depth, and there is no need to repeat the arguments here. The role of public-sector housing and the changing levels of local-authority provision are, however, also pertinent to the debate, and as such will be considered below.

Public-Sector Housing

Debate concerning public-sector housing in rural areas has recently centred around the issue of council house sales. Phillips and Williams (1983: 328) fear that research may have been dominated by the actual conditions and mechanisms behind sales, and comment that this 'emphasis on sales may have been rather misleading, since their real significance lies in their relationship to the low level of provision of public sector housing in rural areas.' Sales are clearly important, in that they reduce the size of the existing stock in the period when local-authority building has ground to a halt in most rural areas. While an average of 21 per cent of the rural housing stock is local-authority rented (Shucksmith, 1981), many rural parishes have significantly lower proportions than this, and some have no council housing at all (Clark, 1980). Where stocks are so small, the sale of even one or two houses can seriously reduce the chances of applicants being housed. The sale of rural council houses constitutes a particularly emotive issue, especially since many of those who do buy their council houses have occupied them for a good number of years, and are therefore eligible for very advantageous discounts.

Traditionally, the other source of housing for the rural working classes has been the private rented sector. A sharp decline in the availability of this type of accommodation, however, has been witnessed in recent years. Private rented housing in rural areas is very often in the form of 'winter lets' or tied accommodation. Neither type of rental offers security to the tenant, and both types of property are frequently in a state of disrepair. Larkin (1978) describes the problems faced by rural residents who are, through low wages and lack of alternative choices, obliged to opt for such housing, suggesting that, in some areas, such residents are by no means rare. Similarly, Dunn *et al.* (1981) draw attention to those members of the rural poor forced to rely on caravans as the only available source of housing.

The exact extent of housing need created by the combination of middle-class competition and limited alternative development is difficult to establish. Incidences of overcrowding, of young couples and families living with in-laws, are a clear indication of housing shortage; but often those in real need are forced to leave rural areas and seek alternative accommodation in towns. For those on low incomes, rural housing offers little if any choice. There is some evidence of the development of alternative forms of tenure in, for example, the provision of housing association lets (Richmond, 1985) but these are, as yet, limited. Consequently, old people seeking sheltered accommodation or single parents requiring small houses or flats are disadvantaged by the basic scarcity of property other than the classic, family-style, detached house or converted cottage. Such need cannot simply be attributed to the effects of competition from middle-class owner-occupiers, but must be assessed in the light of state policy on housing provision and the growing influence of private developers. These issues are discussed in greater depth in the following chapters, and in particular in Chapter 4, where the direct relationship between policy and need is identified in the local context.

Employment Need

Although the major reduction in the agricultural work-force in Britain took place during the 1950s and 1960s (Rural Development Commission, 1987), jobs continue to be lost from agriculture at a significant rate today (the Rural Development Commission estimates as many as 7,000 for 1986/7). Reduced spending on agricultural machinery, buildings, and equipment has also resulted in employment loss 'downstream' of the farm, while the increasing vertical integration of different parts of the food industry has encouraged the decline of small-scale food processing firms— traditionally important employers in rural areas, especially for women. The loss of jobs from agriculture and related industries has been accompanied by a decline in employment elsewhere in the primary sector, the only major exception being forestry—although even here employment opportunities are more limited than is sometimes assumed (see Johnson and Price, 1987). Over much of rural Britain the work-force is having to rely less and less on the traditional forms of employment and to turn instead to the secondary and tertiary sectors.

Changes in the employment structure of rural areas have also been initiated, as was discussed above, by a shift in the location of manufacturing industry and, in particular, by a growth in the service sector. McLaughlin (1986) has drawn attention to the relocation of firms away from major towns and cities into smaller towns and rural areas. His arguments are supported by other authors (Gould and Keeble, 1984) who identify the existence of such trends in, for example, East Anglia and mid-Wales. Despite the obvious validity of these trends, questions must be raised concerning their role in employment provision amongst the existing rural population in general and particularly amongst those traditionally employed in primary industry. It has been argued, for instance, that the relocation of firms does not necessarily provide a great deal of local employment but relies instead on the migration of existing skilled and professional employees. As, in part, a reaction to the residential preferences of the middle classes, the movement of, for example, high-tech industry to rural East Anglia is much less about the provision of jobs for rural people as it is about the satisfaction of demands from an existing qualified work-force.

There is clearly a need to identify the effects of the changing spatial distribution of the service sector and manufacturing employment on the job opportunities of different groups in rural areas. Initial impressions are that it has simply served to fuel the movement of middle-class, professional people into rural areas, rather than addressing the problems of employment need amongst the working class. Similar questions need to be asked about the much publicized 'diversification' of the rural economy (Cloke and McLaughlin, 1989). It is claimed (see Rural Development Commission, 1987) that the development of small workshops and the diversification of farm-based activities provides considerable scope for new employment in rural areas. Whether the reality lives up to these expectations is, as yet, a matter for speculation. It is clear, however, that *levels* of employment creation in relation to such initiatives are not high, and that their success relies to a considerable extent on factors such as the availability of capital and skill, factors which restrict potential opportunities to certain groups. Again, as with housing need, it is not simply provision *per se* which is important but also the quality of that provision and the degree of choice it offers to different groups. Conventional analyses rarely consider the needs of those who have jobs but whose experiences are far removed from their aspirations (an exception being Dench, 1984).

The role of the local and central state in employment location in rural areas has been relatively limited. While organizations such as CoSIRA and the Development Board for Rural Wales have contributed significantly to the creation of jobs in rural areas, it is arguable whether the work of these agencies goes very far toward tackling existing needs. It is suggested, for example, that they encourage job creation in very specialized fields, and attract firms with poor linkages into the existing rural economy (Philips and Williams, 1984). Moreover, while these agencies may be state-financed, they are dependent upon initiatives from private companies or individuals; they do not themselves create jobs but simply respond by offering incentives where initial moves are made. These points will be taken up later in this book, when attention will be drawn to the direct relationship between state policy and employment provision.

Rural Transport Need

Another well-publicized area of social need is rural transport and general accessibility. The problem faced by the less mobile groups within rural society have been well documented, providing the subject of a number of detailed empirical studies at the local level (Gant and Smith, 1983; Moseley and Packman, 1983). Again, it is not the intention here to embark on a lengthy discussion of the different types and degrees of need relevant to rural transport, since that has been done quite adequately elsewhere (Banister, 1980; Moseley, 1979; Cloke, 1985). It is, however, necessary, given the significant role of transport in the lives of those living in the countryside and, consequently, the importance of transport policy, to look briefly at the inequalities which occur amongst different social groups. In this way the critical examination of resource allocation in relation to rural transport will be more realistically informed, as will be any suggestion of 'alternative' transport solutions.

The long history of cut-backs, including the spectacular axing of railway services following the Beeching report of 1963, has left many rural areas seriously lacking, or even totally devoid of, any form of regular public transport. According to figures presented by Moseley (1979), Norfolk, for example, lost a total of 70 per cent of its rail network during the 1960s. In the case of buses, the decline has been more complex. Banister (1980) estimates that the percentage of all rural vehicular-passenger kilometres travelled by bus has declined from 40 per cent in 1952 to about 8 per cent in 1982. Declining demand, due in particular to increasing car ownership, has led to a reduction in the *levels* of services by bus operators (especially in terms of frequency) as well as cuts in the services themselves. The result has been fewer, emptier buses on rural routes. Despite such declining demand, however, there still exists a section of the rural population who are totally dependent on public transport, and the needs of this group appear to be increasingly overlooked in the face of expanding private provision.

There is no doubt that amongst those groups experiencing particular accessibility problems are the elderly and rural poor. The influx of retirement migrants has meant that, in certain areas, this former group constitute an increasing proportion of the total population. Research (e.g. Gant and Smith, 1982) has shown that as a group the elderly are characterized by low levels of car ownership, giving them limited access to essential services. Frequently, moreover, elderly people become disabled and their mobility is thus further restricted. Moseley (1979) draws attention to the occurrence of multiple deprivation, suggesting that those who experience accessibility problems belong in many cases to those groups (for example, the poor, the infirm and disabled, and the elderly) whose general level of need is relatively high. There are a number of other, possibly less visible, groups within rural society for whom accessibility also constitutes a problem. Amongst such groups are the young, for whom social activities may be restricted, especially at evenings and weekends, due to the lack to public transport. Women whose husbands use the household car for work may also experience difficulties of mobility (Little, 1986). A lack of access to transport may leave such women very isolated during the day and present problems in the carrying out of even routine domestic tasks.

The remote location of many villages means that transport is a particularly important service. The decline of many other rural facilities and the concentration of, for example, shops, health services, and entertainment in the larger villages and towns further increases the dependence on transport of those living in the countryside. The reduction or disappearance of public transport may put a whole range of facilities out of the reach of certain groups, and serve to limit employment opportunities. The 1968 Transport Act went some way towards recognizing the extreme importance of rural transport, bringing the operation of bus services under the authority of the county councils and enabling them to provide subsidies for the maintenance of essential, non-profitable routes, many of which were in rural areas. Since that time, however, a shortage of resources has led to a severe reduction in subsidized routes; and as a part of the general movement towards private- rather than public-service provision, the 1980 Transport Act has sought to encourage the extent of private investment in inter-urban bus services. An increase in private operators and hence competition has a detrimental effect on rural services in particular, since such operators compete successfully with public services for the profit-making, mainly urban, routes but are less interested in maintaining rural routes— many of which run at a loss.

The 1985 Transport Act takes privatization several stages further, with the dismembering of the National Bus Company into smaller units to be sold to the private sector, and the deregulation of local bus services. A likely outcome in rural areas is that the very few profitable routes will attract some competition from operators, but that most of the existing network will be thrown on the mercy of local authorities for subsidy (see Knowles, 1985;

Banister *et al.*, 1985; Bell and Cloke, 1988). After the phasing out of the four-year transitional grant from central government (£20 million in the first year), the ability of local authorities to finance unprofitable routes will be subject to severe financial restrictions. It may well be that rural county councils will find this an ideal opportunity to reverse previous commitments to the provision of rural public transport.

Retail, Health, and Other Services

It has been suggested above that those groups experiencing high levels of need in relation to one service area may also be those with greatest need in another. Poor transport facilities, for example, may result in certain sections of the population being denied adequate health provision. In a climate of decreasing public expenditure, it is not surprising that services are becoming increasingly concentrated in the more populated areas. Again, it does not necessarily follow that, because a large proportion of inhabitants in many villages are easily able to reach nearby towns, giving them access to all essential services, and because they may indeed prefer to use these facilities, that the lack of local services does not seriously disadvantage certain groups.

A detailed description of reductions in the levels of, for example, rural health, education, or retail services is not appropriate here. What is important is to draw attention to the wide range of original empirical evidence (see Tricker, 1983; Banister, 1983, in addition to work previously referenced), supported by work undertaken in rural Gloucestershire (see Chapter 4), clearly illustrating the existence of rural deprivation. The fact that those 'in need' frequently constitute a minority in many rural communities means that their problems may easily and conveniently be overlooked. Moreover, such groups are often those with poorest access to the decision-making process and their views least likely to be represented politically.

The relationship between need and social class in rural communities is undeniably strong (see Chapter 4). It is the low-paid who suffer from a lack of public transport, whose access to services and employment is limited, and who cannot compete in the market of rising house prices. Clearly, need is not exclusively confined to the working class—the disappearance of the village post office or school, for example, may provide problems for a wide range of village residents. Superior resources, particularly access to private transport, allows the middle classes, however, to adapt to the inconveniences of falling service provision. For them choice may be restricted, but access to essential service facilities and comfortable housing is rarely denied. Indeed, as noted, the growing presence of the middle classes in rural society may serve to reinforce the needs of the poor.

The primary purpose of this chapter has been to argue the need for the adoption and development of political-economy approaches in the study of rural society and the analysis of rural decision-making. Rather than making endless direct comparisons between different approaches to demonstrate the value of political-economic analyses, we have chosen to focus on some of the major strands of such analyses, and to establish their relevance and importance in contemporary rural research, an approach that remains as yet poorly developed in existing texts. In so doing the chapter has provided a framework for the discussion that follows, establishing in particular the importance of locating rural social change within the context of the broader state/society relationship. It has been suggested, moreover, that insufficient attention has hitherto been paid, in the study of rural economy and society, to the role of class in resource allocation. We have attempted to demonstrate the centrality of class to the evolution of rural social relations, particularly in terms of contemporary trends, and to argue the importance of adopting a class-based analysis in the interpretation of social need and the allocative process. The following chapters build on these arguments, exploring decision-making in the context of various levels of state activity and analysing the relationship between the central and local state in the formulation and implementation of policy.

2

The State and Rural Policy

In this chapter we aim to stress the importance of the state in rural planning and policy-making, to review the theory and operation of the central and local states, and to analyse the relevance of the state to changes in rural areas. We believe that the reluctance of many rural researchers to grasp the admitted complexities of state theory has been a major contribution to the persistence of traditional wisdoms about rural planning which are now becoming increasingly untenable.

The traditional approach to rural planning is evident in the proliferation of recent studies which have adopted a kind of blinkered rationality:

select a policy for analysis;
find out what the policy-makers' objectives are for this policy (as stated for public consumption);
compare these objectives with some form of empirical study of what happens on the ground;
conclude that any difference between what should have occurred (according to published objectives) and what has occurred (according to positivist techniques of measurement) is 'the problem' with the policy;
suggest another policy which may overcome or ameliorate 'the problem' (but which may equally fail the 'blinkered-rationality' test).

Although this approach has in some senses been successful in raising the level of available information on some aspects of rural change and planning, it is beset by some obvious inadequacies. First, it accepts policies which are written down for public consumption at face value. Second, it assumes that state policy objectives may be adopted as a realistic illustration of the underlying roles and functions of the state and its various agencies. Third, it minimizes or even ignores the social, economic, and political contexts of planning and policy-making. Fourth, it offers an internal logic which suggests that policy 'problems' are caused

by faulty implementation techniques, and that technical solutions to these faults will lead to policies which will be more successful in responding to rural problems.

In the analysis of *urban* policy and power relations, this orthodoxy of approach has largely been superseded in the consideration of the state as the pivot of policy analysis (see e.g. the reviews by Ambrose, 1986; Brindley *et al.*, 1989; Harvey, 1989; Lawless and Brown, 1986; and Rees and Lambert, 1985). In studies of rural localities, however, there has until recently been a widespread rejection of socio-political theories of the state as too impractical, too political, and too disruptive of the technical role of applied positivism inherent in the traditional wisdoms described above (Cloke, 1989*a*; Cloke and Moseley, 1989). This rejection is well illustrated in a review of the work of Clavel, Forester, and Goldsmith (1980) by a leading American planner:

A curious conference and ensuing publication took place recently. About 300 persons, primarily people calling themselves radical planners, convened to discuss planning in the present, which they consider to be an age of austerity. They argued that this age is a time of new opportunities for planners radically to affect the role of government, since it indicates that the private enterprise and capitalist system had failed . . . . *This kind of thing gives planners a bad name.*   (Catanese, 1984: 155–6; author's italics)

One of the major hindrances to the adoption of political-economy approaches in general, and theoretical discourse on the state in particular, is the fear that studies of rural change will lose the political neutrality which is perceived to be offered by more 'orthodox' ways of evaluating planning and policy-making. We believe that this fear is ungrounded. Traditional positivist approaches, as Hoggart and Buller (1987), amongst others, have argued, are as flawed in their assumed objectivity as are explicitly theoretical and ideological perspectives. Using the example of Andrew Gilg's (1985) discussion of rural geography, they highlight an unstated but highly important set of assumptions inherent in the orthodox approach of applied positivism. Thus, Gilg's viewpoint (p. 266):

the future for rural geography should be an applied one, where it integrates its own research, relates this to the real behavioural world and to policy formulation, and thus attempts to produce a rural environment that is not only physically attractive but also a lively and prosperous place to live.

is seen by Hoggart and Buller (pp. 266–7) to rest on clear but implicit value judgements:

it assumes a consensus (or integration) view of social organisation, since it rests on the idea that agreement can be reached over what constitutes a 'physically attractive', 'lively' and 'prosperous' environment . . . . There is an underlying acceptance of the view that governments principally are there to serve the people; that they listen to suggestions which serve to promote the 'common good', that they act on these suggestions and, in doing so, are neither self-interested nor promote biases in the distribution of socio-economic benefits . . . . It implies that researchers should primarily restrict their attentions to identifying the most appropriate means of 'tinkering' with existing socio-economic conditions in order to weaken the impress of 'malevolent' trends. This fails to recognise that the processes which brought about current maldistributions or malpractices . . . . are inherent in policy procedures which have to be relied on to alleviate the problems researchers have analysed.

Clearly, the use of contemporary theories of the state *is* overtly political. Wolfe (1977: ix), for example, stresses that 'to resurrect the state is to make a political declaration about the centrality of organised political power in modern societies'. Perhaps, however, it is as well to declare and substantiate a favoured theoretical approach rather than to mask it (sometimes unwittingly) with a veneer of supposed neutrality.

The explicit acknowledgement that planning and policy-making by local authorities and other agencies with decision-making jurisdiction over rural areas are aspects of state activity, and therefore experience the constraints imposed on other state activities, seems to be a better starting-point for analysis than the mere search for better techniques of policy implementation. Equally, the recognition of policy-making and implementation as complex political phenomena, grounded within the overall context of the state and structured by power relations between the centre and the locality, between public and private sectors, and between different agencies and interests, appears a more realistic frame-work than an assumption that policy-making is, in fact, a kind of neutral arbitration procedure.

The remainder of this chapter makes the case for theories of the state to be central in studies of rural change and planning. First, it explores the different conceptual perspectives on the role and the function of the state, and thereby on the socio-political context of planning and policy-making. Of necessity, the account of state theory given here is a somewhat simplified conflation of themes which themselves are the subject of many books (e.g. Clark and Dear, 1984; Cooke, 1983; Dunleavy and O'Leary, 1987; Ham and Hill, 1984; Johnston, 1982; Saunders, 1984*a*; Urry, 1981*a*; Vincent, 1987), but nevertheless the conceptual choices for researchers interested in rural planning may clearly be derived from these themes. We then turn to a conceptualization of the local state, and outline the context, nature, and operation of the state at this sub-national level. Finally, we discuss the question of the local state in rural localities, and assess the possibility that there might be some recognizable *rural* component on the state in these areas.

CONCEPTS OF THE STATE

If we accept that planning and policy-making in rural (as in other) localities are integral parts of the activities of the state, then there is a need to understand the basics of state theory in order to realize the implications of this state context. Initially it should be stressed that state is not synonymous with government. This assertion appears unnecessary, and yet many who have been drawn to state theory as a basis for research have subsequently tended to apply theory only to the work of government agencies. By way of definition, we should recognize that the state includes both institutions and functions, and that the institutions concerned relate to administrative, judiciary, and enforcement functions as well as governmental and political activity.

Secondly, it should be stressed that the functions of the state are not static. This is not to suggest that the changing state is synonymous with party politics in government (for the same reasons expressed above). The institutions and functions of the state are far more enduring than the terms of office of particular political leaders, but nevertheless change does occur. For example, the social-welfare and economic functions of the state were the subject of vast expansion during the late nineteenth and twentieth centuries, such that the contemporary state is made up of institutions and functions which impinge on most facets of life. Thus in 1979 Peter Saunders was able to point out that the distinctiveness of the modern state . . . lies not in the fact that it is interventionist, but in the character and scope of its intervention. More specifically, its character has become increasingly positive and directive while its scope has broadened to encompass areas of economic activity which have traditionally been considered private and thus inviolable. (p. 140)

The 1980s have witnessed an ebbing of this interventionist tide, with major political programmes of privatization and deregulation which have been concerned to transfer some of the state's functions to the private sector (Bell and Cloke, 1989). Despite the seeming radical and rapid nature of these policies, however, the overall functions and institutions of the state as a whole remain *relatively* unscathed, although the accelerating rate of change is seen by some contemporary commentators as illustrating a crisis of legitimation for the state within conditions of advanced capitalism. Here, with monopoly capital generating surplus labour and production, the state is seen to intervene or withdraw according to the perceived requirements of maintaining or reviving its own credibility.

The notions of a state that is wider than government, and which undergoes change, but at a more enduring pace than that of party political turnaround, are basic starting-points for understanding the context of state activities. There are, however, a series of more complex conceptual choices available to those researchers wishing to theorize the nature and organization of the state. It is not our intention here to discuss these choices in the detail which they warrant. Rather, we present in outline form a framework for considering policy-making and planning for rural areas in the context of the state. Here we use the work of Gordon Clark and Michael Dear (1984) who subdivide the state into three inter-related aspects:

(i) *form*: the structural link between social formation and the state;
(ii) *function*: the hierarchy of roles which are integral to that form;
(iii) *apparatus*: the mechanisms through which functions are operated.

Each aspect is discussed in turn, as our contention is that analysis of planning and policy-making will vary enormously according to which concepts of form, function, and apparatus are accepted and adopted as the basis for interpretation.

The Form of the State

Merely to discuss the structural links between the state and social formation is sufficient to risk alienation from those who would seek to depoliticize the study of rural change. Part of this alienation stems from the distracting over-use of jargon in some state-theory writings, and part refers back to the wish to perpetuate a kind of applied positivist approach wherein a 'neutral' stance may be taken in areas of class, power, and politics. Nevertheless, the form of the state fundamentally influences the outcome of all state activities, including processes and procedures of planning and policy-making in rural areas. To ignore state form is to render superficial any appreciation of state or governmental activity. In order to illustrate the importance of theorizing state form, we have isolated two important issues from the multitude of conceptual options in this area of the theory of the state. Both these issues serve to highlight the hidden assumptions which are being made by rural researchers claiming to be neutral or atheoretical. The first issue is the broad but crucial matter of just how the state should be conceptualized *vis-à-vis* the very visible policy-making agencies of government. Two major theoretical pathways emerge from the literature on the state. It has been conventional to envisage state form as a *summation of government institutions*. Thus study of the state focuses on those agencies which perform political, administrative, judiciary, and enforcement functions (see Miliband, 1973*a*, 1977), and in overview the state represents the collective being of these institutions. The alternative is to theorize the form of the state as a *condensate of class-based social relations* (Poulantzas, 1978). The state, therefore, is formed beyond the visible government agencies, and is inextricably linked to the dominant form of social relations at any particular time.

This distinction between a summation of agencies and a condensate of social relations poses an important conceptual decision for those seeking to understand the state's policy activities in rural areas. One view suggests that power is vested *in* government agencies themselves. Analysis of the whys and wherefores of the output of state form would therefore focus on power relations within government agencies, and between these agencies and client groups within society. The other suggests that power is exercised *through* government institutions, which are seen as vehicles for the output of dominant social, economic, and political fractions within society. Explanation of state output here relies on an understanding of power in society, wielded through state agencies and affecting particular fractions within society.

Most investigations of power relations in the state by rural researchers have reflected a form of the state which assumes power within a collection of government agencies. There seems to be considerable scope for studies which attempt to link social relations with the policy-making bodies through which they operate and the social groups which experience benefit or disadvantage as a result (Cloke, 1986*a*; Goldsmith, 1986). Such an approach would also suggest a greater emphasis on the inter-nationalization of the state rather than confinement to the conventional boundaries of nation-states. This would certainly reflect the internationalization of capital and of political allegiance which are currently features of the political economy of developed nations.

Power and State Form

The second of the two issues of state form which illustrate the unwritten assumptions of many studies of policy analysis concerns the configuration of power relations within that form. Again, classifications of power relations are numerous, and here we confine our discussion to four categories which appear to be of particular relevance to contemporary rural studies.

Pluralist/Representational Concepts. This group of concepts centres around the notion of dispersed and fragmented power within the state. Representational perspectives suggest that the state is an independent institution which acts as a neutral regulator of conflict within civil society. The original work of Dahl (1961) and Polsby (1963) served to generate the pluralist theoretical position along these lines. Power within the state is not controlled by any one fraction of society but is available to different contenders through democratic processes of electing represent-atives and public participation. Thus power is widely distributed amongst individuals. This concept was extended by Beer (1965) to cover the role of pressure groups in representing the interests of like-minded individuals, and later by Richardson and Jordan (1979) who advanced the view that pressure groups are now able successfully to negotiate with government agencies over policies.

The key facet of pluralist thinking is that any group in a democratic society can participate in public policy if it is sufficiently determined. Although interest groups and individuals are not involved with equality of access to power, even the least powerful are not powerless. Moreover, the distribution of power within the state is not cumulative, so that the state cannot generate any consistent bias towards particular classes. According to these concepts, the causes of state activity stem from the wishes of the contemporary majority and not from the state itself.

Most analysis of rural planning and policy-making has been set, deliberately or, in some cases, possibly unwittingly (following the automatically derived concepts of others), in the pluralist mould. Electorally, rural areas in Britain have been shown to be Conservative in national terms (apart from isolated Liberal strongholds in west Wales and south-west England) and conservative in local terms, the latter predicated on low turn-outs, established local political configurations, and an increasingly conservative electorate with the inmigratory trends of gentrification and geriatrification. Certainly the role of pressure groups has been an active one (Lowe and Goyder, 1983) although the successful partnership of such groups with government agencies (along the lines suggested by Richardson and Jordan) has been in areas such as agriculture, and (where this does not conflict with agriculture) conservation. In socio-economic sectors contributing to material hardship and deprivation in rural areas (Shaw, 1979; McLaughlin, 1986) no interest group has had sufficient access to power (or has been sufficiently determined, according to pluralist analysis) to enter into similarly successful negotiations. True, the 1982 Conservative Government did partially reverse the previous trend of disproportionate fiscal aid in favour of metropolitan local authorities. The gains made by non-metropolitan areas in this move, however, did not stem from democratic bargaining on behalf of rural individuals or groups. Rather, it was central government's hostile attitude to metropolitan authorities which led to their depletion (and ultimate demise), to the benefit of their non-metropolitan counterparts.

Pluralist concepts have been widely criticized (MacPherson, 1977), in particular because the democratic state in fact sits on top of considerable apathy and non-participation from its electorate. As Saunders (1979: 156) puts it:

People are not expected to show any great interest in the way in which their lives are governed, and any effective increase in the level of political participation is seen as pathological, a threat to the stability of the system and an indication that the system is not functioning properly.

Pluralism, therefore, breeds an attitude of contentment, with an independent state serving as a market-place for political consensus. Gilg's (1984) analysis of political changes in central government and their impact on the countryside illustrates something of the application of this theme. He describes four periods of socio-political thought (Table 2.1) and the trends in rural planning which resulted during these periods. Several trends are espoused by different forms of central government, and for most of the post-war period the gap between the Conservative and Labour parties has been narrow. Indeed, the period from the mid-1950s to the 1970s is described in terms of the emergence of 'a consensus type of politics'. At the close of his analysis (p. 250), Gilg is able to list a series of positive achievements of the post-war planning system such as:

an agriculture which provides a high proportion of Britain's dietary requirements at a reasonable price, many villages have been attractively developed or conserved, large areas of open countryside remain scenically beautiful, much bad development has been prevented and much pollution of the air and water has been cleaned up.

Pluralism would suggest that political consensus has achieved these attributes for the benefit of all. Critics of the pluralist concept point out that planning activities and agricultural policy have generally aided farmers, and those other households, whether indigenous and adventitious, with sufficient wealth and income to buy their way into and maintain their access to highly competitive housing markets, labour markets, and shrinking public- and private-sector service frameworks. Conversely, less advantaged rural inhabitants have encountered apparent state insensitivity to their needs, in the form of inappropriate actions or inapplicable policies from those agencies whose ostensible task it is

Table 2.1. Gilg's Socio-political Periods and Planning Trends

Government	Socio-political period	Agriculture and forestry	Settlement	Conservation and recreation
1945–51: Labour (Socialist)	Nationalization of major public services, state intervention, and post-war recovery.	Agriculture Act 1947. Expansion at all costs. Price guarantees and grants. In forestry, dedication agreements and felling licences.	Town and Country Planning Act 1947. The state to act as developer, the production of end-state plans.	National Parks Act 1949. Agriculture the natural conserver of the landscape and wildlife. Recreation, health outdoor type.
1951–64: Conservative (one-nation consensus)	Gradual relaxation of state control, increasing prosperity and growth—'Never had it so good'.	Agriculture Act 1957. Limitation of change in guaranteed prices to ± 3% p.a. Quotas and standard quantities. Forestry as rural employer.	Town and Country Planning Acts 1953, 1954, and 1959. Allowed free market in land and the re-entry of the private developer.	Designation of National Parks and Nature Reserves.
1964–74: Labour and Conservative (social democrat)	The flowering of economic and social freedom. Everything thought possible, but limits perceived by the early 1970s.	Accession to the EEC, 1972. The problems of over-production begin to appear. But expansions still the goal. Economic return on forestry queried.	Town and Country Planning Acts 1968 and 1971. Replacement of end-state, land-use plans by flexible structure plans. Re-organization of local government into two tiers.	Countryside Act 1968. Growth of recreation leads to positive provision, e.g. Country Parks.
1974–82: Labour and Conservative (Centre and right)	The oil crisis and world recession. Strict financial controls forced on to Labour, gladly espoused by new Tory right.	Surpluses appear in a number of products but overall the UK not self-sufficient. Expansion leads to landscape damage. Re-assertion of forestry expansion.	The production of structure plans, against a background of counter-urbanization, urban decay, and rural growth.	Wildlife and Countryside Act 1981. The conservation decade ends with a voluntary process for conservation, backed by compensation payments.

Source: Gilg, 1984: 852.

to ameliorate their situation. The evidence in Chapter 1 of the distribution of need in rural areas suggests that pluralism alone will not offer a full explanation of the interaction between rural problems and state policies.

Élitist/Instrumentalist Concepts. Élitist concepts maintain that state power is vested in minority élite groups within the institutional setting. This concentration of power leads to a manipulation of state policies in favour of the élite and its interests, and therefore challenges the twofold pluralist expectations of useful public participation and no group being the consistent beneficiary of state decisions. Instead, participation is seen as more of a window-dressing exercise, and policy outcomes are viewed as benefiting particular sections of society.

The classic élitist studies (e.g. Hunter, 1953) were of local communities where local power was found to be held by an élite of, for example, business, financial, and industrial leaders. A more sophisticated view gradually emerged with the disaggregation of this broad idea of the 'élite'. Bottomore (1966), for example, differentiated between a *political élite*—those exercising power in society— and a wider band of the *political class* constituting the political élite plus élites from social and economic sectors—those directly benefiting from political power. Instrumentalism is seen to occur when individuals in key state positions are members both of the political and of the socio-economic élites. The clear outcome of this situation is that the state becomes instrumental in upholding the particular interests of the élites who exercise power within it. A biased distribution of state power can be exerted both by influencing the policy decisions which are made and by non-decision-making (Bachrach and Baratz, 1970), whereby the policy items brought before institutional decision-making processes can be limited by the élite so as to omit those which would not serve their interests.

Concepts of power involving élites have been accommodated into other concepts in very different ways. For example, the occurrence of élites might be seen as compatible with a pluralist view of power. Ham and Hill (1984: 31) express this notion succinctly:

regular elections based on competition between the leaders of political parties, together with participation by pressure group elites in between elections, and interaction between these elites and the bureaucratic elites are the ways in which democracy operates in the modern state. The fact that different elites operate in different issue areas is a protection against domination by one group.

This last phrase is crucial. Are different élites operating in different areas of influence? Instrumentalist components of élitism tend to suggest not, and therefore it is unsurprising that élitism may also be viewed as one form of class rule, thus linking with more structuralist concepts.

The best-known advocate of such instrumentalist concepts is Miliband (1969; 1973a; 1977), who has produced strong evidence to suggest that the configuration of élite individuals in positions of state results in policy outcomes beneficial to the interests of capital. The functions of the state are therefore viewed as biased in three ways:

(i)   the character of its leading personnel;
(ii) the pressures exercised by the economically dominant class;
(iii) the structural constraints imposed by the mode of production.

Saunders (1981) takes issue with several points in Miliband's analysis. First, there is some discrepancy between the acknowledgement that different economic élites sometimes demonstrate divergent interests (for example between monopoly and competitive sectors of capital—see Lojkine, 1977) and the parallel notion that these élites share common class interests. Second, Miliband's suggestion that local government is merely one part of the state's apparatus conflicts with the tensions in central–local state relations and in the discretion exercised by the local state. Third, Miliband suggests that political élites, although constrained by their socio-economic and political environment, do have discretionary powers. As Saunders (1979: 162) notes: 'If the state can act to some extent autonomously, then we need to know how to draw the line between determinism and autonomy, constraint and discretion, action and structure'.

The notions engendered by instrumentalist concepts and the concept of élites are of direct relevance to the analysis of policy-making in rural areas. Certainly the existence of élites in rural society has been recognized at both national and local levels. In the East Anglian context, Newby (1981: 221) describes a traditionally class-divided society:

Farmers and landowners formed an easily identifiable rural ruling class which held a near monopoly over employment opportunities, housing, the magistracy and local politics. Against their extensive domination of rural institutions farm workers and other members of the rural working class were relatively powerless.

Similarly, Buchanan's (1982: 18) analysis of the preparation of the Suffolk structure plan reflected 'the power of a small elite in SCC to order the contents of the plan and control the involvement of councillors, officers, non-governmental organisations and the public through various non-decision-making processes'. Non-decision-making by élites is also evidenced in McLaughlin's (1986) analysis of the state's policy response to rural deprivation. He suggests that public and policy interest in the underlying causes of deprivation have been succcessfuly deflected by state élites by the legitimation of 'softer' issues such as rural services, which are unlikely to challenge societal *status quo* in the way that extensive exposure of, for example, policy prescriptions for the redistribution of wealth and income would.

Moreover, the selected policies of these acknowledged élites have certainly been distributional. Newby (1981), drawing from his earlier research findings (Newby, 1977; Newby *et al.*, 1978), reflects that both agricultural policy and rural planning have been selectively beneficial. He traces a chain of events from the political economy of modern agriculture to the problems encountered by disadvantaged rural groups, and notes that 'the formulation of agricultural policy has mostly ignored the possible external consequences and at best been indifferent to them'. (p. 226). In the same way, strategic planning is seen to have contained strong elements of planning for the better off by restricting the rate of economic growth in rural areas. It can therefore be strongly suggested that political and socio-economic élites (which occur together) have been instrumental in biasing state policies for rural areas. To this extent, instrumentalist concepts are most relevant to rural policy analysis. There remains, however, the incongruity of the instrumentalist view of autonomy and discretion within the state. These notions may be pursued in other conceptualizations of the state, and again later in this chapter, when specific considera-tion is given to the local state in its rural context.

Managerialist Concepts. As with the other concepts described

here, managerialism was developed in the urban milieux. The
work of Rex and Moore (1967) and notably Pahl (1975) served to
highlight the role of the managers who ran state systems of policy
and implementation. These professional bureaucrats are characterized as 'gatekeepers' who, through the use of technical expertise
and manipulation of the mechanics of policy-making processes,
are able to engineer outcomes which reflect their own interests and
those of the social and economic fractions they belong to:

> The controllers, be they planners or social workers, architects or
> education officers, estate agents or property developers, representing the
> market or the plan, private enterprise or the state, all impose their goals
> and values on the lower participants in the urban system.
> (Pahl, 1975: 207)

In his original thesis on managerialism, Pahl recognized that
managers operated in a constrained socio-economic context but
nevertheless saw them as the crucial explanatory factor in the
outcome of state power. This underplay of the importance of
surrounding societal structures was addressed in his reformulated
analysis (Pahl, 1982), in which he maintains the emphasis on the
values and objectives of gatekeepers who control the allocation of
resources but insists that any such emphasis must be firmly
founded on specific recognition of the political economy in which
the state operates. Managers are thus viewed as mediators
between the central state and the local population and between the
private sector and the welfare state. They allocate, but have little
control over what is allocated.

An important facet of Pahl's concept is that the nature of
managerialism is changing as the relationship between the state
and the private sector changes. He notes:

> It could certainly be argued until fairly recently that the state was
> subordinating its intervention to the interests of private capital. However,
> there comes a point when the continuing and expanding role of the state
> reaches a level where its power to control investment, knowledge and the
> allocation of services and facilities gives it an autonomy which enables it to
> pass beyond its previous subservient and facilitative role.
> (Pahl, 1977: 161)

Basically, Pahl's reformulated managerialism is corporatist in
nature, with the state increasingly managing the affairs of the
nation for its own purposes (Winkler, 1976). The problem remains

of differentiating between situations of external constraint, autonomy, and discretion within state activity. Managerialism can only form part of this differentiation, and cannot theorize the entire relationship between state and society.

Although the managerialist thesis was developed in urban contexts, Pahl (1970) recognized that access to resources such as education, employment, and housing are structured in a local context, and that such contexts may be 'physically, "urban", "rural", or a mixture of the two' (p. 203). The rural context of managerialism has been the subject of considerable substantive research. Heller's (1979) analysis of managerialism in rural health services and Phillips and Williams's (1982) work on housing management are just two examples of an increasing body of managerialist research in the rural context. Equally, there have been detailed managerialist studies of policy-making and planning. In one important case study of structure plan-making processes, Flynn (1981: 61) concludes:

The structure planners studied appeared to be creating a 'culture' within which bureaucratic and political values were operationalised. Both inside and outside county hall, the officers used various strategies and rationales. Whether such strategies and rationales were employed consciously or not, their effect was to establish a pragmatic consensus which reflects two dimensions of policy. Firstly it translated explicit political prescriptions (and tacit assumptions) into 'technical' policies. And secondly, it supplied the norms through which intra- and inter-organisational conflicts (both political and bureaucratic) could be managed.

Flynn's study is revealing in its analysis of the role of managers, but comes up against the same stumbling-block of political 'prescriptions' and political 'norms' which form the nub of wider critiques of managerialism. To what extent are outcomes attributable to manager bias, local political discretion, central state economy, or societal constraints according to the prevailing political economy? Managerialist concepts seem to provide only one piece of the jigsaw.

Structuralist Concepts. Structuralist concepts dictate that classes rather than individuals should constitute the real disaggregation of political analysis. Thus the individualistic orientation of pluralism, managerialism, and instrumentalism is rejected in favour of a model which views the state as representative of the current balance of class influence. In Britain this balance favours the interests of monopoly capital, and therefore the state, in reflecting this balance, will favour this dominant class. Structuralist concepts of the state (Poulantzas, 1973*b*; 1975; Castells, 1978) recognize the major function of state policy as being to furnish the needs of the interests of capital, with an accompanying short-term function of providing limited reforms for the dominated working class so as to break down the unity and solidarity of this potential political force. According to this model, the state will only adopt an interventionist role so as to institute short-term reforms with the explicit intention of preserving the long-term interests of the dominant class.

Two problems arise when the attempt is made to apply structuralist concepts to the empirical evidence of state activity as it affects rural areas. First, and most obviously, structuralist analysis claims to account for all empirical phenomena, and therefore effectively renders itself immune to falsification. As Saunders (1979: 184) suggests,

> from this perspective, observable phenomena merely contribute to the raw materials of the thought process; scientific knowledge is the result of the correct theoretical tools (derived from a particular reading of Marx) to these raw materials, and it follows that such knowedge cannot therefore be assessed for validity by resort back to observable phenomena.

Secondly, Poulantzas has stressed that the ruling class, which is protected by state activity, is itself divided into different fractions. Thus state intervention, as well as representing short-term reforms for the proletariat, may also constitute aid for one particular fraction of the bourgeoisie against another. The state therefore has *relative autonomy* which permits it to regulate between these different areas of intervention.

Few attempts have been made to place rural policy-making in these contexts, perhaps because the 'rural' scale of analysis is so often rejected by structuralists who have preferred to concentrate on international, national, urban, and regional spheres (see Chapter 1). Nevertheless, the planning system has been viewed as part of the state's internal survival mechanism for capitalist interests (Ambrose, 1986; Knox and Cullen, 1981; Reade, 1987), and there does appear to be some scope for the application of structural concepts to rural localities. This point is discussed further in the analysis of the rural local state later in this chapter, but a brief example illustrating short-term reformist policy might be the wholesale espousal of self-help and voluntary initiatives as agents of welfare in rural areas. Regardless of any intrinsic benefits arising from these activities, they have been seized by policy-makers as high-profile, low-cost signals of activity in the absence of more serious investment on behalf of the rural disadvantaged (Cloke, 1983).

A Plurality of Power?   These four categories of power relations are neither exhaustive nor necessarily mutually exclusive. Indeed, there have been recent moves by some political scientists both to extend the range of theories of the state and to suggest areas of overlap between different concepts of power and the state. For example, Dunleavy and O'Leary's (1987) text on theories of the state accepts the categories of pluralism, élitism, and Marxism (falling within the structuralist approach discussed above), but adds two further theories:

(i) the new right: 'a set of theorists whose intellectual origins lie in the mainstream traditions of western liberal and conservative philosophy, but who add novelty and rigour to these ideological positions by mounting a developed social-science based critique of pluralism' (p. 72). While the influence of new right thinking on Western governments has certainly provided the context for radical political change, particularly in areas of privatization and deregulation, the new right's theory of the state is less easy to disentangle from the categories of power already discussed. Perhaps one central concern is that pluralist power is seen as inefficient in its restriction of the 'best outcomes' as dictated by market forces. New right theories of power thereby suggest a portfolio of 'neutral', positivist, and largely economic techniques for arbitrating between competing bidders for resources. These techniques might be viewed as more efficient than pluralist responses to democratic demand or pressure group activity.

(ii) Neo-pluralism: a different direction of attack on pluralist concepts which rejects anachronistic and ideological theories and suggests an analysis 'centring on the operations of large corpora-tions and the modern extended state, sensitive to the problems and deficiencies of current social arrangements, but coldly realistic about the limited scope for reform' (p. 272). The state here is seen as a *deformed polyarchy*, responding both to electoral mandate and interest group pressures and to the economic pressures from business interests.

In the cases of both the new right and neo-pluralism, it can be argued that these concepts illustrate governmental politics rather than more fundamental theories of the state and power relations. Nevertheless, it is interesting to follow Dunleavy and O'Leary's analysis through to the point where they discuss the overlap between their different theories of the state. They clearly suggest that different theories are not isolated from each other, and, using concepts of élitism and pluralism as core elements, they differentiate six areas of theoretical convergence (Fig. 2.1):

(i) Instrumentalist Marxist accounts of the state overlap with

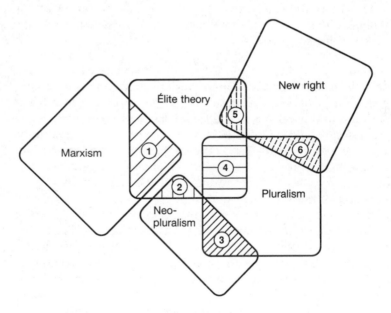

1. instrumentalism/external-control model (business domination)
2. liberal corporatism/professionalized state
3. deformed polyarchy/radical pluralism
4. democratic élitism/revisionist democracy
5. public-choice interest group model/new class
6. demand-side model/governmental-overload thesis

FIG. 2.1. Overlaps between Theories of the State
Source: Dunleavy and O'Leary, 1987: 323

élitist theory in stressing that state policy in capitalist society is controlled by capital so as to sponsor profit. Ordinary citizens are excluded from power.

(ii) Élitism and neo-pluralism converge in the idea that representative politics has been usurped as the determinant of public policy. Élitism stresses corporatist arrangements in which élites implement their own interests; neo-pluralism suggests that power can also be exercised by groups whose professional knowledge places them in crucial decision-making positions within government agencies. Such groups can also be seen as a kind of élite on account of the specific professional credentials. Although Dunleavy and O'Leary do not devote much discussion to the managerialist thesis, there is an obvious overlap here also.

(iii) Pluralism and neo-pluralism retain some common ground in accepting that there is little point in making small-scale incremental changes to democratic participation in policy-making processes, because the agenda for political action is dominated by the control which business interests have over economic resources (as accepted in the deformed-polyarchy model mentioned above).

(iv) Some aspects of pluralism and élitism come together in revisionist accounts of democratic processes which suggest that apathy amongst some voters actually aids democratic stability by preventing some less socialized and perhaps more authoritarian individuals from 'spoiling' the political process.

(v) The new right idea that there are public-sector professional élites overlaps with élitism (and managerialism).

(vi) Some pluralists agree with the new right notion that public-sector policy-making processes are unable to keep up with the public's demands for government.

These overlaps give some idea of the richness and complexity of different theories of state form and power relations. Perhaps more importantly, they reiterate how difficult it is to take a neutral or atheoretical view of the state and its constituent functions and apparatus. Rural researchers can gain much from the specific espousal of one or more of these theoretical perspectives. Some will seek to mediate between concepts, and work such as that by Dunleavy and O'Leary helps to isolate areas of convergence. Others will forsake a plurality of theory. Again, it is noticeable that no overlaps were found between Marxism and the new right (unsurprisingly), between Marxism and neo-pluralism, and (perhaps a little surprisingly) between the new right and neo-pluralism.

An awareness of the concepts of state form seems to be an essential prerequisite for understanding policy in the rural context. The status quo (by accident or design) is represented by variations of the pluralist model. Our view differs from this. By viewing the state as a condensate of social relations, and by recognizing that the state derives from the economic and political imperatives of capitalist production, we (along with many others) assume that the state is bound up both in the process of capital accumulation and in the social and spatial impacts of economic restructuring. It follows that policies stemming from state agencies are not unbiased, and so the pluralist status quo misrepresents power relations and state form. We would therefore look to the overlapping aspects of structuralism, élitism, and managerialism for a theoretical basis for informing research into policy-making and planning for rural (and other) areas.

The Function of the State

State form is inextricably linked with state function. Form provides the overriding context within which planning and policy-making occur, and function dictates the roles which planning and policy-making are to perform. An understanding of state function will uncover the hidden agenda for planning. Again, it should be stressed that the literature on state function is of massive proportions, and that we have selected what we think to be the basic theoretical choices for this particular context, dovetailing into the questions raised about state form.

Several theorists (e.g. Mandel, 1975) have defined the function of the state as that of acting to protect and reproduce the existing structures and relations of society and production. At a simplified level, the discussion of state form begs the question of whether protection and reproduction of interests are available to all societal segments or only those of a particularly powerful fragment or combination of fragments of society. In other words, are state functions *aggregate* in nature, and potentially for the benefit of any group or interest, or are they *selective*? Devotees of pluralism will presumably accept an aggregate function of the state. In combination, therefore, these theoretical perspectives suggest a state which is *in* but not *of* capitalist structures, and a portfolio of roles in terms of planning and policy emerges:

regulating the market for the common good;
deregulating public sector intervention so as to stimulate competition for the common good;
neutral arbitration of competing bids for resources, and so on.

Those accepting other explanations of state form and power relations, particularly élitist and structuralist concepts, will tend towards the idea of selective roles for state function. This conceptual pathway could take the form of assuming that the state functions in favour of professional élites and managers in a way which is separate from capital or class interests. Or, perhaps more realistically, this conceptual stance suggests that research relating to planning and policy-making has to deal with the *capitalist state* rather than the state of capitalism. In this case, a different series of state policy functions emerges, ranging from the state as parasite, with no real role in economic production, to the state as an instrument of class rule, buttressing the political domination of labour by capital.

Once again, the emancipation of rural research according to state theory can be purist or pluralist. It is possible to follow through from, say, a Marxist/structuralist perspective of form to a pure distillation of state functions in the capitalist state. Equally a pluralist view of form can be linked with a range of state functions which are democratically derived. However, such polar views of the state can tend to oversimplify the complexity of the functions performed through the state and by its agencies. In our view, any general theoretical portrayal of the state as some kind of puppet dancing to the tune of capitalism, and reacting only to the pulling of strings by dominant social and capital fractions, belies the apparent ability of the state in some circumstances to generate its own autonomous energy and power (Jessop, 1978; 1982). There may well, therefore, be a need to develop a multiple concept of the state which accounts simultaneously for functions which are set by the social relations of capital and for functions generated within a policy environment of localized autonomy and discretion.

Something of this dualism has been discussed by Saunders (1979; 1981*a*). Following on from the work of O'Connor (1973), he sees the state as performing three main functions (Saunders, 1979: 147–8):

Sustenance of private production and capital accumulation:
provision of necessary non-productive urban infrastructure (e.g. road developments);
aiding the reorganization and restructuring of production in space (e.g. planning and urban renewal);
provision of investment in 'human capital' (e.g. education in general and technical-college education in particular);
'demand orchestration' (Holland, 1975) (e.g. local-authority public-works contracts).

Reproduction of labour power through collective consumption:
by means of the material conditions of existence (e.g. low-rent local-authority housing);
by means of the cultural conditions of existence (e.g. libraries, museums, recreation parks).

Maintenance of order and social cohesion:
by coercion (e.g. police);
support of the 'surplus population' (e.g. social services and other welfare support services such as temporary accommodation);
support of the agencies of legitimation (e.g. schools, social work, 'public participation').

From these functions, Saunders discerns two major elements of state intervention:

(i) The corporate level, where the state intervenes on behalf of specific capital interests, either (as historically) by means of regulating the market using policies of social investment such as those relating to agricultural subsidies, or (as recently in some sectors) by way of permitting more freedom to capital accumulation and restructuring through policies of privatization and deregulation.

(ii) The competitive level, where the state intervenes in a less predetermined manner to provide services such as housing, education, and health for dependent populations.

This corporate–competitive division reflects to some extent the theoretical decisions relating to state function. At the *corporate* level, intervention is intertwined with the functions of the capitalist state, and might therefore be regarded to a significant degree as pursuing a selective *reproduction* of the structures and relations of society and production. At the *competitive* level, state activities reflect more of the seemingly autonomous power of the state, and might therefore be seen as more liable to pursue the potential of an *aggregate* state function as suggested by pluralist concepts. Two important caveats should be introduced here. First, intervention at the competitive level operates within the boundaries set by the corporate level, so it can be argued that the state in capitalism is significantly constrained by the capitalist state where conflicts occur between these two functional roles. Second, Saunders made a distinction between the scales of corporate and competitive activity, with the former being located at national and regional scales and the latter being largely a local phenomenon. This distinction has fundamental implications for Saunders's concept of the local state, and we present a critique of this viewpoint in 'Concepts of the Local State' below.

Rural planning and policy-making can be seen in terms of corporate and competitive levels of activity. It can be suggested that the supposedly 'successful' elements of rural planning in the post-war era have been at the corporate level, where strong policies have been generated to provide the infrastructure for capital accumulation in rural areas, notably those favouring agricultural capital. More recently, the conflicts between different capital fractions with interests in rural areas have become more apparent—for example, with industrial, commercial, construction, and agricultural interests all operating in the same arena. Nevertheless, the corporate function still prevails. The slow changes in agricultural policy have been combined with a continued strong emphasis in rural development planning on the provision of infrastructure for industrial and commercial capital activity. Even the recent state intentions in Britain to limit the powers of development planning (see Cloke and McLaughlin, 1989) should be viewed in the context of a state response to those capital interests whose idea of government support takes the form of reduced public spending (thus lowering taxation burdens on capital) and reduced state regulation of private-sector economic activity (thus releasing constraints on processes of accumulation).

Competitive policies of provision have proved somewhat less important than corporate controls, and so policies in the competitive arena may be counted amongst the apparent 'failures' of social planning in rural areas (see e.g. Lowe *et al.*, 1986). Indeed, policies of intervention at the competitive level are of reduced importance in contemporary Western capitalist nations, where the previously established welfare state is being rolled back as governments seem less willing to indulge in policies of social consumption for the purposes of legitimation.

In the past, rural planning issues have sometimes been characterized as a battle between the aims and enactment of physical planning and those of socio-economic planning. The result of this tussle has been declared as a win for physical planning, with state policy systems being shown to be better adapted to land-use control than to regulation of the causes and effects of socio-economic change (Davidson and Wibberley, 1977; Gilg, 1978). The discussion of the theories of state function presented here offers a different interpretation. In these terms, it would be more accurate to explain the relative success of rural land-use planning as a result of the higher priority given by the state to corporate intervention for production compared with competitive intervention for consumption.

The Apparatus of the State

Consideration of the apparatus of the state inevitably reflects the foregoing discussions of form and function. Conceptual choices ranging from pluralism (and therefore an acceptance of a state within capitalism) to structuralism (with an assumption of a capitalist state) lead on directly to a view of the mechanisms through which particular state functions are operated. Briefly, the literature on state apparatus suggests four broad functional categories:

(i) *Consensus*: the apparatus of participation in the processes of society through access to law, democratic government, and so on.

(ii) *Production*: using state apparatus for securing suitable conditions for capital accumulation. Mechanisms within this category range from participation via public-sector production to the regulations of social investment and consumption and, latterly, to the deregulation of various areas of private-sector production and privatization of public production activities.

(iii) *Consumption and legitimation*: a complex interrelationship of apparatus designed to secure both the continued willingness of active and surplus labour to go along with the current social contract and the well-being of society in traditional areas of welfare such as health and education. Various mechanisms of information are also relevant in this category.

(iv) *Administration*: a bureaucratic machine which is given the task of ensuring the smooth running and mutual compatibility of other areas of state apparatus.

Clear implications for the study of rural planning and policy-making arise from this categorization. In particular, the traditional sectoral view of policy—that is, that particular strategies have been specifically designed for use in rural localities, and that researchers should therefore treat these policies as having 'rural' objectives, 'rural' implementation, and 'rural' results—is demolished by the recognition that such policies are spread right across the different categories of state apparatus. So, instead of analysing one seemingly unidirectional policy for, say agriculture or rural communities, we have to take full account of a set of apparently unified planning and policy-making apparatuses which in fact is being used to pursue several different state functions simultaneously.

Examples of the functional overlap of planning apparatus in rural areas abound. Public participation, for instance, (of which we say much more in Chapter 6), is now a statutory part of planning and policy-making procedures following the report of the Skeffington Committee in 1969 (Committee on Public Participation in Planning, 1969). Many would regard public participation as part of the apparatus of *consensus*, representing part of the wish for greater public involvement in policy matters. Such a view might stem from pluralist concepts of power relations and state form, whereby greater formal participation would be an obvious approach towards achieving a wider availability of information about policies and an increased input into policies from a range of interesting parties. Structuralist, élitist, and managerialist concepts point towards public participation more as apparatus of *legitimation*. The ineffectual nature of formal participation in influencing policy decisions adds weight to this view.

Rural planning and policies can also be seen as part of the state's apparatus of *production*. Indeed, there are many policy mechanisms which have contributed towards the creation and maintenance of an environment for capital accumulation in rural localities. The underpinning of agriculture through policies of subsidy and land-use planning controls; the attempts to ensure a continuing supply of land for housing construction; the interpretation of planning regulations to permit industrial and commercial activities on green-field sites; and the relaxation of planning opposition to major developments in rural areas such as nuclear power stations, mineral workings, and transportation routes are all examples of the apparatus of production in rural areas. Production functions have in fact been afforded high priority and some financial stability by the state, particularly in comparison with the expenditure restrictions imposed on implementing policies of consumption. Despite these constraints, the apparatus of *consumption* in rural areas has retained a high profile. Issues of village schools, post offices, health services, and so on receive regular lip-service from decision-makers in state agencies. It could be argued, however, that consumption policies (especially those directed towards welfare functions) have been designed to legitimize the wide operation of the central state and to pre-empt criticism of policies of production rather than to provide a specific response to the problems of rural deprivation (McLaughlin, 1986).

Of equally high profile in the analysis of rural planning and policy-making have been elements of the *administrative* apparatus. Indeed, one of the main perceived objectives of strategic planning has been to co-ordinate the activities of different decision-making agencies in rural areas. Researchers (e.g. Smart and Wright, 1983; Smart, 1987) have noted the problems stemming from the breakdown of inter-agency co-ordination; but, again, the concepts of the state presented here suggest that such a breakdown does not necessarily reflect a need for more rational and all-embracing planning mechanisms. The incompatibility of different areas of state policy could be viewed as the result of conflicting capital interests at the corporate level, or as the outcome of the search for a suitable minimum level of investment in the competitive sphere for the purposes of legitimation. In this context, the lack of co-ordination in planning apparatus might be viewed as a good excuse for not doing more.

Those particular examples of the different functions pursued by the state apparatus are admittedly partial to the British case, and may be more arguable in the context of different nation-states at different times. They do, however, underline the point that seemingly sectoral policies for rural areas do, in fact, represent a multiplicity of functions within a seemingly discrete apparatus. Planning and policy-making are not holistic. Rather, they reflect the broad functions of the state, and thereby represent an amalgam of apparatus through which these various functions are carried out.

It should be stressed that, in this brief review of theories of the state, we are *not* arguing that the outcomes of policy decisions will be constrained to the point of predictability by deterministic concepts of form, function, and apparatus. Clearly, particular policies in particular contexts will be worked out within complex and iterative procedures of bargaining which will shape the final outcome. This mediation of structural precepts by participatory agencies has been strongly illustrated by many researchers, for example, Elson (1986) in his work on the derivation of green-belt policies. These processes will be discussed in detail in Chapter 3. We *do*, however, contend that rural-policy researchers need both to acknowledge the varying assumptions about form, function, and apparatus of the state which underlie their work and to allow their work to be fully informed by the theoretical decisions which they make regarding the state.

CONCEPTS OF THE LOCAL STATE

Thus far in this chapter we have argued that 'rural' policy apparatus should be viewed against the wider political economic background of the form and function of the state. We now turn specifically to local policies which beg similar questions to those already discussed: what is the form and function of the state in its local guise, and how do theories of local government inform policy analysts of the constraints and potentials of decision-making in the local arena?

One of the initial problems with this area concerns semantics. Just as government has been substituted directly for central state and vice versa, the terms 'local government' and 'local state' have tended to be used interchangeably in analyses of local policy arenas. The reason for this is partly pragmatic, in that the most visible and accessible unit of local policy-making is indeed local government, which—being both democratically elected and neatly parcelled into departments with specific functions—is ripe for research activity. Thus, even those who claim a theoretical difference between state and government will often be found conducting their empirical study within the confines of government. For example, Cynthia Cockburn (1977), who coined the term 'local state', focused her empirical work on elected local government, and subsequent commentators have seized on this trend to suggest that 'this makes it relatively unproblematic to interchange the terms local state and local government since in practice they have come to mean the same thing' (Stoker, 1988: 218).

There are, however, as clear theoretical differences between local state and government as there are between central state and government. It should therefore be reiterated that the state relates to functions and agencies dealing with administration, justice, and enforcement as well as those dealing with government and politics. Clearly, there are significant problems of research design and enactment in analysing policy beyond the sphere of local government—as our study in rural Gloucestershire illustrates (see Chapter 4). Nevertheless, there is a clear conceptual distinction between state and government, and this becomes particularly apparent in discussions on the relationship between the centre and the locality.

A second problem with conceptualizing the local state is also linked to this area of central–local relationships. There have emerged, during the 1970s and 1980s, a series of holistic images concerning the local state which revolved around the idea of a consistent political opposition from the periphery to the centre. In this manner Dunleavy (1984: 63–4) highlights two perspectives on local government and central–local relations:

The dominant Marxist view of local government stresses its potential utility as a defence of working-class interests against central government attacks, fiscal retrenchment, and attempts to re-introduce 'market disciplines' into areas of social life previously dominated by 'welfarism'. . . . The second strand of local state literature takes a diametrically opposite view of local government pointing out that working-class mobilisations into local politics . . . were frequently disruptive—designed to force issues such as social insurance, pension provision and hospital care on to the central state's agenda by exposing the limits of local government as a forum for progressive redistribution . . . . A fragmented local government system and the continued decentralisation of functions to local authorities serves mainly to break up this process to the benefit of dominant class interests.

Both these perspectives are predicated on a significant level of working-class involvement in local government activities and a wider participation in other local state institutions.

Indeed, a review of the major trends of central–local relations (Saunders, 1984*a*) suggests that the local state has neither acted as much of a defence against central state attacks nor been successful in influencing the central state agenda in favour of progressive reform. The opposite seems, in fact, to have occurred. Institutions of local government have been restructured so as to enforce uniform, centrally derived policies; local-expenditure support has been revised so as to enforce reductions in social-consumption spending; local corporatist strategies have been designed so as to outflank local democracy; and anti-state sentiments and support for private enterprise solutions have been mobilized to break down popular expectations of social-welfare provision.

In similar vein, Saunders summarizes the plight of local councils. They are faced with an organizational problem of avoiding the enactment of central policies often backed by the law. Attempts to participate in the management of the local economy have usually floundered because of the strength of central controls. The mobilization of groups of consumers of council services so as to raise political opposition to the centre have proved extremely difficult because of the fragmentation of consumption, which is not distributed along the lines of either class or gender. Finally, the advancement of collectivist principles of consumption has been somewhat undermined by the increasing rate of individual aspiration towards private ownership.

In terms of planning and policy, central–local relations have more recently been intertwined with the rise of *anti-planning* ideology, and particular forms of planning deregulation have occurred and are proposed. For example, the day-to-day practice of planning within the apparatus of the local state is being changed significantly, with a reduced role for stategic planning (and thus greater opportunity for developers to bring direct pressure on lower-tier councils, often through the attractiveness of 'planning gain'); with the easing of development restrictions on some agricultural land; with the (as yet) vague ideas for simplified planning zones in some rural areas where a general permission for development might be granted; and with the reduced importance of major planning inquiries. Housing and commercial development is also being deregulated, with the removal of limits in development; with the increasing obligation on planners to nominate suitable development land; and with the increasing success of developers in their appeals against local-authority refusals to develop (Blowers, 1987).

Our understanding of the local state is therefore bound up with aspects of central–local relations in general, and with matters of autonomy and discretion in particular. To what degree is the local state able and willing to make autonomous policy decisions, or to exercise significant discretion in its implementaion of centrally derived policies? The answers to this fundamental question are closely related to the form and function of the local state *vis-à-vis* the central state. Different understandings of emergent policy and planning decisions will come from different conceptual choices. For example, Cooke (1983) offers three interpretative analyses of the degree to which discretion is permitted by the central state:

(i) the local state is a mere agency of the central state, carrying out centrally prescribed duties and policies as part of the overall maintenance of an environment in which capital accumulation is permitted to flourish. Here, the local state has no significant autonomy and discretion and is functional for capitalism. Localized decision-making is 'mainly engaged in legitimizing exercises which hoodwink the public' (Cooke, 1983: 181).

(ii) the local state has occasional autonomy, exercising discretionary powers, but always within the heavily constrained and strictly prescribed limits of the overall state–society relationship (Hirsch, 1981).

(iii) the local state has considerable autonomy in the competitive sector of consumption policies (Saunders, 1979). Referring back to the distinction between corporate policies of production and competitive policies of consumption discussed earlier in this chapter in the context of state function, it is suggested that the local state's activities are primarily in the consumption arena, where activities reflect local pluralist and élitist pressures from individuals, pressure groups, and others involved at the interface between democracy and power.

These conceptual choices are certainly not all-embracing, particularly for those wishing to follow pluralist concepts of power relations through into the local context. They also blur the two rather different strands of interpretation which are available for rural researchers seeking conceptual guidance in this area: central–local relations and the local state.

Central–Local Relations

Traditionally, concepts of central–local relations tended to stagnate around the inter-governmental question of whether local government should be seen merely as an extension or agency of central government, or whether a partnership exists between autonomous but collaborating governments at the central and local level. Within this debate, two concepts of local government have emerged in the pluralist and new right moulds of power relations.

Localism. The localist model is founded on the merits of local democracy, and views local government as the vehicle for such democracy. It has become the rationale for fending off attacks from the centre on local government, and is particularly associated with research and publications commissioned by local authorities and their constituent organizations (Jones and Stewart, 1983; SOLACE, 1986; Widdecombe, 1986; Young, 1986). Indeed, localism has almost become a kind of ideology for those participating in local government. Jones and Stewart (1983) outline four aspects of the ideology:

(i) It is necessary to diffuse power amongst decision-makers and localities so as to represent the dispersion of political power in society.
(ii) *Local* government is the best response to *local* needs. Diversity of response also sponsors innovation, for which there is less scope in centrally directed policy-making.
(iii) Local government is more open to challenge and citizen pressure than centralized government.
(iv) Local government is better able to earn citizen loyalty and involvement than its more remote counterpart.

This localist model esentially follows a pluralist genre of power relations. Although recognizing that local governments cannot give equal status to all the resource demands they receive, localists suggest that, as long as decisions are made by democratically elected representatives in an open and accountable manner, then this is a legitimate and enfranchising form of local power. Localists also acknowledge the organization difficulties which prevent a full responsiveness to the needs of the locality (Greenwood and Stewart, 1986) but adopt a 'something is better than nothing' approach.

In many ways localism seems to reflect what might be, and not what is. Rather than concentrating on a discussion of the constraints which prevent widespread pluralism and local autonomy (as do other approaches), localism makes a series of assumptions about the current anatomy of local power and representation, and about the ability to reform local government. For example, it assumes that local representation will not be usurped by élites or managers for the pursuit of their own interests. It assumes that local representation can adequately deal with the prejudices associated with class, race, and gender. It assumes that social and territorial justice are compatible with democratic representation. Even if it does not assume these things (making these assumptions into aspects of legitimizing the current situation), it assumes that these matters can be put right through the reform of local government at some point in the future. Ultimately, the localist view runs away from its point of origin in central–local relations. Reform is not in the gift of local authorities themselves, but is constrained by the apparent power of the centre over the locality. Only a real partnership between autonomous central and local governments could fulfil these expectations, and there seems to be little available evidence of such partnership, certainly in contemporary Britain.

Public-Choice Theory. Public-choice theory (e.g. Niskanen, 1973) represents for new right followers, at least in part, what localism is for pluralist thinkers. In essence, the market-place is seen as the central mechanism for decisions regarding the allocation of goods and services, and the efficient operation of the market is seen as being hindered by representative democracy and public-sector bureaucracy. As Stoker (1988: 226) has summarized:

Party competition builds up public expectations about what the state can provide as self-interested politicians, seek to maximise their vote. Once in office it is possible for them to disguise the consequences of decisions, with the true economic and fiscal situation being hidden from voters . . . . Politicians and bureaucrats may seek to establish constituencies to support existing and increased levels of spending. Vocal and highly organised interest groups are formed which constantly push for more and better provision to meet their special interests. The losers are the disorganised and silent majority who finance this expenditure.

Thus local government is tagged as being wasteful, inefficient, and profligate (Henney, 1984), characteristics which can be ameliorated through centrally imposed policies of privatization (especially contracting out), deregulation, and the fragmentation of adminis-trative units.

Again, there are some rather obvious and well-known criticisms which can be levelled against the public-choice thesis when applied to local government. First, the approach seems to ignore in-consistencies and defects in the market as the core decision-making arena. Any view of local government as having a welfare function for those with needs, as opposed to those who can pay for services, will clash with the market-place philosophy. Equally, this view of local government ignores any discrimination against the consumers of welfare services on the grounds of class, race, or gender. Such discrimination is assumed not to exist in a situation where ability to pay supposedly transcends class, race, and gender boundaries. In addition there have been serious attacks (e.g. Dunleavy, 1986) on the public-choice assumption that bureaucrats will artifically maximize their budgets. Rather, there seems to be evidence that bureaucrats are just as likely to pursue self-interest through the promotion of self-beneficial work practices and structures as to attempt to secure inflated spending power.

Finally, and perhaps most crucially, the question of just who decides on governmental profligacy must be asked—in simple terms, which tier of government so dominates central–local relations that it can make judgements and implement tactics to reduce the authority of the other? New right and public-choice thinking appears to favour the centre for this role, and it is thus not unfair to suggest that a public-choice view of inter-governmental relations is founded on a dominant centre foisting its own market-driven disciplines on to the locality. This being so, the conceptual judgements made as to the form and functions of the central state are crucial. A non-neutral state will presumably bring its inherent biases into the sphere of local-government reform. This appears to be the case with current new right governments and their dealings with local authorities.

Policy Networks. Not all the conceptualization of central–local relations falls into the localist or public-choice categories. Many researchers, in their critique of central–local directions, have moved into the conceptual arena of the local state (see below); but others have sought to widen the debate to include the broader organizational influences of inter-governmental relations. Key figures in the conceptualization of policy networks have been Dunleavy (1980; 1984) and R. Rhodes (1981; 1985; 1986; 1988). Dunleavy highlighted the need to understand local councils as part of a 'national local government' system. He stressed that relations between central government and local government are intersected by other agencies such as political parties, professional organizations, quangos, and trade unions. While central government influence is paramount, these other agencies also contribute to the form of policy within local government. Rhodes, too, has argued that research should be directed to the ways in which central and local agencies of government bargain with each other through a mesh of individual political, professional, and constitutional links. In effect, he takes the concept of a national system of local government and identifies within it a range of *policy networks*, each of which represents a discrete policy, service, or territorial interest. Analysis is then focused on the individuals and agencies that interact within a particular network. Research on particular networks is illustrated by G. Rhodes (1986) on environmental health and trading standards and by R. Rhodes (1988) on education policy networks.

   Although an interesting and fruitful advance on more traditional themes of inter-governmental relations, the concept of policy networks clearly overstates the importance of organizational power within governmental decision-making. Duncan and Goodwin (1988: 32) point out that this approach

leaves many other key questions unasked—let alone answered—questions about the stakes that the various institutions are bargaining over; about the origin and maintenance of the ideology that pervades the 'rules of the game'; even about the development of the institutions themselves, and why and how they work as they do.

For a wider understanding of the political and economic context of local decision-making, we must turn to theorists who have explicitly attempted to conceptualize the state (as opposed to government) in its local form.

The Local State

Again, there is a danger of undue simplification of the local-state literature within a brief review. Nevertheless, despite the extensive commentary available on the subject, the original contributors to the debate may be represented by three progressions of thought from the late 1970s to the present day.

Cockburn: The Local State as a Functional Part of the Capitalist State. Cockburn (1977) presented empirical evidence of local government in the London Borough of Lambeth. More importantly, however, she presented a theoretical account of the local state based on Marxist principles, as translated in particular by Poulantzas. Her view is conditioned by the existence of a capitalist state which functions as a relatively autonomous mechanism of class domination, and which manages economic and social reproduction in the interests of capital as a whole. The local state is an integral part of the whole, and performs a role in the overall functions of domination and management in its local territory. In particular, the local arm of the state was responsible for the reproduction of the local labour force, including the provision of those welfare services required to maintain a co-operative and accessible group of workers and thus to ensure the continuation of local production.

Cockburn's view of the local state suffers from its functionalist acceptance of the central state as some kind of immovable given phenomenon. If the central state has no history of change, conflict, confusion, and contradiction, then the local state cannot be theorized as exhibiting these characteristics. Here there seems to be a major problem, as there *is* evidence of continuous conflict in inter-governmental relations throughout the twentieth century. If local government were a static mechanism of class control, there would seem to be no justification for granting it any aspect of electoral control or any element of autonomy or discretion. We are being asked to believe that central and local governments, and other institutions, willingly collaborate to promote the interests of capital, and that local agencies willingly subordinate themselves to the centre. There is little evidence to support these contentions.

Cockburn's view of the local state has been much criticized by commentators of various ideological persuasions. Duncan and Goodwin (1988: 34) again get to the heart of the matter:

Cockburn thus reduces two contradictory social processes of the local state—that it is simultaneously agent and obstacle for the national state—to those of a one-way agent. Not only does this ignore a whole aspect of local state activity—that which opposes the centre—but it also reduces social relations between active human agents to purely functional operations. This results from the search for a universal model of a thing—the capitalist state—which can be applied to all places at all times using one 'model' of activity as the basis of understanding. This line of reasoning is thus misleading, historically and conceptually.

Saunders: The Dual-State or Dual-Politics Model. Saunders (1981*a*; 1982; 1984*a*; 1985; 1986), sometimes in collaboration with Cawson (1982; Cawson and Saunders, 1983) has introduced and gradually reformulated the dual-state thesis. Basically, it takes the two roles mentioned above (p. 55) in the discussion of the function of the state:

(i) The *corporate* level of state intervention in the arena of production: Decisions here are made by state officials, along with a small, privileged selection of producer groups, professional bodies, and trade unions whose co-operation is required in order to ensure the successful enactment of policies of social investment to aid capital accumulation.

(ii) The *competitive* level of state intervention in the arena of consumption: Decisions here represent a more open and democratic process of competitive lobbying between different interest groups, and elections and public opinion are far more important than at the corporate level.

and suggests that each takes place at a different level, with policies of social investment for production being a *central* function, and policies for social consumption being a mainly *local* function (Table 2.2). The local state is thus characterized both by this consumption role and also by distinctive political processes, incorporating a wide range of competitive struggles between interest groups who are mobilized around issues of consumption.

Table 2.2. The Specificity of the Local State

	Level		Tension: Central control versus local autonomy
	Central/regional	Local	
Economic function	Social investment	Social consumption	Economic versus social-policy priorities
Mode of interest mediation	Corporate bias	Competitive struggles	Rational direction versus democratic accountability
Ideological principle	Private property	Citizenship rights	Profit versus need

Source: Saunders, 1981c: 32.

An open and democratic access to power within the local state is envisaged, and hence a very different concept of the local state from that of Cockburn emerges. Saunders argues that pluralist concepts are generally most appropriate in the arena of the local state, and that local politics tend to revolve around the ideology of need because of their preoccupation with consumption issues. However, he is careful to stress that pluralistic potential in the locality is tightly constrained by the very different power relations of corporate politics within the central state, where the ideology of need is replaced by the ideology of property (or greed?).

Several criticisms of the dual-state thesis have been made during the conceptual debates of the 1980s. Two assumptions have been particularly scrutinized. First, the assumption that there is a clear distinction between the corporatist politics of the centre and the competitive politics of the locality has been questioned. Any inflexible categorization of the political functions which characterize the state in its national and local form can be repudiated by examples of corporatism in the locality and competition at the centre. Although the strength of Saunders's argument is that the local state is *typically* concerned with competitive issues and politics, he himself admits: 'Since most state policies will involve some relevance for both production and consumption, it can be difficult to disentangle the two and to distinguish empirically between primarily-production orientated and primarily-consumption orientated interventions' (1986, 44); and the work of Dunleavy (1984) has shown that only about one-third of local-authority expenditure can be seen as directed towards consumption issues, the remainder being in the areas of housing, education, and highways, which all contribute to production and capital accumulation.

A second questionable assumption concerns the pluralist nature of local politics. Again, Saunders (1981*b*: 271) admits that, in some areas of the local state, 'one particular section of the population may achieve a virtual stranglehold over the local political process'—conditions which are not particularly conducive to pluralist power relations.

A third area of debate highlights the focus of the dual-*state* thesis on *government*, rather than explicitly dealing with the functions of administration, justice, and enforcement which collaborate in the wider view of the state. Saunders's work has been criticized because it underestimates the role of the administrative professions in decision-making (Dunleavy, 1984). Equally, any local functions of justice and enforcement are not brought into the competitive thesis. Indeed, they appear to be strongly motivated by the ideology of private property, and the politics of corporatism.

To be fair, Saunders has revised much of the early rigidity of the dual-state thesis in his later work. In particular, he has replaced the idea that state function determines state politics with the notion that it is 'the saliency of a given area of producer interests' (1986: 35) which explains whether an issue is resolved nationally or locally. Stoker (1988: 237) captures the irony of this revision of the concept:

this (new) approach appears to lead to a crude instrumentalism and determinism—of the form that capital interests 'get the state and the politics they want'—which the dual state thesis was initially and consciously designed to avoid.

Duncan and Goodwin: Social Relations and the Local State. The contribution of Duncan and Goodwin (1982*a*; 1982*b*; 1985; 1988) to local-state concepts has been to relate the local state to wider understandings of social relations and social change, and to view the local state as a process of social relations rather than as a static phenomenon.

Rather than concentrating on descriptions of things or structures that are essentially outcomes of social processes, it may be more useful to focus on the causal processes themselves. It should then be possible to *explain* the nature of state actions and changes therein, rather than just describe them. State forms and actions can then be linked to changing relations between groups of people instead of being left as socially inexplicable organizational forms or bundles of given functions. Just as the capitalist state is a historically formed social relation, so are state institutions at the local level. (1988: 38).

Successful pursuit of a concept of the local state relating to social relations therefore requires answers to two sets of questions:

(i) What is the nature of those social relations which are institutionalized in the capitalist state?
  'Why are relations of gender and production, and other social relations taking place outside the state in workplaces, households and communities, not sufficient for the reproduction of

society in advanced captialism? Why must there be states?'
(Duncan and Goodwin, 1988: 38)
(ii) What is the particular local dimension of institutionalized
social relations?
'Do local social transactions take place in local state institutions,
specific to local areas and autonomous from those taking place
in the national state?'   (pp. 38–9)

In answer to the first group of questions, Duncan and Goodwin
argue that capitalist states transform important social and economic
differentials and relations between, for example, gender, class,
and race groups into legal and artificial relations of supposed
equality. Consequently, state representatives can define and
discuss 'the public interest' when in reality there is only a
collectivity of interests arising from different social relations.
Neither is the state's involvement static. Its *interpretative* role of
artificial relations is continually under threat from the organization
of particular social groups (for example in industrial action, public
demonstration, and so on). Such threats inevitably result in
changing social relations in the state to ensure the upkeep of the
state's legitimacy (and suitable overall conditions for accumulation).

The second question relating to the local dimension of state
social relations is answered in terms of the uneven development in
capitalist nations. Duncan and Goodwin stress that class relations,
gender roles, political cultures, and so on differ according to
localities. Therefore there is a need for different policies in
different localities, and local state agencies are required to
administer these various policies. Nevertheless, uneven development also means that social groups will be spatially constituted,
and that particular groups can dominate these local state agencies,
using them to promote their own interests, even if these are out of
line with centrally dictated requirements. Hence, Duncan and
Goodwin suggest that local states have a *representational* role in
addition to the interpretative role discussed above. Trade unionists
or farmers, perhaps lacking a constant privileged access to the
central capitalist state but able to muster considerable support in
particular localities, can use the local state to represent their own
interests, even if this means opposing central decisions. The centre
will wish to neutralize these local representational interests but,

equally, will have to support a local-state structure so as to continue intervening in locally differentiated social relations.

With the widespread and rapid economic restructuring and social recomposition in Britain in the 1980s, the conflict between interpretative and representational roles has increased. New local coalitions have emerged, most starkly in metropolitan areas, and so the need for central interests to curtail local powers has become more important. The 'crisis' of central–local relations, therefore, is seen to stem from changing social relations:

> It is clear that there is no given need for housing provision, education, police, social welfare or anything else that is managed by the state, to be mixed up in a local electoral system based on universal franchise. In many capitalist countries this is not the case and an equal or greater part of capitalist history, Britain included, has been without such a system. Indeed many state functions fluctuate to and from the local electoral orbit. It is thus not its functions that give the local state its specificity, but the contradiction inherent in its representational and interpretative roles, a contradiction that is activated and sustained through uneven spatial development of social relations.   (Duncan and Goodwin, 1988: 43)

Duncan and Goodwin's work has its critics. Dunleavy and Husbands (1985) suggest that it overemphasizes local experience in the alignment of political viewpoints; this, however, might be contradicted by evidence that national issues sometimes dominate local elections owing to the dominance of the national press and national political parties. Stoker (1988) regards the alliance of representational and interpretative roles in the local state as being uncritical and unduly deterministic. Do central authorities not introduce major social welfare reforms in the interests of non-capitalist groups? How do particular interest groups achieve domination of local authorities? Does not the translation of ideology into policy mean that more emphasis should be placed on the mechanics of administrative policy-making? In the end, Stoker rather rudely dismisses Duncan and Goodwin's work as a 'rationale for "gesture" politics' (p. 240).

Despite these criticisms, it is our contention that concepts of the local state and social relations as outlined by Duncan and Goodwin are of specific relevance to those who are interested in the local state in rural localities. The concepts relating to central–local relations, discussed above, leave much to be desired. Localism tends to be more concerned with potential than explanation, and leaves the door open for uncritical pluralism. Public choice, in its focus on market forces, merely presents a legitimating disguise for capital interests, not explaining the constraints, functions, and relations of the state, but merely espousing sectional interests and hoping to persuade that these are in the general interest. The work on policy networks is interesting and rewarding, but only when placed in a social and political context which is wider than that of government institutions.

Concepts of the local state attempt to provide that wider context. Structuralist concepts appear too deterministic and instrumentalist for those seeking to understand differentiation within the local state. The dual-state thesis is valuable in highlighting the different functions of the state, but encounters major problems of interpretation when attempting to attribute the specificity of the local state of particular competitive politics and consumption functions. The dilemma of the dual state—the apparently simultaneous roles of the local state as an arm of the central state and as an autonomous local policy-making phenomenon—are directly addressed in Duncan and Goodwin's work. Their focus on social relations emphasizes change and diversity, and provides a framework for understanding potential differences between localities.

THE LOCAL STATE AND RURAL AREAS

The final question to be addressed in this chapter concerns the possibility of identifying particular characteristics of the local state in rural areas. It is not our intention here to repeat a discussion on the definition of *rural* and the parameters of the *rural–urban relationship*. Our position on these matters is clearly stated in the preface of this book, and elsewhere (e.g. Cloke, 1989a). There are, however, several unresolved issues relating to the localized character of the state. Do local states differ? Are spatial characteristics an important factor in this difference, and if so, what effect do they have? Is it possible to discern any commonality in rural local states, and if so, how much internal variation occurs? These questions need to be tackled using the foregoing discussion of theories of the local state as a foundation for analysis.

Reference to most theories of the local state will suggest that local states *do* differ. For example, the work of Duncan and

Goodwin is predicated on the unevenness of capital development being reflected in social relations, which in turn are important in shaping the local state. Empirical evidence appears to support this contention. Whichever indicator of the local state is selected, it will, when mapped out, display variations between local state units. Fig. 2.2 illustrates this variation with regard to expenditure by county councils in England and Wales. For whatever reason,

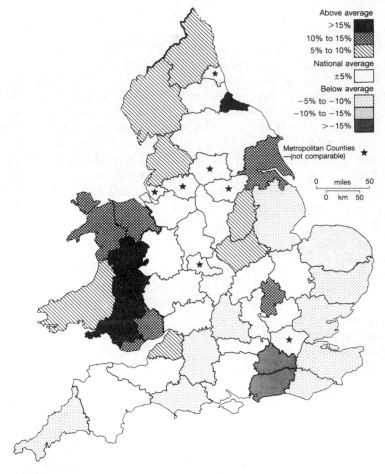

FIG. 2.2. Variations in Expenditure by County Councils, 1984–1985
Source: Duncan and Goodwin, 1988: 7

different local authorities demonstrate varying levels of public expenditure, despite increasing controls over spending by central government. Studies of local government (e.g. Alexander, 1982; Byrne, 1983; Gyford, 1984) are littered with evidence that local authorities do possess some leeway in their relations with the central state. These variations between local states suggest that fundamental structuralist models can only represent part of the picture, and that local states do reflect characteristics of locality, local political economy, and local social relations.

The second question addresses the relationship between space and localization of the state. This has been a core issue in discussions concerning the *raison d'être* of human geography in recent years (Gregory and Urry, 1985), and is no less relevant when the focus is specifically on the geography of the state. The broad outcome of these discussions is that there do appear to be legitimate reasons for looking at local state activities in particular localities. Taylor (1985), for example, has traced a series of recent spatial and aspatial perspectives on state activity. Dealing with the work (predictably) of urban researchers, he highlights Pahl's (1970) managerialist thesis as reaffirming the traditional urban spatial unit. Moving on to the work of Castells (1977), he notes that the city has come to be viewed as a unit of collective consumption, and that urban problems in reality reduce to localized conflicts over public management of that consumption in particular spheres of housing, planning, and so on. Dunleavy (1980) has described this as a *content* definition of the urban field, on which basis the *spatial* manifestation of the urban unit is unnecessary. The complete banishment of the spatial frame of reference is argued by Abrams (1978), who contends that urban areas are merely arenas for social interrelations rather than being socially relevant themselves.

These comments on the aspatial nature of social studies are themselves cogent reasons for including rural areas in the broad domain of the political-economy approach which has thus far been so urban-centred. The work of Urry (1981a), however, has to some extent revitalized the spatial unit in social science by demonstrating that the spatial form of social phenomena can influence social relations. Thus, in particular localities the political mobilization of class interests may differ, just as the representation of classes in that part of society itself differs. Localities, therefore, might reflect variations in the nature of activity by the local state in these different social and political contexts.

The important thing to avoid here is what has become known as spatial fetishism, whereby the contingent effect of the variegation of social relations is confused with the effect of spatial relations—the latter leading to 'urban' or 'rural' local states. As Duncan and Goodwin (1988: 52) stress:

> The hidden supposition is that particular spatial arrangements, in this case the distinction between urban and rural areas, have some independent causal power. This is not the case, and by speaking of 'the urban' we are really talking about social relations like access to housing, racial discrimination or the costs of traffic congestion, or even natural processes like the physical effects of pollution. Unfortunately, calling these urban only confuses the issue.

It is, therefore, the social relations for which we use the shorthand 'rural' which might give the local state a distinctive character in the localities we are dealing with, and not the independent causal powers of rurality which do so. This reinforces our discussion of rurality in the preface of this book.

Duncan and Goodwin's analysis clarifies the debate over social relations and spatial structures so far as 'rural' researchers are concerned. Space makes a difference in social processes in three main ways:

contingent local variation, where spatial contingency affects how social mechanisms operate in practice;
causal local variation, where social mechanisms are derived locally;
locality effects—a rare occurrence where 'a bundle of complementary and locally derived processes and outcomes produce some sort of local social system. (Duncan and Goodwin, 1988: 61)

A search for a 'rural' local state, therefore, should be replaced by an attempt to understand the collective effects of contingency, causality, and locality in particular areas. We will not be looking for a deterministic connection between particular levels of development and forms of social relations on the one hand and certain kinds of local state policies on the other. We cannot, therefore, predict that a locality, for example, with a longstanding agricultural tradition will have evolved a particular form of local state. Although agricultural labour is easily characterized as deferential, there are agricultural areas where significant labour struggles have occured (Dickens *et al.*, 1985). Production and development will be mediated through local social practices and immersed in local cultures, whether real or imaginary. Thus any deterministic representation of a collective 'agricultural' or 'rural' local state will ignore the rich diversity inherent in these mechanisms.

Our view, then, of the shire counties, for example, as some kind of relatively homogeneous block of local-state institutions is as quaintly old-fashioned as some of the images of rural Britain which still pervade popular culture. Thus the changing social relations in one shire, or even within different parts of one shire, should not be expected to determine similar local-state character-istics to those in another. These variations can be simply illustrated. Newby (1988: 39) has painted a graphic picture of social relationships in suburban rural England:

Many newcomers value the presence of the farming population, if only because it serves as a reminder that the village remains truly rural rather than a kind of rustic suburbia. But the locals can be assigned a definite place in the scheme of things. They can be 'characters', sources of quaint bucolic humour or homespun rural philosophy on such matters as the weather, but not expected to put forward views which intrude on the newcomer's sense of how things should be done. What are demanded are pet locals who adorn the landscape along with the fields and the trees.

Although this is obviously a stylized account, not all social relations in rural localities fit this pattern. In rural Wales, for example, where the influx of commuters has in places been smaller, where local culture is vibrant, and where there is no 'newcomer' hegemony over local government, a very different formation of development, social relations, and local state might be envisaged.

The risk is, then, that rural researchers will swing from an extreme interest in spatial fetishism to an equally extreme concern for the unique and the particular. Is there a middle ground? One way forward is to seek out the contingent local variations, causal local variations, and locality effects which commonly affect social mechanisms in rural areas. Traditional analyses do suggest some specificities for rural localities. Fig. 2.3, for example, illustrates Moseley's (1980*a*) succinct summary of these urban–rural relation-

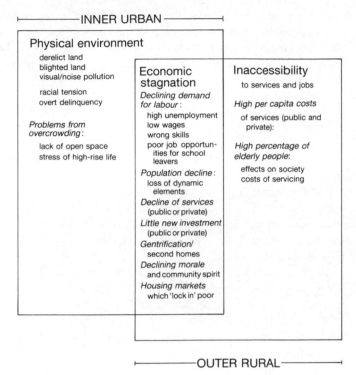

FIG. 2.3. Urban and Rural Britain: Overlapping Sets of Problems
Source: Moseley, 1980*a*: 97

ships in which it is suggested that a particular *rural dimension* is made up of three basic characteristics:

(i) a pleasant environment—which will attract the willing or unwilling unemployed;

(ii) a 'spaced-out' geographical structure—leading to accessibility problems and costly public services;

(iii) a distinctive local political ideology—favouring the market, the volunteer, and the self-helper rather than public provision.

These characteristics are not the cause of social relations in rural areas, and problems such as socio-economic deprivation are fundamentally the same as in urban localities. Nevertheless, the rural dimension does impose at least a façade of specificity which potentially serves to influence the activities of the local state.

The links between the façade of specificity in rural areas and the underlying social relations which help shape the central state and its activities require particular emphasis. For example, the 'spaced-out' nature of rural areas present obvious servicing difficulties, which can only be overcome by state intervention in service markets, or by accepting that only those who can afford to pay can expect to live in this kind of locality. Power from dominant social relations centrally can alter the equation between state provision and market-centred provision (witness the current drive towards privatization—Bell and Cloke, 1989) and locally can dictate the local state's use of autonomy and discretion to provide or subsidize services. The pleasant rural environment is increasingly attracting affluent residents who are fuelling the distinctively conservative local political ideology referred to by Moseley. This ideology is translated into local policies, for example in the planning sector.

An illustration of local power relationships is provided by Buller and Hoggart (1986), who have studied the links between rural residents of 'higher socio-economic status', attempting to preserve the quality of their living environment, and both developers wishing to build and planners in local authorities who are able to grant or refuse planning permission. They argue that power is exerted in two important areas of 'nondecision-making':

First developers are reluctant to submit applications for residential development in areas dominated by groups of higher social standing for 'fear' of invoking local opposition. Second . . . local planning authorities are similarly reluctant to approve applications for residential development in such areas. What makes this a nondecision effect is that the restraint demands of the higher status areas need not be stated overtly for any particular planning application. Rather it qualifies as nondecision-making since both developers and local planning authorities anticipate, and then act upon their anticipation of, possible negative consequences should an application be made or approved.   (p. 197)

Chapter 1 introduced a number of different aspects of social relations in rural localities which might also be regarded as contingent and causal variations affecting broader social mechanisms. One example of contingent local variations is the operation of local class relations in rural society. Clearly, such relations, as noted in Chapter 1, are a function of the historical evolution of the wider relationship between capital and labour in contemporary industrial society. Specific local variations in, for example, the ownership of property or the organization of land tenure may have ensured, however, that class relations in one particular community have evolved in a unique way. The fundamental principle of social division, in such cases, is class, but the way in which this principle has shaped the well-being and personal relationships of individuals within the rural community is a function, not of class alone, but of its interaction with other national, international, and local variables. Such interaction will inevitably be locally specific.

In contrast, causal local variations imply the local derivation of social mechanisms. Examples here are more difficult to identify, since the majority of social mechanisms operate at a broader spatial scale and are derived at a national or global level. Local status systems may, however, fit this classification. Notoriously strong in rural areas, status systems generally evolve around highly specific local historical customs and roles. It may be argued that such systems operate independently of social class, being more dependent on, for example, the possession of skills in relation to rural crafts, kinship ties, and local authenticity rather than the outward display of personal wealth. The influx of large numbers of 'outsiders' into rural areas—people with no background in or knowledge of local status systems but with (very often) an entirely different set of values, is helping to break down traditional systems and to introduce new values based, to a much higher degree, on conspicuous consumption.

Examples of Duncan and Goodwin's third category, locality effects, are even more difficult to present, since such examples incorporate, supposedly, a complete local social system, not simply individual social mechanisms. It could be argued that the evolution and operation of local kinship relations does produce a very specific social system in its own right. Kinship networks pervade all aspects of rural life, incorporating ideological, political, and practical characteristics from the notion of 'belonging' to the operation of community care. Such ties also act to exclude certain members of rural society, and can prove powerful mechanisms for commanding social status and local recognition.

Another way forward may be to trace any common themes in local states in rural localities which might then suggest some commonality in underlying social relations. This is not to ignore previous warnings about the rich diversity of social relations and uneven development in different localities. However, there are some very interesting features of the local states with jurisdiction over rural areas, and these do beg questions of commonality at some level or other. One obvious common theme is manifest in central–local relations in rural localities which, in aggregate, have been politically conservative. For example, it has been suggested (Dearlove, 1979) that the 1974 reorganization of local government in Britain represented a specific measure to reduce the domination of urban councils by working-class representatives. Larger districts, which entailed the abolition of the specific urban–rural administrative divide, gave the opportunity for increased business and professional representation on local authorities, and in this way the teeth of socialist councils in urban areas could be drawn. The mid-1980s, of course, have seen a much more direct method of dentistry, namely the abolition of the metropolitan county councils where socialist administrations generally held sway.

What, then, was the impact of these measures on *rural* areas? Central state would have expected little change in the political constitution of rural locality councils, since old-style agricultural conservatism should have been compatible with professional and commercial Toryism. This expectation was borne out to a certain extent, but as Taylor (1985: 220–1) notes:

Traditional organization within councils was to be streamlined. An integrated approach was required and necessitated a corporate management structure. This strengthened the unelected officers at the expense of councillors . . . . Streamlining organization simply meant making local government operate like a business . . . . In many ways this reorganization back-fired on the central government. Business organization is geared for expansion and this is what happened in local government.

Central state manœuvring of the local state in rural localities therefore actually increased the probability of disharmony. Counties and districts in rural localities became subject to the central state's programmes of financial austerity in just the same way as their more urban counterparts. Reductions in funding for service provision were followed by increasing central control of local budgets, either by diverting funds through centrally derived agencies (such as the Development Commission and CoSIRA) or by direct penalties for overspending (Boddy, 1983).

Whereas it might have been expected that a sympathetic

political partnership might have been struck between conservative local authorities in rural areas and the central state (particularly when the latter was under Conservative party control), these local authorities have in fact suffered a double handicap within the central–local relationship. First, they have been passive agents in the central state's primacy of power over important rural resources. Most obviously, matters concerning the major land-uses of agriculture and forestry represent significant gaps in the power and responsibilities of the local state. There resources certainly constitute important exclusion zones in the planning of rural localities. Other areas of potential control such as the promotion of individual development have, without undue quibble, also been channelled into non-democratic organizations such as the Development Commission and the Development Boards in the Highlands and Islands and Mid-Wales. The second handicap has been that, for all their passivity in these matters, rural locality authorities have been just as subject to the central-government penalties of the 1970s and 1980s as their more radical and progressive urban counterparts.

The platform for the conservatism of the rural local state lies in the democratic consistency of political representation therein over the last thirty years or more. Even taking account of the transition in some areas from the dominance of farmer-landowner groups to coalitions with newcomer populations, rural localities are ruled by the middle class, for whom the accessibility problems caused by a spaced-out geographical environment are not considered a problem. Pressure groups, where they exist, reflect agricultural and conservation issues rather than those of the socio-economic problems of the working class. As Gilg (1985: 107) states:

the majority of rural inhabitants are very satisfied and happy with their life-style, and have consciously chosen to live in the countryside. Many of these people are moreover less concerned with the socio-economic issues . . . but more with the changing environment of the countryside and the increasing pressures being placed upon it.

This state of affairs merely reinforces the existing central-state constraints on progressive policies for the rural deprived. Newby (1981: 239) notes:

the deprived section has found it increasingly difficult to obtain recognition of its requirements, let alone feel capable of diverting a larger proportion of resources in its direction. The economics of public service provision have suffered from the self-reliance of the newcomers, who, as ratepayers, have demonstrated an understandable reluctance to foot the rapidly rising bill on behalf of their less fortunate neighbours. All too often this is the political reality (and it seems unlikely to change) which underlies the neglect of housing, public transport and the whole range of social, health and welfare services in rural areas.

The current social structure and political allegiances of most contemporary rural areas merely reinforces existing central-state constraints on progressive policies for the deprived. Clearly, the exercise of any available discretion by the local state will be far more circumspect in rural localities where these political conditions exist than in other localities.

Within these broad generalizations there exists, inevitably, a degree of variation between the local governments of rural localities. For example, Glover (1985) has illustrated considerable differences between shire counties in terms of their socio-economic and transport expenditure. What is clear, however, is that the political conservatism of rural localities presents an ideal breeding-ground for élitist policy-making within local states (Hoggart, 1981). Here again, some form of commonality emerges in the links between local social relations, power, and the local state in many rural areas. Glover's research in Bedfordshire and Devon uncovered consistent vesting of decision-making power with key council officers. In the Bedfordshire case he notes:

the officers clearly demonstrate an awareness of how to use council rules and procedures to exert influence in the political process and how to further their aims with persuasive and sound technical arguments. The record of stability in public transport policy is one that they are proud of and indeed this stability appears almost to be seen as an important goal to aim for in itself. It merits an effort to 'educate' the politicians about it, and convince them of its values . . . . (Glover, 1985: 145)

These senior professional actors, when working in tandem with political gatekeepers, are the key to understanding the degree to which available discretion is exercised by the local state in rural localities. Buchanan's (1982) review of the preparation of the Suffolk structure plan confirms this view, illustrating the way in which a small élite (namely the two chairs of the planning committees and three senior officers in the county planning department) 'exercised considerable influence' over all aspects of the preparation of the plan.

Perhaps the most cogent and succinct summary of power relations in the local state in rural localities is provided by Blowers (1980: 37):

Planning is a dependent activity, subservient to the needs of the state, and therefore the potential for independent action is severely limited. But, within the limitations prescribed by the necessity to ensure the maintenance of the prevailing pattern of social relationships, planners exert considerable influence and power. And it is a power that is unequally distributed, being concentrated among a few officals and politicians . . . the distribution between administration and politics becomes irrelevant, what matters is the relationship between those leading politicians and officials who are responsible for the development of policy and its implementation, and their interaction with the powerful interests in society at large.

So far as rural planning and policy-making is concerned, therefore, the likelihood of adoption and implementation of progressive redistributive policies to counteract rural deprivation depends on the motivation of these key actors—the degree of paternalism and beneficence amongst councillors and the degree to which politically motivated officers can exercise the 'art of the possible' in their working environment—and on their ability to overcome central-state equilibrium procedures within the confines of structural constraints operating on the working of the local state.

This picture of the local state and rural areas falls into two distinct halves. First, the theoretical view is that to think of a *rural* local state amounts to spatial fetishism, because of the unspoken expectation that rurality itself acts as a causal factor in the differentiation of local-state activity. Rather, we might conceive of a series of local states which exist and act in response to a series of different local contingencies and locality effects. By contrast, the empirical evidence of local government in rural areas suggests some broad similarities in terms of political conservatism, central–local relations, and the nature of local power relations. Clearly, much more work needs to be done to bring these two halves together. Are the commonalities of local-state policy in rural areas the result of common forms of social relations, or is local social differentiation, as expressed through the local state, sufficiently constrained by central-state policy for differentiation not to be transferred into variations in decision-making? In the next chapter we look in depth at the theory and practice of implementing policies for rural areas, and in Chapter 4 we attempt to bridge the gap between concept and empirical study with an account of policy derivation and enactment for rural areas within one particular part of a local state.

3

Planning, Policy, and Implementation

INTRODUCTION

As the subtitle of this book suggests, our overall objective is to consider the constraints applied to planning and policy-making in rural areas. In Chapter 2 it was strongly argued that planning and policy are aspects of state activity, and should therefore be understood in terms of theories of the state, both central and local. Although the notion of a *rural* local state is rejected *per se*, it is suggested that particular commonalities of social relations exist between different non-urban localities and that, as a consequence, the local state in these areas can display some similar characteristics so far as policies and planning are concerned. These common phenomena are associated both with the strong central-state constraints on local-state activity in some sectors (which can reduce local variation to a kind of apparent uniformity) and with the power relations enjoyed by locally dominant élites (which, although potentially different in different localities, exhibit a common bond of conservatism so far as land-use and socio-economic planning issues are concerned).

This chapter builds on the theories of the state presented in Chapter 2. Here we seek to understand the more localized mechanisms by which policies for rural areas are made and enacted. Later in the chapter we present a detailed study of policy implementation issues in a specific arena—that of structure plans for rural areas. First, though, there is a need to take a critical look at concepts of planning and implementation. Just as a particular view of the form and function of the state will colour an understanding of policy apparatus for rural areas, so a particular standpoint on the nature and process of planning will determine any subsequent analysis of the capabilities and constraints associated with current mechanisms in any particular nation-state or sub-national area.

PLANNING AND IMPLEMENTATION

In 1983, a review of rural-settlement planning concluded that it is far easier to pin-point the faults in current rural planning than it is to offer potentially realistic improvements (Cloke, 1983). It suggested that many of the policy alternatives being evaluated by rural researchers actually bore very little relation to the way in which rural resource management decisions were being made. Equally, it presented substantial evidence that policy changes were necessary because of progressive trends of imbalanced resource distribution and social inequity in rural communities. Four groups of potential policy options were offered as an agenda for a more realistic debate on the identification of possible rural strategies:

(i) Continue with a *laissez-faire* approach of exclusive rural conservationism. Resource rationalization will then continue under free-market promptings, and small rural settlements will thus be conserved, eventually, only for those who can afford to live there. Rural areas will thus be subject to rampant gentrification and geriatrification.

(ii) Recognize the need for some additional opportunity provision in rural settlements to tackle rural disadvantage, but only within strict budgetary limitations. Emphasis here will be on the prompting of self-help and community action schemes, perhaps through the formation of a comprehensive system of local administrators and community workers, acting as initiators for local efforts. However, such actions are often insufficient to provide more than temporary first aid for the symptoms of rural problems.

(iii) Realize that low-cost solutions are only a small part of the answer, and bring about a resource reallocation in favour of measures directed towards the opportunity deficiencies suffered by certain disadvantaged groups in all locations. In rural areas, indirect action through subsidy of partnership and direct action by government bodies can do much to provide essential services to such groups where the need exists, provided that sufficient resources are found for the task. This option requires that traditional views of rural-settlement planning should be swept away and a new social welfare-orientated process be substituted, in which the goals and objectives of planning are directed at the well-being of rural communities.

(iv) Take the structural view that, even if a combination of government action, subsidy, and self-help were able to provide a satisfactory opportunity base in rural areas for all rural residents, some of the underlying causes of deprivation will remain. This is because certain sections of the rural community will have insufficient disposable income to make use of the opportunities, regardless of whether they are on site, peripatetic, or at the other end of some form of accessibility link. Such a situation requires radical policies of personal subsidy and wealth redistribution, so that satisfactory incomes are available both to those in full employment and to those who choose the voluntary simplicity of life-style which may be one corner-stone of the future of rural areas.

This review, although only based on the events of the 1970s and early 1980s, reveals two long-standing truisms in the analysis of planning and policy in rural areas. First, that planning has not proved capable of achieving the socio-economic and land-use objectives which some commentators have expected of it. This might be thought of as 'the problem'. Second, it is usual to disentangle planning from its political roots by way of a pragmatic assessment of what is possible in particular governmental circumstances. Thus the options listed above are presented as a kind of stepwise progression, each requiring a greater lifting of political constraint in order to enable more radical policies to be adopted. These might be thought of as 'political pragmatics'.

We would argue that the ways in which the 'problem' and the 'political pragmatics' are conceptualized is of overwhelming importance in the treatment of policy shortcomings and the implementation of alternative policies. The yawning divide between planning intentions and planning practices has been discussed elsewhere (Cloke, 1987). Planning has been strongly criticized for failing to regulate the market-based changes which have exacerbated the problems of social polarization and disadvantage amongst rural communities and the problems of land-use associated with landscape and wildlife conservation. But how many of these shortcomings can be blamed on planning? There are two broad ways of looking at this issue (Cloke and Hanrahan, 1984).

First, it can be suggested that the impact of existing planning policies in rural areas has been significantly restricted by problems with the actual procedures of implementation. For example, Blacksell and Gilg's (1981) research on planning permissions and refusals for housing in parts of rural Devon highlights the existence of a 'policy–implementation gap' whereby the planned location of new housing did not match the actual location of planning permissions. The suggestion prompted by such a gap is that an *implementation problem* exists, and that if only better techniques of implementation could be devised, the problems of planning response to the social and economic needs of rural areas could be dealt with. Implementation problems thus perceived are ultimately capable of resolution as long as logical and rational planning procedures are pursued. From this viewpoint, then, better technical implementation will result in more successful planning.

Secondly, the apparent failure of planning in rural areas may be viewed in a context whereby suitable policies are being precluded within the complex political arena in which the planning is situated. This idea of a *policy problem* hinges on the treatment of what constitutes a 'suitable' policy (considered by whom suitable for whom?), and may therefore be avoided by those who wish to retain a technical form of policy analysis devoid of implicit or explicit connotations.

Our discussion of planning and policy in their state context (Chapter 2) reinforces our argument that the first, technical viewpoint has little to offer. Even those who are content with current planning objectives in rural areas, and who therefore are not acting as advocates for change to more 'suitable' policies, might be criticized for looking at policy and implementation as some kind of dichotomy which ignores the practical complexities of how things actually get done (or don't get done) in contemporary rural planning. Certainly, those seeking to interpret 'suitable' policies as those which in some way aim to tackle issues of uneven development, social disadvantage, and class struggle will consider a policy–implementation dichotomy as an inadequate and misleading portrayal of the various internal survival mechanisms working within the planning process to repel socially progressive policies (Knox and Cullen, 1981).

In commending the second of these two approaches, we suggest that far too much has been expected of planning and policy-making in rural areas, which are unable to attain the objectives required of them because there is no straightforward dichotomy between policy and implementation. This turbulent conceptual relationship between rational and political approaches to policy is clearly demonstrated in the debate over whether policy is 'top-down' or 'bottom-up'—or indeed some hybrid of the two. The conceptual dilemma has been succinctly summed up by Gordon (1984), who has outlined three basic problems in understanding the nature of implementation:

(i) *recalcitrance*: assuming the execution of clear intentions;
(ii) *concretization*: translating abstract ideas into desirable actions in specific but often unforeseen circumstances;
(iii) *immobilism*: securing concerted action which transcends the status quo.

These problems illustrate a shifting core of conceptual concern in implementation studies, starting with the idea of implementation as a practical management exercise and progressing through the unpredictability of general ideological notions in practical political arenas to the difficulties of overcoming entrenched power relations intent on maintaining the status quo. These concepts are briefly discussed in turn.

Top-Down Models: The Rational Approach

The phrases 'top-down' and 'bottom-up' applied to approaches to implementation have been popularized by Hill *et al.* (1979). Top-down approaches entail two essential and interrelated assumptions. First, policy-making procedures are thought of as separate from policy administration mechanisms (thus reflecting the policy–implementation gap, and a rational separation of policy formulation and policy enactment). Secondly, top-down approaches imply that there are explicit policy objectives at the start of the process, and that implementation procedures can be measured against these objectives in terms of successfully (or otherwise) meeting policy goals. In this way, top-down models were first associated with attempts to describe implementation as one discrete stage in the rational process of decision-making. Thus *policy* represents what should be done, and *implementation* represents how to get it done (Baker, 1972).

The rational decision-making model describes a logical sequence of events such as that suggested in Fig. 3.1. With policy at the top and implementation towards the bottom of this chain, implementation is characterized by decisions from above and constrained by the pre-selection of options which are no longer available when the nitty-gritty of enactment at ground level is reached. Thereby, implementation may be defined as:

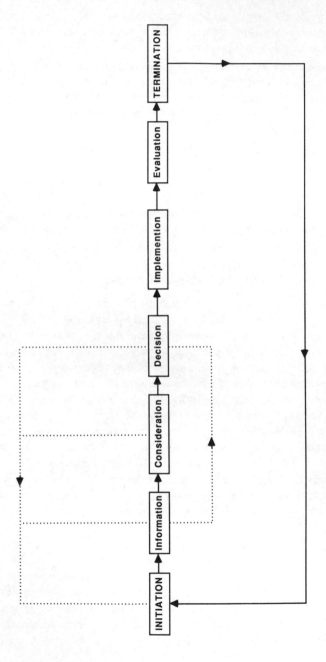

FIG. 3.1. A Rational Decision-Making View of the Policy Process
Source: Jenkins, 1978: 17

'Those outputs (actions) of an agency which derive from a particular decision sequence, the outputs being supposed to achieve, or implement, the policy' (Healey, 1979: 5);
'The ability to forge subsequent links in the causal chain so as to obtain desired results' (Pressman and Wildavsky, 1973: 15);
'Those actions by public and private individuals (or groups) that are directed at the achievement of objectives set forth in prior policy decisions' (Van Meter and Van Horn, 1975: 447).

A grossly oversimplified view of policy and implementation can emerge from this concept. If actions follow logically from decisions, and clearly identifiable policies can be translated into planning activity, then it is to be expected that planning aims and objectives can be fulfilled at the implementation stage. Any gap between policy and implementation thus becomes an illogicality in a logical system. According to this, new problems with the outcomes of policies are caused by the technicalities of implementation rather than by the political context of decision-making elsewhere in the process. The focus thus becomes a technical one, and the diagnosis of problems reflects this. For example, Dunsire (1978) recognizes three areas of implementation failure:

  (i) when the outcome of implementation differs from expectation, even though the actions taken were predicted to achieve the desired outcomes;
 (ii) when the prescribed actions were not carried out;
(iii) when the prescribed actions were carried out but the desired outcomes were not achieved because there were errors in predicting the results of the prescribed actions.

By this analysis, the problems with planning and policy are technical hitches at the implementation stage. The top-down policy itself is not to blame in any of these instances; an improvement in the techniques of implementation will lead to a restoration of rationality in the process, and desired outcomes will be achieved.

   Rational decision-making models dominated policy studies until the last fifteen years, and continue to be granted significant credence by some actions in and commentators of planning processes. The reasons for this domination are partly to do with the desire for a depoliticized form of analysis and partly associated with a preoccupation with policy and plans as ends in themselves.

For example, Smith (1973: 197–8) has noted that 'there is an implicit assumption in most models that once a policy has been "made" by a government, the policy will be implemented and the desired results of the policy will be near those expected by the policy-makers'; and Healey (1979: 5) similarly suggests: 'Planners, no doubt because they see their task as the normative one of designing "good policies", have tended to emphasise the stages of the process which are concerned with policy design'. Implementation, then, has been relegated to the technical back room. At the same time, there has been a tendency to see the process as a scapegoat for the inadequacies of planning and policy-making.

The efficiency of rational decision-making models will depend on whether the 'failure' of implementation can continue to be legitimized in technical, as opposed to political, terms. By laying the blame for rural problems at the door of technical planners, powerful interests in the state representing particular fractions of capital and class can direct interest away from their own influences on the function and apparatus of planning and policy-making. Critics of rational decision-making models have therefore sought to focus on the political and organizational context for planning action as a more fruitful framework for understanding policy and implementation.

Bottom-up Models: The Organizational Approach

Bottom-up models assume neither a separation of policy-making from policy administration nor the existence of clear policy goals against which the success of planning outcomes may be measured. United in their rejection of rational decision-making, these approaches explore the localized realities of how decisions are taken and how implementation occurs.

The purest form of bottom-up model highlights managerialist power relations within the behaviour of decision-makers. Lewis and Flynn (1978; 1979), for example, have presented a model of policy-making where implementation is seen as 'getting things done', and where the different commitments and goal orientations of individual actions in the planning process are analysed as a major influence on how things get done. Using evidence from interviews with individuals working in a range of planning agencies, Lewis and Flynn conceptualize the individual in the context of two principal working concerns: the institution in which they operate, and the world outside that institution (Fig. 3.2), and stress:

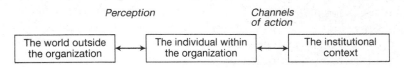

FIG. 3.2. A Behavioural Model of Policy-Making
Source: Lewis and Flynn, 1979: 11

an individual actor is not just a cog in a machine but is the mediator between the world outside the organization and the organizational structure which channels the available responses. The way in which the individual, and the multitude of individuals within an organization mediate between these two sets of concerns are key processes in the understanding of what 'gets done'. (1978: 11)

Their work did not expose a rational decision-making process. Indeed they reported disagreements over policy goals, vagueness about policy details, uncertainty about how policies should be put into operation, procedural complexity, mismatches between powers and perceived problems, and conflicts stemming from pressure group activities, public participation, and political dissent. In these circumstances, getting things done becomes a matter of pragmatic feasibility.

In some cases it is practical for action to follow previously defined policy goals. More commonly, however,

actions result from the resolution of conflicts between two sets of priorities and policy areas; may precede the formulation of a procedure for dealing with similar cases in future and therefore the policy; or may result from what is feasible in the circumstances rather than the fulfilment of the original objectives. (1978:)

The importance of this type of concept is to highlight the understanding of localized action, rather than merely seeing it as the end result of a longer chain of decision-making, only to be understood in the context of its source in a previously constituted policy. Rocke (1985) has stressed that this behavioural and organizational framework helps to break down the psychologically conditioned association of implementation with policy. Bottom-up approaches are useful, then, in identifying areas where action does not conform to policy expectations, and indeed where action bears very little relation to parent policy. Hambleton (1981) goes further in stressing the importance of understanding how and why actors and agencies make the decisions that they do, but pointing out that policy is but one of a range of potential influences on action.

Bottom-up approaches can, however, be taken too far. There is a point when studies of localized action will get so bogged down in the day-to-day minutiae of decisions that they lose sight of the overall political constraints within which those decisions are made. At this point, the understanding of implementation becomes as tunnel-visioned as the rational, top-down approaches.

Hybrid Models: The Political Approach

It will be clear from the preceding discussion that neither the top-down nor the bottom-up model of policy and implementation is compatible with a conceptual framework which views planning and policy as an apparatus of the state which itself reflects both the constraints exerted over power relations at the centre and the variety of social relations in particular localities. Somehow, the constraints from the top and the variety at the bottom must be made to meet somewhere in the middle in order to recognize the political economic reality of decision-making as suggested by state theory.

There have recently been several attempts to combine the most useful elements of top-down and bottom-up approaches into hybrid models of the policy implementation phenomenon. By stressing the influence of political and economic institutions on the activities of policy-making agencies (Healey, 1982), the policy implementation gap comes to represent the changing balance of influence between different socio-political and economic élites, and decision-making procedures reflect the bargaining and negotiation which takes place between different interests. Add to this analysis the role of managers, professions, policy networks, and policy communities in structuring and influencing these procedures of negotiation, and a more realistic appreciation of the political realities of policy and implementation should result.

One important advance in the fleshing out of hybrid models is found in a collection of essays on urban policy and action edited by

Barrett and Fudge (1981). The editors outline four top-down factors which underpin the localized enactment of policy:

(i) knowing what you want to do;
(ii) gaining access to the required resources;
(iii) marshalling and controlling these resources;
(iv) communicating with and controlling the performance of other agencies involved in the process.

They recognize, however, that from a bottom-up perspective these top-down factors are mitigated by local responses to dominant social relations, ideological and professional leanings, environmental pressures, pressures from other agencies, and so on. Implementation is therefore inextricably linked to the power relations stemming from influence and control over the allocation of resources at both central and local levels. Thus elements of both top-down and bottom-up approaches are required for a full and politically realistic understanding of policy enactment and the policy–action relationship.

Hybrid models of policy and implementation have sought to identify the exact nature of the relationship between policy and action. Hambleton (1981), for example, suggests that in practice it is difficult, if not impossible, to distinguish where implementation starts and policy ends, and Barrett (1980) refers to a policy–action continuum which consists of iterative negotiations between actors and agencies who control the means to action and those whose task is to enact policy (Fig. 3.3). The broad conclusion is that policy and implementation are not sequential, but are instead dynamic and interactive processes each influencing the other. Anderson (1975) has described this as a process whereby 'policy is being made as it is being administered, and administered as it is being made' (p. 98).

Policy ⟶ Reformulation

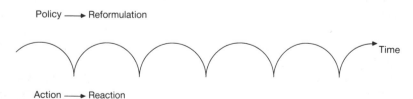

Time

Action ⟶ Reaction

FIG. 3.3. The Policy–Action Relationship
Source: Barrett and Fudge, 1981: 25

These interactive negotiations function within clear, although often implicit, political constraints. Barrett and Fudge (1981) have described this as 'bargaining within negotiated order'. Here is the essence of the hybrid model approach. *Policy* is not a fixed entity. Rather, it represents a series of intentions which are subjected to bargaining and modification during negotiations with relevant agencies and local interests, each seeking to pursue their own goals and impose some control over the process. *Implementation* is the continuum of these policy–action interactions, taking the form of iterative bargaining between those with power to control change, and various interests wishing to promote their own objectives through change.

Hybrid models of policy and action seem to offer a framework for understanding the complex realities of decision-making. They will not, however, be favoured by those wishing to assess policy implementation in terms of success or failure. The continuum concept incorporates delays, altered objectives, parts of policies being given priority over other parts, and so on. Implementation of one policy will be affected by the pursuit of other policies. All these factors mean that success or failure will depend on who is doing the assessing. It is useful, therefore, to follow Alterman (1982: 229) in regarding implementation as a relative concept:

To talk about an implementation process usefully, one must state what is the 'policy of reference' and what are the 'persons, groups or agencies of reference' from whose point of view implementation is described and assessed. One policy's implementation is another group's failure.

It follows that, rather than evaluating implementation by some measure of overall success or failure, it is more profitable to think in terms of the *constraints* on the operation of the policy–action continuum, and of the relationship between dominant social relations in a locality and the control of any unconstrained autonomy and discretion available to the local state. The roots of constraint and control are to be found in the theorization of the form, function, and apparatus of the state discussed in Chapter 2. In order to understand these matters of constraint, discretion, and control, we have to marry these concepts of power relations and the state with an appreciation of the pragmatic arena for policy and action in the local state. We therefore turn first to a discussion of the context for implementation, and then apply the concepts introduced in Chapter 2 and the first part of this chapter to specific studies of implementation in the rural-planning sector.

CONSTRAINTS ON POLICY AND ACTION

It should be stressed at this point that the *primary constraint* on rural policy and action stems from the state–society relationships discussed in Chapter 2. Rural policy-makers are constrained by an artificially limited range of options by the need to conform to the existing form, function, and apparatus of the state. Any thought of policy-makers starting with a clean slate is entirely misleading. Before beginning their negotiations within the policy–action continuum, policy-makers implicitly accept an externally imposed definition of the 'art of the possible' which is dictated by these primary constraints.

There are, however, a series of what might be termed *secondary constraints* which represent restrictions on the already limited range of options open to policy-makers (Cloke and Hanrahan, 1984; Hanrahan and Cloke, 1983). These secondary restrictions present practical difficulties to actors in the policy–action continuum, and serve further to shape the outcomes of turbulence both between top-down and bottom-up elements of implementation and within the local state arena, caused by frictions of structural managerial, élite, and pluralist power relations within broader social relations. The three subdivisions used here to represent arenas of struggle are a useful framework in which to discuss secondary constraints, but they are neither mutually exclusive or exhaustive. Indeed, the theme of social relations and the local state runs through each.

Central–Local Relationships

Investigations into central–local government relations have consistently demonstrated that, with functions being ever-increasingly assumed by government, and with government power consequently penetrating ever deeper into all aspects of society, so ever more complex institutions of government have arisen. This complexity not only involves the traditional central and local elements of the state, but has also spawned mediating agencies between these two levels. Indeed, Saunders (1985: 161) has theorized the existence of a *regional state* as an often-forgotten dimension of central–local relationships:

The establishment of regional state agencies is part of a long-running and fundamental attack on local democracy and on the ability of ordinary people to defend their interests as consumers in the face of demands by dominant class-based producer interests at a time of economic decline.

Using empirical evidence from studies of water and health authorities in southern England, Saunders suggests that two forms of political power are in operation. Politics of production at this regional level are seen to be characterized by class domination organized through forms of corporatism, while the politics of consumption rely more on managerial aspects of bureaucracy and professionalism in trends of closure. Clear issues of accountability and inter-tier conflict and domination arise here, and reverberate throughout the study of central–local relations.

From the point of view of understanding the constraints on policies and plans for rural areas arising from central–local tensions, much of the evidence from urban sociology tends to be ill-suited to the types of localities which interest rural researchers. Typical perspectives of a monetarist Conservative central government, aiming to subdue the resistance of a combination of Socialist local government, trade unions, and consumer organizations (Saunders, 1982), rarely apply in rural areas. Similarly, the converse approach of Labour-controlled local councils seeking to counteract centrally derived policies of contraction is ill-suited to local politics in rural areas, which themselves tend to be dominated by conservatism which can act to neutralize the ideological conflicts between local and central government in urban localities. Yet central–local relations are clearly influential in rural areas, particularly in the allocation of resources through fragmented channels of public administration at various spatial levels (Association of County Councils, 1979). Moreover, local political movements frequently transcend traditional class boundaries, such that Conservative-controlled rural authorities may unite with local socialists against the Conservative central state.

The key issue, therefore, is that of the discretion available at local level. What degree of discretion is permitted by central government to its usually politically sympathetic local counterpart? To what extent are discretionary powers channelled through quangos such as the Development Commission, which lack the democratic 'safeguards' (if so they be) available to local government with which to bolster local policy against central domination? Indeed, how vigorously is available discretion taken up by the politics of rural localities?

The answers to these questions might be 'less than it seems' to the degree of discretion, 'increasingly' to the use of mediating agencies, and 'variable but certainly not radical' to the take-up of discretionary powers. Local government continually finds itself in a position of subordination to external definitions of priorities, rather than being free to follow its own policy agenda. Evidence from the work of Phillips and Williams (1982), for example, suggests that local-authority building programmes in rural areas are largely constrained by the national Housing Investment Programme, although within this constrained local discretion some authorities have even failed to meet the available limited quotas. Similarly, Wright (1982: 6–7), reporting on a widescale study of decision-making in education, transport, housing, and other sectors in rural areas, suggested that local programmes of investment are constructed 'with at least one eye on the central department's policies and priorities, and are implemented with the knowledge that the central department monitors the implementation of programmes closely'.

This central overseeing of local policy-making is highly formalized. Development plans have to be submitted to the Secretary of State for his approval, and the usual outcome of this procedure is for a shift of emphasis to occur. Chapter 4 outlines the modifications thrust upon Gloucestershire's policies for rural areas by the Secretary of State, and a wider survey of structure plan policy modifications reveals a widespread rejection of rural policy initiatives by central government (Cloke and Shaw, 1983). Hambleton (1981) has suggested that the apparently widespread devolution of planning and policy responsibilities to the local level represents a move 'more concerned with regulation than with spawning new initiatives'. This view is borne out by Miller and Miller (1982) in their analysis of the role of local authorities in stimulating the local economy. They stress that the nurturing of the indigenous economy is now the primary local task, as against previous emphases on attracting footloose employers. Yet just when it appears that local authorities can begin to perform this useful nurturing role, central government proposed legislation 'expressly designed to prevent the adoption of this type of approach and to restrict local authorities to a relatively narrow and largely ineffectual field of action' (p. 155).

Aside from these regulatory controls, legal restrictions are imposed by the centre through the application of the *ultra vires* principle by which, if local authorities are deemed to have acted illegally, individual members of that authority are liable to appropriate punishment. Although rarely used, this principle represents strong potential control by the centre, and serves to modify the actions of local government accordingly. To legal controls are added financial ones, which have become increasingly important over recent years, with vigilantly monitored (some would say oppressive) financial restrictions being placed upon the activities of local decision-makers. The sum total of these restrictions is that the severe tenor of central–local relations will have an overbearing effect on the policy decisions of members and officers at the local level.

Inter-Agency Relationships

The plethora of agencies involved in the overall tasks of policy-making and planning for rural areas has been stressed by all the major studies of rural decision-making (e.g. Smart and Wright, 1983). Difficulties of co-ordination and co-operation between these agencies have been a central plank in the critique of post-war rural planning. As such, inter-agency relations are viewed as imposing constraint on the pursuance of state activity.

The duplication of responsibility for rural decisions is necessarily accompanied by a duplication of specific agency definitions of priorities. These priorities rarely match, and thus the activities of agencies are not easily co-ordinated. Organizational theory suggests that agencies will tend to guard their own decision-making domains jealously, and will automatically oppose outside inter-ference in the manner in which their responsibilities are dispensed. Friend *et al.* (1974) and Clegg and Dunkerley (1980), amongst others, believe that it would be naïve to suggest that agencies seeking to legitimize their own independent existence and resources will wish to enter into anything more than loose and temporary liaisons in the name of corporate planning. As Leach (1980: 293) states, 'authorities will only co-operate when it suits them, or when they have to, and then very much on their own terms, and in line with their own interests'.

Evidence has frequently been cited for inter-organizational conflict in rural areas. For example, district and county councils are required to liaise over the provision of various public services, and over the integration of structure and local plans (Leach and Moore, 1979). Specific difficulties have occurred in these inter-relations (Healey, 1979; Bruton, 1983), with tensions arising between strategic and development control activities. Often, district authorities (with the approval of central government through structure plan scrutiny and appeals procedures) will push available discretion to its limits, so that local decisions can stretch, distort, or override the strategic consideration. With some notable exceptions, these tensions constrain the advancement of pro-gressive policies in many rural areas.

Inter-organizational conflict, however, is by no means limited to the duplication of the town and country planning function. The allocation of resources—employment, housing, and especially service opportunities—is also subject to the need for corporate policies which bind together several individual agencies. Packman and Wallace (1982) report on a general failure on the part of all agencies concerned to take positive direct action against the demise of rural services in East Anglia. Their explanation for this failure revolves around the factors of perceived limitations of responsibility by individual agencies, strong, centrally derived, downward pressure on public expenditure, and an inherent reluctance to innovate beyond established policy procedures. Those progressive ideas which do surface tend to be stifled by the dissipation of initiatives between different agencies, and by the limitations of scope and finance imposed by higher authorities.

The evidence reported by Packman and Wallace tends to reflect the needs of those rural areas where positive action is required to regulate the changing patterns of production and consumption dictated by the market. Thus, in their study of the implementation of development plans in rural areas under more urban pressure, Healey *et al.* (1982) found little evidence of substantial conflicts between public-sector organizations. Similarly, the example of gross lack of co-ordination between water authorities and planners in the implementation of key settlement policies in Devon (Glyn-

Jones, 1979) should be matched against contemporary studies in more pressured locations which suggest a good working relationship between water and planning agencies over the provision of infrastructure (Bell, 1986).

Neither should it be assumed that intra-agency relations are habitually more conformant to the notions of corporate planning (Greenwood *et al.*, 1980) than these inter-agency tensions. Parochialism has to be broken not only between different departments of local authorities but also between full-time professional officers and part-time elected councillors. The distribution of local influence and power between these groups varies according to the functional perception of senior departmental management on the one hand and of committee chairmen and other influential local members on the other. Those agencies which are not established on democratic lines also face conflict from different sub-divisions within the agency itself.

All these factors concerning the inter-agency relationship serve to constrain the advance of progressive co-operative action of any significant magnitude in many rural areas. Again, there are examples of situations in which such constraints have been overcome to some degree. The account of Gloucestershire's 'Rural Action Group' in Chapter 4 is indicative of the fairly small-scale successes which have been achieved in this context. Nevertheless, in general terms corporate planning mechanisms have not succeeded in co-ordinating any policies for rural areas which are radically different from what has gone before.

Private–Public-Sector Relationships

The constraints imposed by central controls over local government expenditure have already been noted, as have current trends towards privatization and deregulation. For a full appreciation of why rural planning has been as passive as it has, however, the dependency of policy-makers on the private sector must be fully realized. Passive planning in rural areas has constituted the granting of permission to private interests for development which is beyond the scope and participation of the planning authorities themselves. The realization of public policy thus becomes reliant on the availability of private capital. This reliance means that the making of policies for rural areas is itself constrained by the necessity to prescribe patterns of development which are likely to attract the necessary private finance. In situations where this expectation may not be realized, the terms by which planning authorities describe apparently constructive policies can turn out to be rather tame rhetoric. Thus the announcement of an authority's intentions to 'encourage', 'promote', or 'permit' (for example) housing development in particular areas cannot necessarily be accepted as a blueprint or even as an expectation that such development will occur.

Private-sector investment in areas within the remit of rural planning and policy-making is substantial. Entrepreneurs and industrialists, independent shopkeepers and multiple retail organizations, independent bus-operators, housing developers and their financial backers are all crucial to the objectives of a progressive rural-planning authority. The direct influence of these private interests is such that planners and policy-makers have an important advocacy function to perform in order to attempt to channel private capital into designated localities. Some commentators believe that increasing partnership between the public and private sectors is the most effective future policy-making mechanism (Mawson and Miller, 1983).

Until now, such partnership has proved elusive in rural areas so far as progressive policies are concerned. Certainly, with diminishing public-sector resources the trend has been to pursue economies of scale in locational terms, and the consequent policies of rationalization appear in tune with market-led forces in the private sector. This, however, constitutes a partnership of decline. Attempts to play a more positive role in selectively channelling private-sector resources into 'needy' locations are often less than successful, as public-sector planners are restricted to a supervisory capacity when dealing with the speculative activities of private-sector developers. Murie's (1980) study of planning control over housing reaches this conclusion:

Much housing planning and policy-making gives little attention to the private sector and perpetuates a myth of competence and control. One consequence is often a very wide gap between plans and practice and between the intention and consequence of policy. (p. 310)

Just such a gap was exposed by Blacksell and Gilg (1981) in their study of local-authority resistance to residential development in supposedly protected areas, and encouragement of development in preferred key settlements.

The impact of private interests transcends these obvious direct channels, and also occurs indirectly through an ability to shape public policies. For example, Austin (1983) argues that corporations will seek out methods of reducing overheads, particularly tax payments, in the pursuit of self-interest on a short-run, profit-maximizing basis. One outcome of this trend is that corporate interests will use every available opportunity to influence public decision-makers towards a minimization of collective expenditure on public services. He concludes that 'to the extent that corporation resources are used effectively to intervene in political decision processes on behalf of corporate self-interest, collective provision of human services is likely to be minimised' (p. 353). These less obvious determinants in the public–private sector relationship are crucial in those rural areas where conservative elected representatives depend on these corporate interests for the furthering of their political and economic status.

Rural planning and policy-making, therefore, are dependent on private-sector co-operation, and can be rendered relatively impotent if public-sector aspirations cannot be matched with the will and motivation of private-sector interests. It should not be surprising, therefore, to find that public policy usually includes a full assessment of known private interests *prior* to finalizing rural-planning strategies. Dominant social and economic relations thereby often become enshrined in public policy without recourse to official procedures for public participation.

The secondary constraints described here are not innovative in that they have been widely recognized in the evaluation of planning and policy-making at urban and regional levels. Those interested in rural planning have, however, been more reluctant to embrace these issues, perhaps because, in general, many analysts of rural-planning practice have favoured rational and apolitical approaches to public policy, and have therefore been unwilling to acknowledge the importance of political and organizational factors in constraining the art of the possible for rural policies. We would argue that the combination of primary and secondary constraints discussed here affords a significant depth of insight into the politics and practice of rural planning. It remains to illustrate these concepts in practical planning contexts, and it is to this task that the chapter now turns.

STUDIES IN IMPLEMENTATION: THE EXAMPLE OF THE DEVELOPMENT OF STRUCTURE PLANS

The issues discussed in Chapter 2 and the first part of this chapter clearly suggests that what we know as 'rural planning' is a multi-faceted use of state apparatus at central, regional, and local levels. Implementation of planning apparatus is subject to constraints emanating both from the state–society relationship and from secondary relationships within and between the state sector and the private sector. Within these constraints, policy and imple-mentation tend to be at the same time iterative, political, managerial, and pragmatic.

Our purpose in discussing the merits of these concepts is to provide a broad framework within which planning apparatus relating to varying agencies and on various scales can be understood. We believe that these concepts relate equally well to the day-to-day aspects of regulating development as to the grander-scale elements of policy design emanating from, say, Brussels or Whitehall. At the small scale, for example, there are a number of studies which have begun to trace the links between the function and apparatus of the state and the localized practicalities of carrying out planning. Herington's (1984) study of planning in what he calls 'the outer city', for instance, highlights the political implications of the triumvirate relations between local planners, housing developers, and central government:

if developers feel local plans are inadequate they may seek to obtain permission for development on land not covered by the plan or try to breach the policies stated in it. Either way there is an increasing number of planning appeals and more conflicts with central government are likely. Indeed, these weaknesses of the development planning system have been compounded by the fact that most structure plans now show demand for additional housing—and the DoE's advice to make more land available for housing makes it more difficult for districts to refuse permission for developments in the outer areas.   (p. 123)

Within this area, day-to-day decisions *are* influenced both by local social relations and by central government constraint, through advice notes and control over appeals procedures. This central regulation, or deregulation of planning (Blowers, 1987, has highlighted the significantly increased upholding of planning appeals against local authorities during the Thatcher era) can in turn be seen in terms of the wider functions of the state, particularly its support of capital interests. In the context of housing development in Britain, particular capital fractions are the beneficiaries of centralized deregulation of planning restrictions, with some 0.5 per cent of developers accounting for some 40 per cent of the development.

It should equally be emphasized that state support for capital through the planning apparatus should be seen as neither deterministically predictable nor homogeneous. Some sectors of capital have been in conflict with central handling of planning constraints. An example of this is given by Healey *et al.* (1988: 125–6), who first note the rejection by the Thatcher administration of clearly articulated strategic policies as consensus directives for the planning system, and then offer evidence of how this rejection has operated against, for example, sections of retailing capital:

Nor is it clear that dealing with the pressure for large out-of-town retail stores through the appeal process has been the most effective way to negotiate the conflicting interests of the retail trade, its financial backers, and concerns of existing retail centres, residents and shoppers. The problem . . . was that the economic changes which have led to the demands for new types of location and site were not foreseen when the main parameters of strategic policy were negotiated. By the time they were understood, central government was ideologically opposed to negotiating strategic policy as an approach to market management. Projects and initiatives . . . were favoured over consistency and continuity in spatial policy.

Other studies, such as Elson (1986) on green belts and Witt and Fleming (1984) on the pressures on local-planning councillors, add force to the idea that concepts of the state, and the constraints and negotiations of implementation, are entirely applicable to local-scale research into planning processes.

In terms of grand-scale rural policy design, the role of the nation state and the international state are again both fundamental and beginning to be well documented. The role of the EEC in the determination of UK agricultural policy has been well reviewed by Hoggart and Buller (1987), and the political corporatism and conflicts between state, capital, and agricultural policy are the subject of lengthy debate by Cox *et al.* (1986). Once again, it is not our intention here to review all potential policy arenas for which political economic concepts of the state and implementation are useful frameworks for understanding. We merely suggest that the application of these concepts to widely differing research issues connected with policy, planning, and rural localities can generate significant insight. For the purposes of the remainder of this chapter we present one more detailed analysis of implementation issues—that of the nature of implementation of county structure plan policies for rural areas in Britain. This example is then followed through in the case of the Gloucestershire structure plan in Chapter 4.

Implementation and Structure Plans

The selection of structure plans for specific examination represents a pragmatic choice of policy arena for study. We do not suggest that structure plan policies are *the* most important policies which impinge on rural areas, neither do we regard county councils as synonymous with the local state. Indeed, we are well aware of the restrictions imposed by studying any specified subset of policies within any subset of local state agencies, and the consequent deficiencies in our research are acknowledged. Nevertheless, we do believe in the need to build bridges between the conceptualization of planning and policy in their state context and empirical information from the realities of ground-level policy-making. The study of structure plans is but one small part of the potential span of such bridges.

There is now a significant historical period between the legislative birth of county structure plans in 1968 and 1972, their subsequent formulation, and the current practice of implementing the policies within them. The Department of the Environment requires structure planners to justify their proposals for development to interpret national and regional policies in the county context, and to provide a framework for local plans. Therefore structure plans have included justifications of how selected policies might be implemented, thus providing useful 'source material' for understanding 'official' interpretations of implementation. Clearly, written source material such as this should not be used out of context. Most structure plans explicitly state that the policies therein are not blueprints for the future. Instead, they are viewed as intended lines of action which are deliberately flexible, so as to cope with socio-economic changes beyond the control of policy-makers. An understanding of action connected with these policies will be heavily dependent on the iterative processes of co-ordination and conflict within the negotiation and bargaining procedures.

Analysis of structure plan material, then,

offers insight into the *initial* intentions and points of conflict resolution between those influential actors and agencies involved; it also acts as a *benchmark* against which subsequent divergence from actual intentions may be measured and assessed; it gives an *impression* of the degree of foresight which is available to forward planners at the development stage; *but* it neither reveals what will happen, nor discloses those aspects of implementation which by consent between members and officers are deemed inappropriate for publication.   (Cloke and Little, 1986: 262)

Implementation: The Official View.   Although most structure plans include a chapter devoted to 'implementation' or 'feasibility', few plans explicitly discuss the relationship between policies and powers on which effective implementation depends. Bracken (1982: 15) notes that

one gains an impression (which may well be unintended) that those responsible for the preparation of Structure Plans do not necessarily share the same degree of commitment and interest in the implementation of those policies.

This disinterest can be explained in different ways. There is a somewhat traditional assumption that planning policies somehow implement themselves. There is the factor of weariness on the part of structure planners that most influential decisions are taken outside their arena of power through non-statutory planning modes, meaning that the structure plan itself is a fragile agenda for action which gets taken over by events (Broadbent, 1979). There is the implicit adherence to rational decision-making models which diminish the importance of implementation until the policy preparation 'stage' is completed.

These suggestions are authentic but oversimplified. In fact, it was the rather slavish following of government advice which conditioned discussions of implementation in structure plans. The 1971 Town and Country Planning Act emphasizes that policies should be designed in the light of resources which are available according to realistic assumptions. There was no question here of policy-makers designing policies according to the needs of the locality, and resources being found to pay for these policies. Rather, policies were founded on the ethic of good housekeeping on a restricted budget, and policy choices were constrained accordingly. Typically, then, discussion of implementation takes the form of financial resource estimates for both the public and the private sectors.

Very little information is given about the political bargaining procedures which must take place over which policy options are or are not acceptable in resource terms. A list of these iterative negotiations is given in the plan for Shropshire (1983: 129) which stresses that

it must be emphasised that although this [feasibility and implementation] section is presented after the policy statements, attention has been paid both to the likely availability of resources and to gaining the greatest benefit from their use at all stages in the Plan formulation process.

These considerations, although usually implicit, are clearly relevant to the development of policy in all other structure plans.

The overall impression of the discussions of implementation in structure plans is that it is dominated by the availability of financial resources for decision-making agencies. A rational expectation would be that more finance would mean improved implementation of desired policies. However, the plans stress that the future allocation of finance not only is uncertain but can be manipulated by shifting governmental relations. Equally, factors other than finance will also impinge on implementation, notably the jealously guarded sectoral control exercised by specific agencies delivering services to their clientele according to their guide-lines. The themes of uncertainty and co-ordination thus dominate discussions of the feasibility of policy implementation.

Uncertainty. The unenviable position of the forward planner seeking to make a realistic assessment of future resource availability is highlighted in the plan for Cumbria and the Lake District (Cumbria County Council and Lake District Special Planning Board, 1980: 137):

Although the use of information on past levels of public expenditure, economic policy and private investment is complicated by the effect of inflation, it offers the only guidelines to the future. Changes of policy, or of Government may have an immediate effect upon the activity of the private sector and upon the effectiveness of local authorities in meeting their objectives. It is against this changing background that the assessment of resources has been attempted and the conclusions tempered by reorganising the uncertainties involved.

Not surprisingly, central-government advice on financial predictions was slavishly adhered to by structure planners. A 1978 government white paper (Cmnd. 7049) on public expenditure was used as the basis for predictions in the bulk of structure plans. Table 3.1 shows percentage changes in the capital and current expenditure of English local authorities over the first six years of most structure plans at 1977 prices. After significant reductions in capital expenditure in 1977–8, a limited expansion was foreseen up to 1981–2, although at the end of this period there would have been a decrease in real terms of 14.1 per cent. Only the trade, industry, and employment sector would receive increased capital expenditure. Current expenditure was predicted to increase in real terms by 5.8 per cent during this period.

It was the task of structure planners to interpret these predictions in terms of their own policy and action expectations. The Devon plan (Devon County Council, 1979: 168) foresaw 'a period during which there are to be severe restrictions in the levels of public expenditure', and the Cambridgeshire plan (Cambridgeshire County Council, 1980: 194), highlighting the slower growth in public expenditure than that in the economy as a whole, concluded that 'these forecasts will significantly affect public expenditure on services provided by the Local Authority'.

By contrast, other county councils were more optimistic, judging that these predictions at the very worst meant no proportionate increase in expenditure as opposed to the 'severe restrictions' foreseen by other authorities using the same figures. Thus, Berkshire's plan (Berskhire County Council, 1980: 89) concluded:

The public sector may therefore find itself in the position of having to complement expanding private sector activity without any proportionate increase in its share of the nation's output. If this happens there may be repercussions on the level and quality of some of the services and facilities provided by the public sector.

Table 3.1. Change in English Local Authorities' Capital and Current Expenditure, 1977/8–1981/2 (1977 prices)

	Changes over previous year					Change over 1976/7 (%)
	1977/8 (%)	1978/9 (%)	1979/80 (%)	1980/1 (%)	1981/2 (%)	
Current expenditure						
Roads and transport	−5.9	–	+1.6	+1.7	−0.4	−3.2
Education, libraries, etc.	+1.5	+1.8	+0.7	+0.9	+0.4	+5.3
Law, order, and protective services	+1.3	+1.6	+1.2	+1.0	+1.1	+6.3
Health and personal social services	+3.5	+2.5	+2.4	+2.0	+3.0	+14.2
Other environmental services	+3.9	−1.4	+2.8	+1.4	+1.6	+8.5
Agriculture service, etc.	–	–	–	–	–	–
Trade, industry, and employment	+6.1	+2.9	+2.8	+2.7	−2.7	+1.7
Housing	−0.6	−0.9	+1.2	+0.6	+1.4	+1.7
All services	+1.3	+1.2	+1.2	+1.1	+0.8	+5.8
Capital expenditure						
Roads and transport	−16.0	−4.6	+4.2	−1.0	+1.5	−15.9
Education, libraries, etc.	−40.8	−14.7	+3.7	+0.4	+1.6	−43.4
Law, order, and protective services	−19.7	−5.3	−31.5	−2.7	–	−49.3
Health and personal social services	−32.4	+6.5	+6.1	+15.2	–	−22.1
Other environmental services	−43.0	+34.0	−5.8	+7.9	−2.4	−22.8
Trade, industry, and employment	+67.0	−20.0	+50.0	−17.0	−20.0	+33.8
Housing	−19.0	+14.0	+4.4	+0.8	+0.5	−2.5
All services	−24.2	+8.8	+2.3	+1.4	+0.4	−14.1

Source: Treasury, 1978.

The treatment of financial uncertainty using government statistics can be judged against what actually happened to expenditure levels over that period. According to SOLACE (1983), three trends occurred:

(i) Local-government capital and revenue, taken together, declined in real terms by 3 per cent 1977/8 and 1982/3.

(ii) Local-government spending represented a declining proportion of GDP from 15.9 per cent in 1974/5 to 13.5 per cent in 1980/1.

(iii) There were significant reductions in the proportion of relevant local-authority expenditure payable in government grants.

These trends suggest that the pessimistic county authorities handled uncertainty the best, but even they underestimated the increasingly severe central-government policies of restricting local-government expenditure. Policy and action may therefore be seen to have been developed in an overwhelmingly restrictive economic environment. The selection of 'practicable' policies must have been constrained by these financial considerations, and the continuing application and enactment of policy is being increasingly structured by central-state financial parameters.

To some extent, rural policy-making has not been too drastically affected by the uncertainty over resource availability. The traditional political tendencies of rural authorities have been conservative, and policy proclivities have therefore favoured environmental preservation and market-orientated servicing patterns rather than local-state intervention in markets to provide normative levels of housing and services. These tendencies are largely compatible with keeping local taxes down and with supporting private-sector interests, although there are conflicts between conservation policies and construction interests. In turn, these conservative policies tend to conform with the strategic necessities of spatial and social rationalization of resources dictated by financial uncertainties and the unwinding climate of expenditure restriction in the 1980s.

In a discussion of the links between financial restrictions and the policies adopted in structure plans, four options have been suggested by which county councils can combine the expenditure parameters inflicted from above and the political preferences exerted from within so that a widely acceptable plan can be submitted to, and approved by, central government (Cloke and Little, 1986: 269–70). These options essentially represent tiers of the same cake, formed into a single structure of policy legitimation in the face of external and internal political pressures.

(i) *Rationalization.* Plans such as that for Norfolk (Norfolk County Council, 1980) claim to reduce the need for additional expenditure on services and to minimize costs by:

restraint on population growth through control of housing development;
restriction on further holiday development;
concentration of urban growth into relatively few well-serviced areas;
avoiding any overload of existing services by adopting phased development (where possible);
controlling the further dispersal of the rural population.

This broad strategy of concentrating the population into centres of existing service provision reflects the 'least-cost' or 'economies of scale' approach which is conformable to market trends and financial restraints, and has been adopted in the majority of non-metropolitan counties.

(ii) *Flexibility.* An adjunct to the resource concentration/ rationalization theme is that of county authorities maintaining an ability to be flexible in the implementation of their strategies according to the financial ground-rules of the time. For example, the Cambridgeshire plan (1980) claims that: 'the strategy is not dependent either on fast national economic growth or upon the success of local policies of severe restraint. It will not involve major new capital investment other than that which, in general, is required to deal with existing problems and commitments' (p. 203).

Heeding the warning given at the beginning of this analysis regarding the degree of credibility to be attached to some of the stated intentions within structure plans, these protestations of flexibility might be interpreted as propaganda-laden. Alternatively, they could be seen as preconditions for the continuance of status quo planning, offering few innovative or even reactive policy options with which to tackle rural problems.

(iii) *Marginality.* A hint of realism, or even scepticism, can be detected in some of the commentaries linking implementation, policy, and resource restrictions. For example, several plans stress that the adopted strategies represent a kind of 'fine-tuning' to an already efficient policy system. Shropshire County Council (1983) are representative of this group, stating that: 'In relation to the existing pattern of land use in the County, any changes proposed in the Plan can be regarded as marginal and no single investment decision will commit a significant proportion of available resources early in the Plan period.'

There is obviously a thin line between flexibility and marginality in policy themes, and it appears likely that there will be direct overlap between them in many cases.

(iv) *Restricted influence*. If all else fails, then it is legitimate for structure plans to fall back on the time-honoured theme that planners themselves lack the direct powers of responsibility which would permit them to exert specific influence on the implementation of their strategies. Berkshire County Council (1980: 89) gives a particularly well-phrased account of this theme: 'By putting forward proposals for the scale, rate and general location of change it provides the framework within which investors in the local economy may plan their future programmes, although investment decisions by private companies and public authorities are to a large extent determined by factors which lie outside the influence of the Plan.'

Financial uncertainties have not been the major constraint on the policy–action continuum in rural areas because rural policies were *already* being geared to public-sector economies through resource rationalization. Enactment of structure plan strategies thus depends to a large extent on the negotiations between planners and decision-makers in resource-allocating agencies in the public and (increasingly importantly) the private sectors.

Co-ordination. The second dominant theme in discussions relating to the feasibility of policy implementation is that of inter-agency co-ordination. Listed below are those resource-allocating agencies which require co-ordinating under the umbrella of structure plan policies (Gloucestershire County Council, 1979: 191).

(i) *The county council*—in its expenditure on the provision of most additional transport, waste disposal, and education (capital-expenditure) facilities, and in future in its contribution to industrial promotion. To a lesser extent the plan will also influence expenditure on social services, fire, police, libraries, and other services, in their relation to the pattern of future development in the county.

(ii) *The district councils*—in their public sector housing activities, particularly in the preparation of housing strategy and investment programmes, and for industrial promotion and the development of recreation facilities.

(iii) *The water authorities*—in assessing their investment priorities (in Gloucestershire) for sewerage and sewage treatment provision, water supply, and land drainage (where related to development).

(iv) *The health authorities*—by setting a context for the formulation and implementation of regional and area policies and programmes.

(v) *The statutory undertakers*—in their planning of investment for telecommunications, electricity, and gas supplies.

(vi) *The private sector*—in its various developments, and in particular any investment decisions which relate to population and employment growth in the county.

Analysis of plan documentation reveals that discussion of the intended relationships between planners and these agencies is brief and superficial. It would be naïve, perhaps, to expect otherwise in the glaring publicity and legal context of written planning documents. Such collaborative relationships are often worked out quietly by way of informal liaison between individuals. Nevertheless, there is evidence of the way in which different forms of co-ordination can represent constraints in the policy action process.

For example, structure plans reveal a strong difference in attitude towards *self-supporting* services (electricity, gas, etc.) where financial restrictions tend not to be imposed from the centre, and *dependent* services (education, social services, transport, health, etc.) which tend to be constrained by fixed budgets. The former are 'partners' in action, the latter can be 'barriers' to action. Partner agencies can offer spare capacity within which planners can operate, and fruitful liaison can occur. Barrier agencies have a backlog of investment, and need to compromise far more to make their priorities conform with those of structure planners. In this case the pragmatic option is for planners to incorporate the need for service centralization (economies of scale for the agencies involved dictate this anyway) with the political need to ensure growth restraint in small villages, and hopefully end up with a policy which smooths over most difficulties.

It is perhaps not surprising that private sector agencies have been recognized as increasingly dominant in the implementation of structure plan policies, given their growing role in the provision of public services. The relationship between structure planning and the private sector is somewhat paradoxical. Planners have no direct control over private-agency resources, but they do provide a context for many investment decisions. Plans can dictate the locations for development, but plan policies are themselves directly influenced by predictions regarding the potential level of private investment. The balance of power between planners and the private sector is ultimately dictated by central-state decisions. Although many counties claim that the means of implementation in the private sector are co-ordination, land-use control, investment, and persuasion (Derbyshire County Council, 1977: 333), there is little or no mention of how co-ordination and persuasion are to be effected. Far more concrete are the decisions of central-government inspectors in appeal cases, and central-government advice notes laying down guide-lines for the contemporary interpretation of town and country planning legislation. By these mechanisms the private sector can be given a helping hand by the centre, and local-government planners have very little right of reply.

Co-operation and co-ordination between planners and decision-making agencies are crucial areas for the understanding of local policy and action, yet there is no 'official' version in structure plan literature of how these are to be achieved. The implication is that vigilant monitoring will uncover agency decisions which are aberrant in relation to strategic policy objectives. But even if agencies are caught out in this way, there is little evidence that influence can be brought to bear by planners to make them change their ways. In general terms, the structure plans confirm McKee's (1984: 7) assessment of what contemporary planning is really all about: 'When stripped to its barest essentials, the activity of planning must address itself to the three basic issues of political choice (policy), the statutory and legal frameworks (alternative options available) and resources (implementation).' This is a pragmatic and very partial view of the nature and context of implementation, but it appears to be widely held by members and officers in local authorities so far as structure plans are concerned. Such a blinkered view, however, confirms the need for a much closer examination by researchers of how things actually get done, in view of both the primary and secondary *constraints* on policy-making and enactment.

Certainly, this 'offical' view of implementation will itself colour and constrain what actually happens. The predominant contemporary nature of implementation in rural planning when placed in the historical perspective of the structure plan era is that policy and action have become increasingly opportunistic. This is marked by the almost universal tendency to legitimize and utilize the 'planning' resources represented by voluntary initiative and community self-help. Although it can be argued that self-help has some intrinsic merits (Rogers, 1987), the style of planning by opportunism has arisen because of the increasing economic and political constraints on a more rational form of planning (McLaughlin, 1987). These issues are discussed in more depth in Chapter 6. To find out more about the local perceptions of planners regarding policy and implementation, it is necessary to go beyond the written word of the structure plans and sample the reactions of individual planners. In the next section we report on a survey which has been designed to do just this.

IMPLEMENTATION: THE PERCEPTIONS OF
STRUCTURE PLANNERS

The conceptual approach to policy and implementation outlined in the first half of this chapter does not as yet marry with the evidence presented so far relating to structure plans. After all, Barrett and Hill's (1984) three ingredients for an approach to policy and implementation were:

(i) *Policy* is complex and ambiguous, often devoid of clear goals, and frequently emerging during as well as before implementation.

(ii) *Implementation* is best seen as a continuum between those putting policy into effect and those upon whom action depends.

(iii) *The interactions* of these processes are crucial, particularly power interest structures and inter-actor of inter-agency relationships.

These factors add flesh to the bare bones of policy and implementation as discussed in structure plans. If these ingredients are acknowledged by actors in the planning process, we can begin to narrow the gap between concept and practice in the representation of the implementation theme and in the understanding of how policy and implementation actually work.

A major survey of planners working in thirty-seven county council planning departments was undertaken in 1985. The details of survey technique, and a critique of this type of survey are presented elsewhere (Cloke and Little, 1986*b*), but for our present purposes we will restrict our description to the four major issues connected with implementation on which planners' perceptions were recorded in the survey.

What is Implementation?

Planners were asked to define the nature of implementation within the structure planning process. In terms of a bald definition, most responses stressed enactment, using words such as 'action', 'putting into practice', 'bringing to fruition', and so on (Table 3.5) and suggested that implementation is viewed by planners within a kind of rational decision-making framework. Definitions of implementation were as follows (Cloke and Little, 1986*b*: 270):

turning the general statements of policy into day-to-day action;
putting into practice planning policies and proposals;
achieving a given set of policy objectives;
bringing permitted planning proposals to fruition;
getting a plan done on the ground: only if a plan is 'implemented' does it progress from being a bound volume of paper on a shelf to a useful economic/social instrument.

However, when given scope to refine these initial definitions by way of attaching particular types of action to the implementation process, planners preferred a wider view of the scope of implementation. Five overlapping categories emerged.

(i) *Land-use control activities*. For some structure planners, implementation activities were restricted to the area of land-use control. This perception was conditioned by central-government instructions that structure plan policies should relate to the use of land rather than to broader sectors of socio-economic activity (Cloke, 1983). Action on implementation therefore equals development taking place, or being appropriately controlled, in accordance with plan policies. This is the narrowest definition to emerge from the survey.

(ii) *Pursuit of agreed policies by county planners.* In expanding the scope of action beyond the narrow limits of (i), planners differentiated implementation according to *who* was doing the enacting. One group of planners were prepared to acknowledge that action carried out by planning authorities at the county level constituted implementation, even if it were not strictly orientated towards land use. Examples of this included the role of co-ordination (see 'Studies in Implementation' above), which includes exhortation, persuasion, and recommendation to other public- and private-sector agencies that certain functions, activities, or investments should be undertaken in the context of plan policies. The broad aim here is to influence the policies of other agencies, although the practical means of achieving this aim are restricted (at least officially) to the establishment of advisory groups, working parties, and corporate planning systems. The wider scope of implementation also includes direct action available to county planning authorities, such as industrial or infrastructural development, recreation development, landscaping, and interpretation for conservation.

(iii) *Pursuit of agreed policies by other agencies.* The view in (ii) of implementation being restricted by what planners themselves can do was itself extended by a further group of planners who saw action in the context of structure plans as including the decision-making powers of other agencies. Essentially, then, decisions made outside planning departments were themselves seen as integral to implementation, which therefore could not be confined within the walls of county hall or within the activity patterns of the officers who work there.

This extension of the scope of implementation carries with it the sentiment that planners are *dependent* on outside agencies for the successful enactment of their policies. One respondent summarizes this feeling of dependence thus:

The County Council as strategic planning authority is dependent, with some exceptions, for the implementation of the policies and proposals of the Structure Plan on (1) the district councils who grant the majority of planning permissions; and (2) the various public agencies, private organisations and individuals who carry out development.

(iv) *Pursuit of wider objectives.* Only one respondent county planner in the survey suggested that implementation included the pursuit of objectives beyond the agreed policies of the structure plan. At one level, this county's representative accepted that implementation consisted of those actions described in (i)–(iii) above; it was further stressed that implementation 'is also any involvement with what is happening in the area. It is a wide-ranging definition that encompasses virtually anything which helps to achieve the objectives of the local authority.' The significance of this response is that it comes from one of the three counties identified by Cloke and Shaw (1983) as attempting to innovate with their rural policies by proposing strategies of wider resource dispersal in the countryside. It might be suggested that this wide-ranging perceived definition of implementation is connected with these attempts to drag rural policy away from traditional resource concentration strategies. If this is the case, the motives and mechanisms which underlie these attitudes will be important to our understanding of how things get done.

(v) *Acceptance of market-led activities.* One other respondent differed from the others by defining implementation in terms of the external constraints within which planning operates. The activities associated with bringing about agreed structure plan policies are seen as 'achieving miracles in a hostile economic and political climate'. Indeed, this particular planner suggests that it is a mistake to regard implementation as synonymous with action. This pessimism (or realism) is spawned by an appreciation of the dominance of the external political environment, where market forces are the predominant influence over those activities which planners seeks to influence. The respondent concludes that 'implementation without power . . . is merely an acceptance of the market mechanisms and their resulting actions, whether in line with policy or not'.

In this one response we see a very neat confirmation of the conceptual analysis of policy and action presented above. Significantly, the response is drawn from a county which has experienced considerable central-government meddling with its policies during the structure plan approval and appeals procedures. Perhaps equally significantly, other respondents begin to adopt the same model of having to accept market forces when questioned further about the problems associated with successful implementation.

Implementation Problems

The second area of planners' perceptions investigated by the survey concerned the nature of those day-to-day problems experienced by planners in achieving what they considered to be successful policy implementation in rural areas. The notion of 'problems' is chaotic: perceptions of a problem are time-dependent, and may vary considerably within the boundaries of a county authority. Nevertheless, a number of different implementation difficulties did emerge from the survey, and each illustrates the conceptual material presented in the first part of this chapter. At the risk of over-categorization, these difficulties are again discussed in turn, although they are not necessarily mutually exclusive.

(i) *Inter-organizational conflicts.* The most frequently identified problem relates to the inter-organizational co-operation which was highlighted in the structure plan documentation. Despite written reassurances to the contrary, there is a real conflict between many county planning authorities and other decision-making agencies. Too often, respondents report that the heavy reliance placed by the county council on other agencies is not matched by any agreement amongst these bodies as to the strategic approach required. Parochial interest often takes precedence over strategic considerations in this policy environment.

This category includes a number of specific problems: the plethora of implementing agencies and resulting fragmentation of responsibilities; the policy conflicts between strategic and resource-specific policy objectives; the lack of formal consultation procedures; and so on. The central problem from the strategic planned viewpoint, however, is clear: 'A considerable difficulty in implementing overall policies for the revitalisation of rural areas is that local planning authorities have not direct control or influence over these other agencies.' This lack of control and influence points directly to the political decisions which have led to the fragmentation of decision-making, and to the nasty suspicion of the employment of divide-and-rule tactics by powerful sectional interests.

(ii) *Lack of finance.* A question asking what is the problem will inevitably, it seems, receive the answer: lack of finance. This survey on implementation problems is no different. The lack of finance response appeared often to be a reflex, of obvious importance, but rarely pursued to the point of specifying from where and for what purpose such finance is required. Those respondents that did take the issue further mentioned two specific financial factors. First, rural areas, particularly the more sparsely populated, offer low rates of return on investment and high unit costs, especially for service delivery. Second, inadequate global expenditure budgets for rural services and rural housing were stressed. These problems point back not only to local financial restraints emanating from central government but also to the central-government restrictions of structure plan involvement with socio-economic factors beyond those connected with land-use.

(iii) *Lack of control over private-sector interests.* A major problem reported by structure planners was a conflict between market forces and planning objectives. It was strongly suggested that profit-orientated development is dominant, and overrules need-orientated development enshrined in structure plans. As a result, strategic policies are often viewed as tangential by major private-sector decision-makers. For example, market pressures on land and housing lead to gentrification and a squeezing out of indigenous residents. Aspirations of house-building and construction interests thus came into direct conflict with planning objectives relating to local housing needs. Equally, the lack of control over agricultural land-use change and quasi-agricultural activities such as 'horsiculture' and waste-tipping can conflict with rural policies concerned with landscape conservation. All in all, what actually happens in rural areas is often dictated by market-orientated private resources, and the direction of this investment is seen by the optimistic as not necessarily concurring with policy goals, and by the pessimistic as openly conflicting with policy goals.

(iv) *Local political and public commitment.* A further 'problem' of implementation was perceived to be the varying political and public commitment to the agreed strategic planning aims for rural areas. This is manifest not only in an unwillingness to designate additional funds for rural projects but also in a kind of 'crisis of confidence' amongst planners and rural community groups because of the inability actively to respond to rural problems which are being identified. Thus, even if progressive policies can be agreed as part of strategic policy, political decision-makers will often instinctively support the status quo when it comes to backing these policies with progressive decisions.

There are clear connections between this political conservatism and the majority view in many rural communities opposing development and rate-based spending on rural services and facilities. Residents, particularly recent inmigrants, might support 'worthwhile' policies in principle but will object fiercely if implementation of these policies is threatened in the vicinity of their property interests. The not-in-my-back-yard (NIMBY) syndrome referred to earlier is deep and long-standing.

(v) *Government policies.* A minority of respondents stressed the fragmentary enabling legislation handed down by central government as a major difficulty in achieving planning objectives. One planner complained of 'weak and uncertain government legislation and advice', citing the draft circulars on green belts, housing, and design as being a form of 'anti-planning influence' in the face of development pressures. Other policy areas affected by these difficulties included landscape conservation and environmental protection. Any legislation, such as the Wildlife and Countryside Act, which involves management agreements and therefore payment by local agencies is rendered extremely problematic because local authority participation is so hampered by government controls over local government spending.

(vi) *Social-planning restrictions.* There are major difficulties in the implementation of social-planning objectives, and these were again stressed in the survey responses, although only by a minority of respondents. These difficulties are partly due to a literal adherence to central-government guide-lines on the core policies for structure plans. Social community and educational policies can be ruled out on these grounds, because they are not strictly land-use matters. In part, social-planning dilemmas arise from the strength of resource rationalization, or 'key settlement' policies (Cloke, 1979), which appear to offer benefits of economies of scale and yet do not sit easily alongside policies of providing housing services and employment in the smaller, non-key settlements.

(vii) *Advice not taken up.* Finally, it is worth mentioning that two respondents considered that a problem with policy information was that advice from planners is often not heeded by relevant agencies and individuals. Such advice covers a range of local issues, from conservation to industrial environments, but difficulties had been experienced in getting the message across to target landowners, councils, and communities. This problem feeds into wider issues of the marketing of planning and the depth of participation in planning by individuals and agencies in the locality.

These examples of the practical difficulties experienced by planners in the implementation of their structure plan policies contain few surprises, in view of our earlier discussion of the concepts of policy and action. They do, however, provide valuable insights as to what goes on behind the scenes of the sweeping legalistic statements in the written structure plans. The picture is one of professional planners being hemmed in both by *external constraints*, imposed by the distribution of administrative power and finance amongst a plethora of sectoral agencies, and by *internal inconsistencies*, arising from the resource conflict compromises necessary to produce and live with a plan which is approvable in both the local and central political arenas. Rural policy and implementation are clearly placed in the political sphere in which political acceptability far outweighs any conventionally conceived, rational planning task of neutral arbitration between conflicting sub-societal interests. There is a demonstrable shift towards an emphasis on private-sector decision-making which has been engineered by central government who have used various means (see (i), (ii), (iii), (v), and (vi) above) to curb any potential comprehensive planning role for local authorities.

Overcoming Problems of Implementation

Judging from the correspondence of concept and practice on the matter, there would appear to be few simple methods available to planners by which to improve their implementation capabilities. It appears that the central state keeps a tight constraint on any possibility of untrammelled comprehensive action by local planners, and that local victories in rural areas tended to be piecemeal and opportunistic. The survey questioned planners on these points and asked them to outline the ways in which they perceived that these problems of implementation could be overcome. Three suggestions (of increasingly remote likelihood) were offered.

(i) *By altering implementation*. This is the least likely category to yield useful suggestions, as improvements to implementation under current constraints have presumably been tried already. Indeed, many respondents clearly saw no realistic way of

overcoming implementation problems while current policy, legislation, and governmental attitudes to local expenditure persisted.
Others, however, did diagnose potential areas of improvement.
First it was suggested that attitudinal changes amongst planners
and politicians can be important (this reflects the 'crisis of
confidence' mentioned above). If actors in the planning system
became too disheartened or negative, then the inability to break
the shackles of central constraint becomes a self-fulfilling prophecy.
Second, it was suggested that better co-operation could be
achieved by establishing more formal joint working groups with
district councils and other agencies, although the degree to which
inter-agency power jealousy would be broken down by these
measures is questionable. Equally, respondents thought that
closer links with the private sector and voluntary bodies might
prompt action more suited to plan objectives. One more sceptical
comment suggested that planners should seek informally to
develop better contacts with 'individuals in high places'—an
expression of the need for greater access to where power actually
lies.

(ii) *By altering policies*. Structure plan policies will already
have been influenced by matters of feasibility and practicality of
implementation, because of requirements laid down by central
government. Policy options are thereby constrained by the
realities of implementation *before* agreement on written policies.
Therefore, apart from the to-ing and fro-ing suggested by the
policy–action continuum concept, it would not be expected that
approved policies would be a target for major change in order to
bring about better implementation procedures. This expectation
was largely borne out by the survey, where the blame for
implementation failures, and suggestions of potential areas for
improvement, were either directed locally (see (i)) or linked to
more structural changes at the central-state level (see (iii)).

Such policy changes that were advocated tended to reflect
particular circumstances in particular localities, relating, for
example, to the perceived requirement for 'housing for local
needs' policies. More generally, it was suggested that the problem
of developing policies for which no resources were available might
be partially overcome by linking specific policies with specific
resources, or by including an 'opportunity purchase' heading in
capital budgets. Also, it was recognized that some rural problems

might be tackled with specific 'policy packages' for small areas. This would be linked with a low-key, incremental, local approach, perhaps overseen by a project officer in the area concerned.

(iii) *By more centralized change.* The easiest target for proposed changes affecting implementation is central government, both in its role of paymaster and with its control over legislation and administrative structures. Predictably, county planners tended to favour reorganization such that county authorities could undertake a much more comprehensive planning role. In this way inter-agency turbulence could be reduced, and additional responsibility would be gained.

Other suggested changes were directed towards particular policy sectors. Respondents favoured a shift of central government and EC policy priorities so as to accord to conservation and amenity an importance equal to that given to agriculture. It was a matter of considerable concern that planning objectives for the rural landscape were not matched by implementation capabilities. In the same vein, an extension of planning controls to cover agricultural and forestry land-use changes was advocated by some respondents as one way of increasing their scope for action.

In general, the survey revealed that planners desired additional powers of intervention in most sectors, backed by appropriate fiscal allocation, in order to make their policies stick. Investment in industrial-site development, and public-sector development of housing and services, was considered in some cases to be the only possible way of achieving policy objectives in rural areas where the private sector was not providing suitable development for the needs of local people. Such suggestions are obviously out of tune with current political trends of deregulation and other forms of sponsorship of the private sector. But it is important to note that a significant group of personnel within local-authority planning has reached the conclusion that rural needs will only be met by more direct intervention by the public sector into the operation of housing, service, and employment markets. Without such intervention, implementation will inevitably fail to reflect the agreed planning objectives of elected local authorities.

Examples of Implementation Problems Overcome

It is noticeable that suggestions as to how implementation problems might be overcome takes the form either of a fine-tuning of implementation procedures or of major structural changes in the political and administrative nature of planning. The final part of the survey of county planners asked them to describe any circumstances in which they considered that implementation problems had actually been overcome in their area. Half of the sample were unable to convey any such example. Of the remainder, some illustrations were offered of each of the three areas of improvement discussed above.

Fine-tuning of implementation techniques had occurred in two counties, where land and finance had been provided for employment promotion by the county authorities themselves. Otherwise, instances of success were attributed to amendments to previous policies. For example, the introduction of local-area needs clauses to housing and settlement policies was reported to have reduced the previous impact of estate developments in small villages, and similar changes to industrial development have meant that small-scale employment developments are now permitted in many rural areas. At a strategic policy level, some counties had withdrawn growth-centre status from settlements where agencies such as the water authorities could not provide infrastructural development adequate for proposed housing developments.

A further area of implementation success was in the area of co-ordination and co-operation in planning. Several counties reported the initiation of rural co-ordination projects, with project officers in a particular locality given the task of linking consumer needs with decision-making channels for appropriate action. Similarly, co-ordination with the voluntary sector had been improved through the auspices of the rural community councils.

By far the largest growth area in implementaion activity, however, was in the *environmental-management* sector. Examples of recent environmental-management schemes (Cloke and Little, 1966: 281) are:

control of vandalism, litter, and access on the urban fringe;
coastal caravan and camping plan;
intensive livestock units plan;
land renewal in worked-out coalmine areas;
joint-grant tree-planting;
environmental-restoration schemes;
countryside management projects to remove eyesores and improve specific areas and landscape generally.

The impetus for initiative here has been the availability of labour through Manpower Services Commission schemes. Local authorities have devoted much energy to devising schemes specifically to make use of this personpower, even though MSC initiatives are temporary and politically sensitive.

There is a strong flavour of *opportunism* in these accounts of the practical implementation of policies and planning objectives. Any available resource, whether directly accessible to the authority, such as MSC labour, or indirectly usable, such as self-help and voluntary initiative, will be fully grasped in order to pursue the planning task. This planning by opportunism pervaded all the responses to this survey, and it is again difficult to escape the conclusion that this form of planning has arisen because of the severe restrictions imposed by the central state on the localized freedom to respond to localized problems.

CONCLUSION

In his study of policy and action in one particular county structure planning area, Flynn (1981: 61) concluded that planners 'appeared to be creating a "culture" within which bureaucratic and political values were operationalized'. They were using 'strategies and rationales' the effect of which was to establish a 'pragmatic consensus' reflecting two elements of policy: 'Firstly it translated explicit political prescriptions (and tacit assumptions) into "technical" policies. And secondly it supplied the norms through which intra- and inter-organisational conflicts (both political and bureaucratic) could be managed.'

The attempt in this chapter to marry together the conceptualization of policy and action and the practicalities of implementation, as stated in planning documents and as perceived by planning officers, reflects not only the overall culture but also both the policy dimensions mentioned in Flynn's analysis. The practical evidence suggests that planners do view implementation as the process of translating written policies into action, but the context in which this translation takes place is both centrally constrained and locally variable. Central constraints are exercised through control of finance, administrative structure, and legislative power. Within these bounds, however, there is sufficient discretion for action to differ according to the political prescriptions of individual county authorities. Although there is a kind of consensus among these prescriptions—basically restricting policy and action to land-use activities centring around key settlement policies—some counties have pursued wider objectives, involving some dispersal of investment.

The evidence presented here of planners' experience of implementation problems focuses on inter-agency conflicts. It might be expected that intra-organization tensions will also contribute to tensions over policy and action, but such factors are unlikely to emerge in a survey of this type. Given the inter-agency theme, it is to be expected that prescriptions for overcoming implementation problems look to a fine-tuning of localized co-ordinative management, although more radical suggestions for restructuring the nature of the interventionist planning by removing central-government constraints on finance and power were also part of the currency of planners' perceptions.

These responses from planners confirm many of the conceptual themes discussed earlier in the chapter. It seems entirely legitimate to view policy and action as one set of activities within the broader sphere of government, constrained by the socio-political environment in which planning operates. Within this framework, a façade of rational decision-making remains as a stylized representation of what is going on rather than as an accurate description of the interactive bargaining which is taking place. Planners responding to the survey perceived implementation as getting things done at ground-level. This suggests that within their broader understanding of the politicization of policy and action there has developed a culture of management in order to get the job done—just as Flynn has proposed.

Although the evidence presented in the second half of this chapter is partial in terms of the types of decision-makers and policy sectors included, it does lend weight to the view that implementation is by no means a straightforward rational process. Indeed, it is characterized by internal inconsistencies and continuous rather than linear processes. The overwhelming majority of respondents concluded that the stage-by-stage rational decision-making model is in practice defunct, even though it is still theoretically acceptable to their authority as the public face of the working framework in which planning operates. One response to this issue deserves a full airing:

Whilst a sequential view may appear rational and have value in justifying or explaining what is happening it does not adequately represent the actual processes of change. Policies of the authority are intentions, desirable courses of action, a base line for negotiation, and implementation can be putting these policies into effect. The distinction between policy and implementation is in practice blurred and artificial when the main emphasis is how can the local authority best respond to the problems that exist in its area.

Accepting this last premiss, the focal question for rural policy and action is how to engineer a response to rural problems when faced with the constraints of inadequate finance and insufficient corporate responsibility for planning. Clearly, the current culture is one of planning by opportunism. Any resource which becomes available to local authorities is pressed into service; the recent universal harnessing of voluntary initiatives and self-help as an integral part of the planning strategy of local authorities reflects this opportunistic use of any available resource. More importantly, it also represents an absence of alternative procedures for enacting policies. Is this how a local authority can best respond to the problems that exist in its area? Or are planners constrained by a knowledge of what they can do (according to the prevailing 'culture' of planning) and building their policies within these limitations at least partly as a legitimation of their function? The latter viewpoint seems difficult to oppose.

But is the premiss that local authorities are trying their best to respond to local problems one which we can accept at face value? We discussed in Chapter 2 the way in which the local state reflects the social relations of the locality. The notion of local problems, then, will be limited to those problems experienced or recognized by locally dominant power groups, unless other needs can be championed by professional officers such as planners within the local state. Equally, we must be careful to take full account of the concepts of the form and function of the central state (see Chapter 1) in interpreting central–local relations and resultant local policy. To what extent can the state's function be mitigated by discretionary local use of power by local élites? A fuller answer to these questions can only come from the study of policy and action in a particular rural locality, where factors of capitalism, state, and social relations can be encountered in one arena. It is to such a study that we now turn.

4

Motives, Mechanisms, and Impacts of Rural Policy: The Case of Gloucestershire

INTRODUCTION

The purpose of this chapter is to apply the theoretical discussions raised previously to the formulation, implementation, and outcome of policy in a specific area, Gloucestershire. In accordance with political-economy perspectives, attention will focus in particular on the role of the state in the decision-making process, and on the implications for different social groups of the resulting policy prescriptions and their implementation. In establishing the value of political-economy approaches to the study of rural planning and policy-making, earlier chapters have drawn attention to debate surrounding the potential incompatibility of broad theoretical analyses and detailed empirical observations. The point was made that, while strong arguments have been constructed to demonstrate the essential inconsistency of applying approaches based on the study of major structural changes at the local level, such arguments are not adhered to here. Instead, we believe that it is essential for original empirical work to be set within a broader theoretical framework which goes beyond the traditional positivist approaches that in themselves perpetuate, almost by default, a pluralist view of the world. Just as important is the belief that original material, drawn from the detailed study of specific localities, is important to the development of theoretical perspectives.

One of the major problems encountered in using locality-specific examples in the context of theoretical and conceptual studies is the need to be selective. In this chapter, much background detail concerning the evolution of policy decisions and the distribution of social need, for example, has had to be sacrificed—space has permitted only certain debates or decisions over policy formulation and particular instances of policy outcome to be recorded. At the same time, it is important that such selectivity does not lead to narrow and misleading conclusions.

In the case of Gloucestershire, the details presented are clearly not comprehensive. One specific casualty of the necessarily selective presentation of research evidence in this chapter is the omission of a more detailed analysis of the day-to-day planning procedures which followed the plan-making motives and mechanisms which are emphasized here. We are not suggesting by this that plan-making is more important than these nitty-gritty development issues. Neither are we assuming that concepts of the state, and of policy and implementation, are more applicable to the former than the latter. Indeed, we have published accounts elsewhere which stress both the local-scale implementation of Gloucestershire's structure plan policies by district councils and other agencies (Cloke and Little, 1987c) and the key issues of change in particular rural communities in the years following the ratification of the strategic plan (Cloke and Little, 1987d). Here it is clear that localized change in rural areas is just as much influenced by central government legislation and advice—concerning, for example, bus deregulation, schools closures, privatization of housing, and the rationalization of policing in rural areas—as by planning decisions made by district councils (which themselves are constrained centrally through appeals procedures and advice notes).

We are, however, convinced that the evidence we present here does accurately reflect key issues and trends in the formulation and outcome of rural policy. In particular, the focus is on a portrayal of dominant conflicts of interest and power relations which percolate throughout the allocative system, and from which other decisions and their implementation (not discussed here) derive. Such material as has been presented stems from detailed and lengthy discussions with policy-makers and residents—much fuller descriptions of both research methods and results can be found elsewhere (e.g. Cloke and Little, 1986a; 1987b; 1987c).

The choice of Gloucestershire as the 'subject' of this study is in some ways important and in others irrelevant to the principal direction and parameters of the research. Many of the issues raised are certainly not unique to the county, but reflect more widespread processes taking place in contemporary rural Britain. As such, they could have been studied in any number of 'examples'. The much cited 'locality' studies in geographical research have, however, demonstrated the uneven development of socio-economic processes and the local specificity of such processes both in terms of space and time (e.g. Murgatroyd *et al.*, 1985; Duncan, 1986). Gloucestershire was selected, then, not only as simply one of many convenient sites for the observation of rural-policy formulation and its outcome, but also in recognition of a number of specific historical and political characteristics which influenced both the decision-making process and the local implications of policy implementation.

STRUCTURE PLAN POLICIES FOR RURAL GLOUCESTERSHIRE

The Background

Probably the most important factor in the initial selection of Gloucestershire as a case study area was the relatively radical stance adopted by the county in the treatment of rural areas within the strategic planning system. Nationally, a survey of the rural policies embraced by first-generation structure plans (Cloke and Shaw, 1983) has demonstrated a near-universal commitment to policies of resource concentration. Gloucestershire was one of only three counties, by contrast, to favour a policy of resource dispersal within its rural areas (the other two being Cumbria and North Yorkshire— see Fig. 4.1). Thus one of the inbuilt objectives of the research was to explain the evolution and significance of this deviation from the widely accepted principles and constraints of rural planning at this time (namely, that the concentration of resources into 'key' settlements formed the most effective use of diminishing public funds). The work sought specifically to identify the extent to which this appearance of seemingly pro-rural policies represented a significant issue in terms of the operation of the policy process itself, and to consider in what way (if at all) that significance was reflected in the outcome of decisions taken *on the ground* within the county's rural communities.

In recognition of the need to be selective, the study of the policy process in Gloucestershire (and consequently the account presented below) was confined largely to structure planning within the county, thus isolating one particular policy community as a microcosm of professional and political interactions (Cloke and Little, 1987*a*). It is worth noting, however, that strategic planning *prior* to the establishment of structure plans demonstrated a

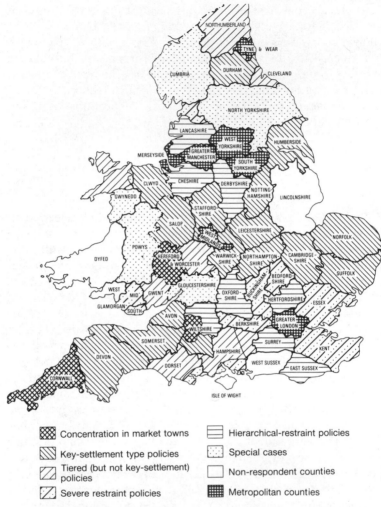

▨ Concentration in market towns		▤ Hierarchical-restraint policies	
◩ Key-settlement type policies		⬚ Special cases	
◪ Tiered (but not key-settlement) policies		☐ Non-respondent counties	
◪ Severe restraint policies		▦ Metropolitan counties	

FIG. 4.1. A Categorization of Settlement Planning Policies within County Structure Plans

Source: Cloke, 1983: 147

predominantly conventional set of priorities for the rural parts of the county. These priorities combined a concern for the conservation of the value and character of the countryside with a desire to meet the needs of those living there. They advocated 'united' and 'appropriate' development with an awareness both of the problems facing some of the remoter, declining rural areas and of the pressures occurring in the more accessible locations. The result was a reliance on somewhat standard policies of resource concentration, tempered by an apparent commitment to maintaining some small-scale rural services and allowing very limited development (Cloke and Little, 1987*b*).

That policy moved from this strikingly conventional set of objectives and assumptions to the actively pro-rural tenor of the draft structure plan is of considerable relevance to the policy process itself. As noted elsewhere (Healey, 1986) there has been a strong tendency for studies of rural policy-making to rely entirely on written policy statements—generally structure plan documents. The details of the negotiations and conflicts which preceded such statements have, as a result, been widely ignored. And yet the complexities involved in the formulation of written policy—for example, the incorporation of central-state directives, or the resolution of tensions between different agencies, or levels of state involvement—are as much a part of the final objectives (and likely outcome) as the written statement itself. Here, the transfer of initial policy objectives and priorities into draft, and into their accepted policy statements, displays a complex set of relationships, constraints, and allegiances, the recognition of which is not only crucial to the understanding of policy for rural Gloucestershire but provides an important insight into the broader mechanisms of policy formulation.

County-Level Commitment to Rural Policy

Fig. 4.2 outlines the programme of policy-making within the Gloucestershire structure plan. An early indication of the growing concern amongst members and officers for the problems experienced by the rural parts of the county was evident in the early 1970s in the first stages of structure plan preparation. A survey based on 1971 census data revealed particular pockets of deprivation within the rural areas, and prompted the recognition that planning action should be targeted towards 'problem areas'. Such recognition was enhanced by two further surveys, the first of district and parish council representatives (1,451 in all) and the second of 2,000 households throughout the county. It is not so much the actual

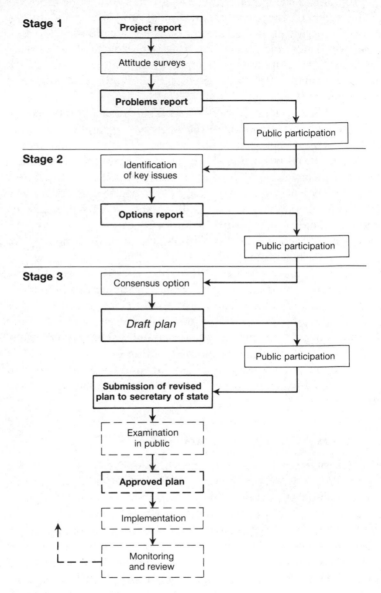

Stage 1

Project report

Attitude surveys

Problems report

Public participation

Stage 2

Identification of key issues

Options report

Public participation

Stage 3

Consensus option

Draft plan

Public participation

Submission of revised plan to secretary of state

Examination in public

Approved plan

Implementation

Monitoring and review

FIG. 4.2. The Stages in the Gloucestershire Structure Plan-Making Process
Source: Cloke and Little, 1987*b*: 961

results of these surveys as their handling by planning officers which is important here. Indeed, public perceptions of the problems of rural areas and of the possible solutions were somewhat disparate of nature, and (again) reflected a general concern with rural conservation and the preservation of natural beauty rather than with the occurrence of deprivation. And yet planning officers were able to use these results as evidence of a need to address the socio-economic problems of rural areas, and to allow the survey procedure as a whole to legitimize (without unduly constraining) their own policy preferences.

Further endorsement of 'pro-rural' objectives was sought in a third structure plan preparation exercise—this time in a series of fifteen technical reports designed to look at physical, social, and economic characteristics of the county (Gloucester County Council (GCC), 1978). Again, the handling of these reports, the approaches and techniques adopted, was important to the endorsement of preferred policy options. The reports gave technical credibility to the view that 'problem groups' existed, and that there was a tendency for such groups to concentrate in 'localities of adverse conditions' (GCC 1979: 2). The establishment of technical justification for the existence of such problems was seen by officers as an important first step towards gaining political support for the introduction of radical rural policies. County councillors were deliberately not included in the earlier surveys, since it was felt that their involvement at this stage might prejudice subsequent decision-making. Clearly, in all three exercises the importance of managing political opinion, of presenting well-researched technical information, and of staging arguments within the 'art of the possible' context of local political control imposed strong, if not overt, boundaries on the conclusions reached by planning officers.

The results and conclusions of these surveys were brought together by the County Council in a document entitled 'The Problems' (GCC, 1976). This report, presented at a meeting of the Policy and Resources Committee in April 1977, provides an important insight into the evolution of rural policy for the county. In particular it demonstrates, in the identification of five specific themes (GCC, 1976) the desire of planning officers to 'keep the options open' as regards the strength and direction of policy response to the problems of the rural areas:

  (i) *Conservation.* This theme summarized concern for the

protection of agricultural land and the outstanding quality of the rural and built environment in the county. It implied the need to resolve planning conflicts in a period of continuing change, exemplified by the working of minerals in areas of high visual amenity, the growth of road traffic in historic towns, and the encroachment of urban development on farmland.

(ii) *Maximum economic growth*. This theme stressed the wide benefits of economic growth, and was related closely to the issue of the scale of population and economic growth in the county. Gloucestershire has a relatively high potential for economic growth, and its encouragement, this theme argued, would lead to greater prosperity and—with expansion in jobs and population—increase the choice of opportunities available to individuals.

(iii) *A more balanced distribution of living and working opportunities*. This theme emphasized concern over the distribution of opportunity within the county, and the need to solve worsening problems arising from existing differences in living and working conditions. Opportunities in the central parts of the Forest of Dean and the Cotswolds, in particular, have been shown to be relatively limited compared with those in most of the Severn Vale. In the more remote rural areas, there are often combinations of economic and social problems.

(iv) *Minimizing the cost of public investment*. The need to continue central- and local-government financial restrictions was a fourth concern emerging at the first stage of structure-plan preparation. This was associated with the need for the efficient and effective use of resources in the context of the national economic situation. The need was re-emphasized for the structure plan to take account of constraints, including the existing disposition of land-use, current planning permissions, and natural resources in the county. Above all, the need for a realistic appraisal of available resources was stressed.

(v) *Continuation of current policies*. Although the first stage of the structure plan process identified the four themes above, the public participation exercises also showed them to be set against a background where the majority of residents were generally satisfied with their present way of life, notwithstanding the range of problems identified. There was little support for radical change, and thus a fifth theme, a continuation of current policies, was introduced.

The themes drawn from the preliminary surveys and arising from the Problems Report indicate a general support for conservative policies of resource concentration. Of the five, only No. 3 confronts the issue of resource distribution or gives any suggestion of a swing in favour of progressive policy changes. Importantly, however, in the endorsement of these themes no attempt was made to water down the potential impact of theme 3 by suggesting 'compromise' themes. Nor was the essential incompatibility of the themes allowed to threaten the concern for distributive issues as expressed in this theme. Thus, the Problems Report at least ensured that the potential for the introduction of more radical policies in response to the problems of rural areas remained viable.

The evolution of the Problems Report (and incorporated themes) into what was known as the Options Report (GCC, 1977) forms the final pre-structure plan preparation exercise to be considered here. The formulation and management of the Options Report represents, essentially, the continuation of attempts by planning officers to retain a commitment to addressing the problems of the more needy areas. From the five major themes identified as part of the Problems Report, the Options Report established four policy options (GCC, 1977). These options were designed as mutually exclusive, with only one, option C, demonstrating any degree of compromise, or willingness to pay attention to the needs of disadvantaged groups within the limitations of 'feasible' levels of public investment:

Option A. Continue the current approach to accommodate trends. This option described the possible effects of continuing with existing planning policies, as in theme 5. It served as a control against which the effects of alternatives in other options could be judged.

Option B. Encourage economic growth. This option primarily stressed the theme of economic growth, but also contained elements of the conservation theme. The option sought to generate increased economic growth in the Severn Vale, but counterbalanced this with greater emphasis on conservation (theme 1) to safeguard the county's areas of high visual amenity from the increasing pressures which development and expansion in the vale would generate.

Option C. Assist areas of limited opportunity. This option reflected the concern (in theme 3) to maintain and improve conditions in areas where opportunities are limited. The option sought to achieve this without involving such an unacceptably high level of public investment (theme 4) as would seriously prejudice overall county prosperity.

Option D. Limit growth. The option covered two of the themes described earlier, with its aim to reduce public expenditure in county population and economic growth. This would then have an effect upon conservation (theme 1)—particularly preservation—in terms of reducing the impact of physical change.

While there is insufficient space here to present a detailed account of the handling of these options, it is important to outline a number of factors which point to the view that the whole options exercise was designed ultimately to produce a compromise which would include a commitment to rural policy:

  (i) The options were clearly structured in such a way as to divide public opinion. They were couched in uncompromising terms that were sure to split different agencies and organizations.
 (ii) The options were given careful guidance through various County Council subcommittees by planning officers—in particular:
(iii) Officers were able to dissuade the influential Policy and Resources Committee to declare, *before* the public participation exercise, its strong predilection for option A.
 (iv) Only a very short time (six weeks) was permitted for the carrying out of the public-participation exercise (this in itself raises a number of questions about the access of members of the public to the decision-making process—questions which will be taken up again in Chapter 6).

Public opinion was indeed, as predicted, divided as to the suitability of each of the policy options. In total, 19 per cent of respondents favoured option A, 11 per cent option B, 34 per cent option C, and 20 per cent option D. A further 16 per cent of respondents suggested a combination of options (Cloke and Little, 1987*b*). No individual option, then, dominated opinion or emerged as a 'natural choice' on which to base county policy. As a result, a consensus option (as opposed to a compromise) was constructed, incorporating parts of all the options, watering down the support given by option C to the needs of areas of poor opportunity—

ensuring that rural areas would not take precedence over urban areas as far as expenditure was concerned—but at the same time retaining some commitment to stimulating rural regeneration. It was this consensus option which formed the basis of the draft structure plan which was presented to central government for approval.

This description of the evolution of a policy option for Gloucestershire has not simply been given to demonstrate the priorities or preferences of local decision-makers. Rather, it has been included as a means of investigating the *management* of the decision-making process and the interaction of individuals and groups within that process. Clearly, the arrival by Gloucestershire County Council at a consensus option was not a matter of chance; its introduction and acceptance were carefully handled by different interests in a way that says as much (if not more) about the policy-making process as about the specific direction of agreed decisions. Thus the next task of this section is to consider the reasons why the consensus was arrived at in the case of the Gloucester structure plan process, and to relate these observations to the theoretical debate surrounding consensus within policy-making. Again, a more detailed account by the authors of the issues raised here can be found elsewhere (Cloke and Little, 1987a; 1987b).

Officer–Member Relations and the Motives for Consensus

It is relatively simple to uncover the *mechanisms* involved in the adoption of consensus amongst policy-makers in Gloucestershire. Some of the relevant explanations have already been alluded to—the presentation of overstated, and oversimplified options that were technically flawed, for example, or the rushing through of the public participation exercise. While such points may be debatable, they are, nevertheless, quite easily identifiable. Far less so are the actual reasons *why* the consensus option was arrived at. In order to attempt to answer this question, it is necessary to pay close attention to the relationship between officers and members during the various stages of the construction of the plan, and, in particular, at the level of involvement of different groups and individuals.

Flynn (1981) has argued that the creation of consensus amongst policy-makers 'reduces the prospect of fundamental conflicts and

engenders a healthy environment or culture for decision-making'
(Cloke and Little, 1987*a*: 33). He suggests that the chief concern
amongst planning officers in pursuit of such consensus is the
identification of policy options which are politically acceptable as
well as technically sound. Such an assumption, however, down-
grades as of secondary concern any ideological commitment that
planning officers may hold to particular policy directions. In the
case of Gloucestershire, there is indeed evidence that senior
planners recognized early on in the structure plan process the
importance of constructing policy in such a way that it was
politically acceptable and would appeal to the majority of
councillors. There is also an indiction, however, that the *motive*
for such tactical orchestration of policy was not simply a desire to
avoid conflict but reflected a genuine concern for the needs and
well-being of the rural people.

Key officers and councillors appear to have been important in
working to achieve consensus—thus lending weight to a managerialist interpretation of policy-making, at this level, whereby (as
explained in Chapter 2) particular actors assume important
'gatekeeping' roles within the decision-making process. General
discussion between the bulk of planning officers and councillors
during the preparation of the draft structure plan for Gloucestershire
was, not uncommonly, rather limited. Instead, dealings with
councillors were undertaken largely by senior management,
primarily, in this case, through a small 'subcommittee' of the
Policy and Resources Committee composed of senior members
and leaders of the opposition parties along with the county
planning officer and his senior officers (Cloke and Little, 1987*b*).
The informality and selectivity of this committee is, again, not
unusual in policy formulation (Davies, 1986). In the Gloucestershire
case, the success and indeed tolerance of this subcommittee relied
heavily on the trust bestowed on the county planning officer
himself, coupled with the fact that the council was dominated by a
large Conservative majority.

For the most part, then, councillors were happy to leave
technical aspects of planning procedures in the hands of the senior
officers. The county planning officer acted in general as the
mediator between the officers and the members, and in particular
forged strong links with the chair and vice-chair of the council. The
relationship which evolved between these key individuals was

clearly important both in the management of policy decisions and in the arrival at the consensus option in the draft structure plan. Also important in these relationships, and in the ultimate direction of policy, were personal preferences of other councillors (primarily the 'Cotswold cavalry'—a group of mainly ex-military councillors from rural constituencies) who were also committed to pro-rural policy initiatives.

This brief account of the formulation of policy objectives for the Gloucestershire draft structure plan has tried to illustrate the key role of planning officers in the management of consensus and in the deliberate shaping of policy within the political 'art of the possible' as perceived by decision-makers.

The particular direction of policy making orchestration in Gloucestershire, however, demonstrates an added dimension to the management of consensus, as officers were able to incorporate some of their policy preferences in favour of areas of rural decline. This achievement occurred only because partnership was available with key committee gate-keepers backed up by a substantial rural lobby within the council membership. (Cloke and Little, 1987*a*: 41)

This discussion has focused entirely on *internal* mechanisms and interrelationships in the formulation of policy. The perception of the 'political culture' of decision-making was strongly influenced, it may be argued, by the existence of a clear commitment amongst councillors to the rural parts of the county.

The submission of the draft structure plan revealed that a similar commitment to rural policies was patently *not* present, however, in the mind of the central state. Thus the following section of this chapter will go on to consider the role played by the central state in the formulation of policies for rural Gloucestershire, and to place this specifically within the debate surrounding the relationship between the central and the local states.

THE ROLE OF THE CENTRAL STATE IN THE FORMULATION OF POLICIES FOR RURAL GLOUCESTERHSIRE

In the preparation of the draft structure plan for Gloucestershire, planning officers had been careful to secure the direction and advice of the local office of the Department of the Environment in terms of the overall limits and expectations of the plan. It would therefore have been difficult to predict the objections raised by the secretary of state when the examination in public of the plan took place in September 1980. These objections essentially challenged the consensus that had been achieved within the County Council, insisting in particular that the emphasis of the plan be directed more firmly towards the type of conservative environmental concerns that had been so efficiently bypassed during previous internal negotiations.

It would be wrong, however, to imagine that the secretary of state's objections related exclusively or even predominantly to the specific character of the rural policies in Gloucestershire's structure plan. Rather, it is more realistic to think of them as clear evidence of the trends outlined in detail in Chapter 2—namely, of the desire by the central state to secure an ever-deepening penetration into local state activity, and also of widespread attempts to confine structure plan influence to matters predominantly relating to land-use, at the expense of more socially orientated policies. Thus the specific demands of the secretary of state must be interpreted within the overall framework of changing central–local relations in contemporary Britain, and in the context of the continuation of strong preservationist attitudes towards the countryside.

While these broader issues are undoubtedly of principal importance here, it is nevertheless interesting to consider the practical implications of the secretary of state's objections and subsequent amendments to the Gloucestershire structure plan, not least to provide a context for the discussion of policy implementation which follows. As discussed elsewhere (Cloke and Little, 1987*b*), it is in the formulation of policies for housing that alterations to the structure plan are most clearly identifiable, in terms both of the aims of the central state and of the likely impact on rural communities. Table 4.1 outlines the submitted and the approved structure plan policies for housing (labelled with an H), as well as selected policies for employment (E), transport (T), and community facilities (CF). The major effect of policy alterations to housing policy is both to simplify considerably policy H3, which was aimed at addressing areas of decline, and (potentially) significantly to reduce its likely impact. In particular, the 'socially progressive' content of policies to encourage residential development have been considerably downgraded in the assertion (by approved policy) that such residential development would be

Table 4.1. Examples of the Secretary of State's Modifications of Policies Submitted by Gloucestershire County Council

	Submitted policy	Approved policy
H2	Residential development will be located principally at the main centres of employment.	Retained unchanged
H3	In areas of rural decline, particularly within the north and south Cotswolds, residential development will be encouraged in villages and groups of villages where additional housing can contribute to alleviating the causes of that decline. The following factors will be used to identify the areas of rural decline where residential development will be encouraged: (a) an actual or threatened loss of important local community facilities and services, including schools, shops, post offices, public transport, health facilities, and library services; (b) a static or declining population including a high proportion of elderly people; (c) an insufficient supply of appropriate housing to meet the needs of the local population; (d) a rural area where the county council or district council proposes to promote employment opportunities.	In areas of decline, residential development normally limited to infilling, and small groups of dwellings, will be encouraged in villages where additional housing can contribute to alleviating the causes of that decline.
H4	In areas not covered by principal policy H3, residential development will be permitted in those villages which have a primary level of local community facilities and services.	In areas not covered by policy H3, residential development, normally limited to infilling, and small groups of dwellings, will usually be permitted in those villages which have a primary level of local community facilities and services.

Table 4.1. (*Continued*)

	Submitted policy	Approved policy
H5	In other villages, residential development will normally be restricted to meet the remaining needs of any policy area.	In other villages, residential development will normally be restricted to infilling.
E5	The establishment of small-scale industry within or adjacent to rural settlements will be permitted, unless overriding problems of traffic generation or the loss of environmental or residential amenity are identified.	Small-scale industry will normally be permitted within or adjacent to existing settlements, unless there are overriding problems of traffic or the loss of environmental or residential amenity. (Particular emphasis will be given to the establishment of small-scale industry within or adjacent to rural settlement.)[a]
T3	The public transport system will be maintained and developed to cater for the educational, social, and economic needs of the community as a whole.	The public transport system will be maintained and developed to cater for the educational, social and economic needs of the community as a whole, and especially in rural areas.
CF1	The county council will determine the priorities for the provision of community services in accordance with principal policies H2, H3, and H4.	Retained unchanged.
CF2	Any further rationalization of county primary schools will take account of principal policies H3 and H4.	Deleted.
CF4	The county council will encourage the area health authority and other agencies to take account of principal policies H2, H3, and H4 in the provision of health and community services.	Deleted.

[a] Added in response to the council's objections to the secretary of state's modifications.

Source: Cloke and Little, 1987*b*: 797).

'normally limited to infilling, and small groups of dwellings'. Policies H4 and H5 have been similarly revised (see Table 4.1), ostensibly with the aim of simplifying policy and its implementation, but more likely in order to perpetuate the conservation ethic and confine the scope of policy more firmly to land-use and physical planning issues.

By amending housing policy in this way, the downgrading of more socially progressive objectives had implications for other areas of policy. In particular, submitted policy CF2, stating that any further rationalization of primary schools would take the aims of policies H3 and H4 into account (GCC, 1979), was deleted, together with policy CF4, which encouraged Area Health Authorities and other agencies similarly to take account of policies H2, H3, and H4 in the provision of health and community services. The principle of resource dispersal, then, was attacked throughout the plan, and renewed emphasis was placed on the protection of the quality of the environment. Thus the direction of the secretary of state's amendments appear generally to be subordinating the needs of rural communities to the aims of conservation.

In justifying the extent and nature of amendments to the structure plan, the secretary of state argued that the detail included in the submitted policies constituted an infringement on the responsibilities of the *district* councils concerned—particularly as regards the implementation of development control and the formulation of local plans. This argument is clearly important in the context of the broader debate concerning local–central relations. At a time when the distribution of power appears, explicitly and implicitly, to be moving towards greater concentration at the centre, it seems strangely inconsistent that the secretary of state should demonstrate such concern for the relative autonomy of the district. To view events in Gloucestershire as some sort of straightforward concern for the authority of the district, however, would be to place too naïve an interpretation on the motives and actions of the central state. Such events should not be interpreted in isolation, but rather in the context of the whole package of directives and controls designed to restrict just this autonomy (see Chapter 2).

Firstly, it must be remembered that the district council represents just one arm of the local state, not its totality. Attempts by the central state to increase the importance of the district in the formulation and implementation of policy have consequently been interpreted (see Duncan and Goodwin, 1985) as an attempt to exploit divisions within the local state as a whole and to draw different factions in different directions, thus weakening its overall effectiveness. Apparent commitment to strengthening the role of the district should, moreover, be evaluated in the light of direct political, financial, and legislative attacks on local state autonomy. The broadening of district functions and influence in written policy statements such as those contained in the Gloucestershire structure plan is meaningless when accompanied by ever-tightening controls on spending power and legislative freedom in the implementation of local policy.

Having said this, it has been argued by many authors (e.g. Gyford, 1984; Duncan and Goodwin, 1988) that local states may demonstrate varying levels of autonomy from the central state. The uneven development of capitalist processes, reflected in the variation in social and political relations in different local states, has led to varying local expressions of central control. If this view is accepted, it is clear that the distribution of power between central and local states is open to a degree of flexibility (albeit within strictly defined limits). In the case of Gloucestershire, such flexibility lies in the implementation of structure plan policy and the potential offered to districts in the interpretation of decision-making.

The approved strategic policies, whilst moving demonstrably away from initial priorities of greater resource dispersal, do at least leave some room for manœuvre during implementation procedures. Consequently, the future of rural areas in Gloucestershire following the secretary of state's structure plan modifications might be seen to lie to some degree in the hands of the district councils. If interpreted to the letter, the modifications could easily render the policies for rural decline impotent. If implemented with greater recognition and respect for the original motives which underlay the submitted policies, the modifications could have less of a restrictive effect on the more idealistic prescriptions for rural problems. Whichever course of action is taken, it is clear that an understanding of the role and influence of the central state in policy-making for rural Gloucestershire rests on the analysis not only of policy formulation but also of policy implementation.

THE IMPLEMENTATION OF RURAL POLICY

The Relationship between County and District

In Chapter 3 we examined the notion of implementation in planning at a theoretical level, and specifically examined some of the constraints operating on the implementation of county structure plan policy. The intention here is to apply some of the ideas raised in that earlier discussion in continuing the analysis of policies for rural Gloucestershire. A principle focus for such analysis will be the 'secondary constraints' referred to in Chapter 3 and, in particular, the relationship between county and district as part of the implementation process. It is worth emphasizing at this point that, despite the pragmatic subdivision of subject-matter during the presentation of the analysis, the view expressed earlier—that policy formulation and implementation cannot be interpreted in terms of a dichotomy, as separate stages in the planning process— is adhered to here.

It was argued above that, following the secretary of state's amendments to the Gloucestershire structure plan, the district councils were left in a potentially powerful position in terms of the implementation of rural settlement policies. Consequently, the extent to which county planners could persuade their district counterparts to adopt county-level preferences in the implementation of policy is of key importance. Clearly, the county authorities were wary of the dangers of overstepping the boundaries of recognized responsibilities and appearing to exert too great an influence on the actions of district councils. It was possible, however, even following the negative impression forced by the secretary of state, for county-level planners to 'reinstate and re-emphasise their own policy preferences through the use of nonstatutory and advisory documents' (Cloke and Little, 1987*c*: 1033).

Rather than attempt to convey their policy values and priorities in *discussion* with other agencies (which would probably have had little chance of success), county planners chose a more practical method of influence through the development of a classification for rural areas. It was the intention that this classification might be taken up and used by districts in the prioritization of resource distribution for rural communities. The classification distinguished between areas of growth, stability, rural deprivation, and rural decline, and was based on relative levels of opportunity and access amongst rural settlements (see Fig. 4.3), and led to county planners producing a map identifying those areas considered to be top priority for planning policy and providing a clear indication of 'preferred' patterns of resource distribution.

In addition, the county council sought further to influence the implementation of policy, firstly, by relating the area classification to the principal settlement policies as contained within the structure plan (H3, H4, and H5), and secondly, by elaborating on each category with 'policy guide-lines'. Such elaboration in the context of H3 policies is most clearly demonstrated in Fig. 4.4. Advice is obviously quite specific with the restriction of housing development to settlements which display a range of services and within groups of villages which can collectively offer a range of services (Cloke and Little, 1987c).

The county defers to local knowledge of the districts by resisting the actual naming of the groups of villages which may be suitable for residential development on the basis of these criteria. It does provide a set of guide-lines to assist in their identification, but these leave room for tactical manœuvre at the district levels.

In practice, this listing creates considerable difficulties for the implementing agency, even if they are fully sympathetic to the planning objectives underlying it . . . . . Certainly, an unco-operative district council would find it a simple task to uncover legitimate reasons for the inability to implement the encouragement of development on the basis of these village groups as defined by the county. Even a cooperative development control agency, if not fully convinced by the concept of groups, would find it easier to follow the traditional pathway of permitting growth in recognisable centres.   (Cloke and Little, 1987b: 1036)

Settlement policies H4 and H5 are similarly elaborated upon by the county, with classifications provided to assist in implementation of policy objectives.

There is insufficient space here to present a full interpretation of county directives for the implementation of policies for other rural services in Gloucestershire. It is important, however, to note the emphasis placed by the county on the establishment of partnerships and co-operation as a means of addressing problems of rural-service provision. Specifically, partnerships between communities are advocated, and between policy-makers and rural residents in

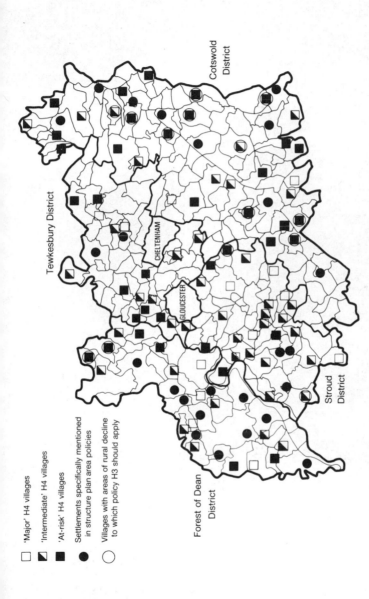

FIG. 4.3. At-Risk Settlements. For comprehensive analysis all villages were examined under the criteria for identifying H4 settlements. Within areas of rural decline, however, policy H3 will apply, and not H4.

Source: Gloucestershire County Council, 1981

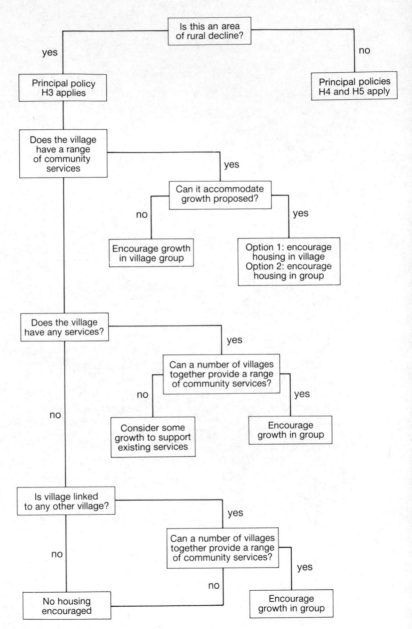

FIG. 4.4. Settlement Framework Options in Areas of Rural Decline
Source: Gloucestershire County Council, 1981

the fostering of self-help schemes. Reference is also made to the need for the implementation of policies for rural services to be carried out in co-ordination with other public- and private-sector decision-making agencies such as the Rural Development Commission (particularly CoSIRA as was), Area Health Authorities, etc. There is a clear indication, then, of the county's recognition of the need to confront the type of inter-agency conflicts which characteristically hamper the implementation of rural policies (see Chapter 3), and to try to harness relationships for the potential benefit of communities.

The need to foster such partnership arrangements for the implementation of rural policies was formalized in the establishment of a Rural Community Action Project (RCAP). This project was established in Cotswold District and involved the County Council, the District Council, major service agencies, and representatives from local communities in an effect to identify both rural problems and possible solutions. Despite the involvement of 'official' organizations, the major role within the group was seen to be with local people. While a reliance on self-help responses to the problems of rural areas does in some ways run counter to the identified county priorities of redistributing public resources to meet the needs of the more deprived rural communities, the creation of the RCAP was supported at many levels, not least by the 'Cotswold Cavalry' whose influence had been instrumental in the initial acceptance of pro-rural policies in the draft structure plan. Self-help appears to represent a politically acceptable means both of distributing limited resources in the context of local and central state constraint, and of presenting, at the very least, the illustration of positive action.

Finally, in this section we will look briefly at the extent to which county priorities and expectations for the implementation of policies for rural areas have actually been taken up by the districts. The second part of this chapter is devoted partly to an analysis of these issues in relation to specific policies and decisions. Here, the intention is rather to consider the more general response of the districts to the advice that has been documented above. Clearly, at the time of the research, only a relatively short space of time had elapsed during which the reaction of the districts to the structure plan policies and the suggestions for their implementation could be assessed. Nevertheless, there are some interesting points to note.

At this broad level, there appears to be a somewhat mixed response by districts to the County Council's objectives for settlement planning. The Forest of Dean District Council, for example, while recognizing their own powers of interpretation, have chosen to adhere quite closely to the framework proposed by the county. Their own strategy thus mirrors, for example, the county planners' identification of areas of decline. Tewkesbury Borough Council, on the other hand, elected to classify settlements according to their own, internally derived criteria of decline. According to this classification, none of the parishes could be identified as an 'area of rural decline, suitable for the application of structure plan policy H3' (Tewkesbury Borough Council, 1984: 11). This conclusion runs counter to that of the County Council, who identified four potential candidates for H3 policy within the same area.

There is thus no automatic uptake of county policy priorities by districts; and even where the two levels of the local state are in general agreement, the flexibility incorporated by the district in the interpretation of county policy can be quite far-reaching in terms of the specific implementation of such policy. Further indication of the extent to which the district is prepared to accept the preferences of the county in a formal sense may also be found in the decisions and allocative procedures outlined in local plans. In Gloucestershire, the lack of local plans (at the time of the research) made such an analysis impossible. The absence of local plans itself, however, could be seen to create a more flexible background for the incorporation of county influences in district policy. 'Indeed, the county planning authority is often in a position to prepare "supplementary planning" documents . . . . in the hope that these will be largely endorsed by the hard-pressed district planning authorities as suitable models for the planning of their own rural areas' (Cloke and Little, 1987c: 1046).

The clearest indication of the district's commitment to centrally derived policies, and, just as importantly, of its *ability* to act on the resulting interpretation of those policies, is gained at the parish level. In this context not only will the specific relationship between different local-state agencies (including the county and the district *and* private organizations) be evident, but it will be possible to identify the broader influence of the central state on the implementation of policy. Thus the following section turns to an analysis of policy implementation in selected parishes in Gloucestershire, the main intention being to apply to the local context the issues raised above regarding the redistribution of resources to areas of rural decline, and to look more directly at the *impact* of policies for rural areas.

LOCAL IMPLEMENTATION AND POLICY IMPACT

While the analysis of the policy-making process, and of the interaction between different agencies within that process, tells us much about the priorities and expectations of rural planning, it tells us nothing about the impact of policies themselves or the extent to which original objectives have been fulfilled. It is thus important that the study of the mechanisms of policy formulation and implementation be accompanied by an analysis of the outcome of decisions made at the parish level. In the past, work has tended to polarize around studies dealing with the construction of policy in rural areas on the one hand and, more commonly, those looking simply at social need and rural deprivation, on the other hand where links between the two have been made it has tended to be at a rather abstract level, in relation, not to *specific* instances of policy implementation, but to broader packages of policy prescription. Here we attempt to explore these links in the context of identifiable key decisions—to consider, in particular, whether there is any evidence in Gloucestershire that the original concern for the rural parts of the county is being reflected in policy outcome within the rural communities.

To return to the theoretical basis of the research, the adoption of a political-economy approach presupposes that the costs and benefits of resource allocation will vary amongst different groups in the rural population. Clearly, then, an essential element of the analysis of policy and its impact is the differential effects of allocative decisions on sections of rural society. Such effects can only be assessed through the use of detailed, locality-based investigations. Here research focuses on ten parishes in north-west Gloucestershire straddling the boundary between the districts of the Forest of Dean and Tewkesbury (see Fig. 4.5). The specific objectives of the study carried out in these ten parishes was to identify particular key issues in terms of policy impact, and to consider the implications of decisions made on different groups in the selected communities. In this way, the hope was to relate levels of need within the rural parishes to policy priorities for those areas.

There are a number of deficiencies present in both the methodology and its application. Most obvious are the potential pitfalls involved in trying to secure too strong or direct a link between policy and its impact. Particular examples of social disadvantage or lack of opportunity, whether experienced by groups or individuals, are frequently the result, not of specific decisions, but rather of the impact of a combination of decisions and of the broader allocative processes within society as a whole. Nevertheless, having made a commitment to tackling rural disadvantage, it is important to examine the ways in which (if at all) policy-makers attempt to address some of the more fundamental issues surrounding resource distribution in the context of individual policies. Another methodological inadequacy is the dependence on questionnaires and all the associated problems concerning bias, interpretation of need, and so on that have been rehearsed elsewhere (see Cloke and Little, 1987*d*). Of key importance in this respect is the failure of individuals to recognize the difficulties they experience, with the mentality of 'making the best of it' being particularly well entrenched in rural society. Finally, it should be noted that the study of key issues and policy impact is, of necessity, selective. There is insufficient space here for a systematic analysis of all areas of policy, and those issues that have been selected are intended to be as much illustrative of wider trends in terms of the outcome of decision-making as interpretations of specific instances of the links between policy and impact. It is important, however, that these wider trends be identified in the context of community-based enquiry.

The Study Parishes: A Background

A brief introduction is necessary to place the study parishes (Fig. 4.5) within a physical as well as a policy-making context, and to establish their background characteristics in relation to socio-economic structures and levels of need. Greater detail on the changing characteristics of the parishes is included elsewhere (e.g. Cloke and Little, 1987*c*; 1987*e*). For the purposes of this discussion these may be summarized as follows.

Population Change. Analysis of population change during the period 1971–81 shows the case study area to be one of significant growth. The population of Tewkesbury District increased by 9.3 per cent, whilst that of the Forest of Dean grew by 10.5 per cent (Office of Population Censuses and Surveys (OPCS), 1981). Both figures are significantly higher than the 8 per cent calculated by OPCS as the 'average' for 'accessible rural areas' in Britain over the same period (OPCS, 1981). The area would thus appear to exhibit the trends outlined in Chapter 1 of this book—the growing desire by certain groups of people to live in rural and semi-rural localities, together with the decentralization of (in particular) service employment.

However, these figures, and such a generalized explanation, must be treated with caution. A glance at the rates of change for individual parishes (see Table 4.2) reveals that the high growth rates recorded at district level mask a variety of trends. As the table shows, two parishes, Chaceley and Hasfield, experienced an absolute decline in population between 1971 and 1981, while four others grew at less than the average rate (Hartpury, Redmarley, Tirley, and Upleadon). All other parishes grew at a substantially higher rate than the district averages, the greatest increase

Table 4.2. Population Change by Case Study Parish, 1971–1981

| Parish | Population | | % change, 1971–1981 |
	1971	1981	
Ashleworth	300	432	41.0
Chaceley	121	114	−5.8
Corse	459	542	18.1
Hartpury	664	685	3.2
Hasfield	163	144	−11.7
Pauntley	138	172	24.6
Redmarley	754	810	7.4
Staunton	396	482	21.7
Tirley	303	326	7.6
Upleadon	230	235	2.2

Source: Cloke and Little, 1987*f*.

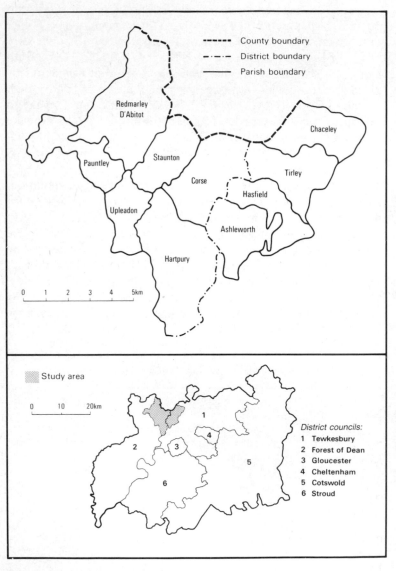

FIG. 4.5. The Ten Case Study Parishes
Source: Cloke and Little, 1987*d*

Table 4.3. Social-Class Structure of Case Study Parishes

Class	Ashleworth	Chaceley	Corse	Hartpury	Hasfield	Pauntley	Redmarley	Staunton	Tirley	Upleadon	All
1 (professional)[a]	14.0	21.4	20.3	15.5	16.6	9.1	12.9	15.3	13.6	3.8	14.5
2 (employers and managers)	24.5	50.0	28.8	20.2	41.7	40.9	32.3	13.4	13.6	34.6	30.0
3 (intermediate)	29.8	21.4	20.3	34.5	33.3	18.2	16.1	22.0	43.2	38.5	26.8
4 (skilled manual)	15.8	7.1	10.2	7.1	8.3	4.5	11.8	16.9	6.8	3.8	10.4
5 (semi-skilled manual)	14.0	0	11.9	7.1	0	9.1	21.5	23.7	11.4	11.5	13.8
6 (unskilled manual)	1.8	0	8.5	15.5	0	18.2	5.4	8.5	11.4	7.7	8.5
Retired	20.5	25.0	36.8	27.1	36.8	24.1	27.6	31.5	20.7	30.8	28.2
Unemployed	1.4	5.0	1.1	1.7	0	0	3.0	4.3	3.4	2.6	2.4

[a] Classes 1–6 as a % of all employed: retired and unemployed as a % of all households.

Source: Cloke and Little, 1987e.

occurring in Ashleworth. Particular reasons for this variation in parish trends are discussed in the context of housing and employment policy below. Here it is important simply to note the different patterns occurring within such a small area, and to appreciate the fact that these patterns may easily be masked in broader interpretations.

Class Structure. A number of assumptions were made concerning the class structure of the case study area on the basis of trends documented in existing work. These trends have been outlined in Chapter 1 of this book and suggest that major patterns of population movement in more accessible areas are class-led (gentrification). Thus we have seen an inmigration of middle-class residents at the expense of the lower classes, especially in the south of England. Superimposed upon these essentially class-dictated population movements is the age-led migration of the retired (geriatrification). The selection of the case study parishes was expected to demonstrate the importance of the first trend particularly, gentrification. It was anticipated that the attractiveness and relative accessibility of the area, together with the importance of service industries to the local economy, would be reflected in the inmigration of middle-class 'newcomers', particularly the rapidly expanding service class composed of professionals and managers (Thrift, 1987*a*).

The study area did indeed demonstrate these established trends (see Table 4.3), although not to the extent that may have been expected. By comparison with national figures, the ten parishes together contained a high proportion of professionals and managers (classes 1 and 2) and a relatively low proportion of semi-skilled and unskilled manual workers. Numbers of retired people in the area were higher than the national average, while there were far fewer unemployed people in the study area than is the case nationally. These patterns were not, however, extreme. More interesting, perhaps, and certainly more important in the context of the present investigation, is the extent to which individual parishes deviate from the broader pattern. Chanceley and Hasfield, for example, appeared as real enclaves of middle-class dominance, while parishes such as Staunton and Ashleworth have retained larger than average groups of intermediate and working-class residents. Furthermore, while accepted wisdom maintains that the

Table 4.4. Perceived Need for New
Employment in the Study Parishes

Parish	%
Ashleworth	61.6
Chaceley	40.0
Corse	66.3
Hartpury	50.8
Hasfield	15.8
Pauntley	24.1
Redmarley	48.5
Staunton	70.7
Tirley	69.0
Upleadon	46.2

Source: Cloke and Little, 1987*e*.

majority of middle-class residents tend to be 'newcomers' to rural communities (in contrast to the working-class 'locals'), the evidence from the Gloucestershire parishes indicated a much more complex relationship between social class and length of residence.

Broadly, the data on social class indicated that, while a net immigration of professional and managerial classes was taking place, these groups did not totally dominate the population structure. There remained a significant contingent of residents from the lower social classes, particularly, as Table 4.3 shows, in certain parishes, of whom not all were long-standing residents. Such characteristics are clearly important, not only in the context of existing population structures and the distribution of need, but also to the distributional impact of present and future policy.

Social Need in the Study Parishes

Before moving on to consider specific examples of policy impact, it is important briefly to discuss general issues of need as identified from within the study parishes. As demonstrated by Figs. 4.3 and 4.4 above, five of the selected study parishes, Redmarley, Pauntley, Chaceley, Tirley, and Hasfield, are amongst those parishes classified by the county as 'areas of rural decline'. Implicit in this categorization is the idea that such areas represent locations of lowest opportunity, with minimum levels of access, job provision, available housing, and services, and are consequently, in the minds of the county planners, suitable targets for planning action. The designation of areas of decline was based on a combination of census statistics and a county-wide report (GCC, 1980), which together identified the demographic and socio-economic characteristics of individual parishes. The case study investigation was designed to place these findings in the context of residents' own perceptions of levels of need in the rural parishes, and to see whether any spatial variation in these perceptions existed.

The problems of identifying and analysing need have been explored on a theoretical level in Chapter 1 of this book. There is no virtue in repeating the discussion here, except perhaps to reinforce the need to recognize the problems inherent in the interpretation of social need, and to stress that the questionnaire dealt specifically with individual perceptions of need, not fixed and quantitative criteria such as income levels.

Employment Need.   While 'official' unemployment rates within the study parishes were relatively low, the scale of employment *need* was perceived by residents as high. As Table 4.4 demonstrates, over half those questioned in the survey (55.2 per cent) believed there to be a need for new employment in the area. In the majority

Table 4.5. Housing Tenure by Parish (% Households)

Parish	Owner-occupied	Tenure		
		Council	Tied	Other rented
Ashleworth	59.3	23.3	2.7	12.7
Chaceley	70.7	0	4.9	22.0
Corse	80.5	11.1	2.1	4.2
Hartpury	71.7	8.7	7.6	11.4
Hasfield	59.6	0	8.5	27.7
Pauntley	83.6	0	5.4	7.3
Redmarley	72.4	8.6	5.2	12.7
Staunton	53.5	40.5	1.1	4.3
Tirley	62.1	18.1	6.0	12.1
Upleadon	72.7	13.0	2.6	13.0

Source: Cloke and Little, 1987*e*.

of cases respondents did not elaborate on the type of employment required, or the groups felt to be most in need; the only reservation commonly expressed by those who perceived a need for greater employment opportunities was that such opportunities would best be met through small-scale workshop development or a similar 'environmentally appropriate' solution. A closer look at the social characteristics of those perceiving a need for the creation of employment opportunities in the locality does, however, suggest that the greatest need lies in the intermediate and manual sectors.

Existing employment opportunities in the study parishes are relatively few, and most of those in waged work commute to urban centres such as Gloucester and Cheltenham. Apart from agricultural work, the majority of village-based employment is provided by local services. In addition, a small workshop in Hasfield employs a few people making engines for exhibitions (Cloke and Little, 1984). Despite the fact that most village-based employment is of a manual nature, it is still manual workers for whom the need is seen as greatest.

The poor mobility of the working-class residents clearly increases their dependence on local opportunities. Also important is the recognition that, although present provision within the study area may be sufficient for existing residents, it cannot be expected to meet the demands made by children of these residents, nor to offer any form of reasonable choice to the working classes.

Housing Need. Chapter 1 has drawn attention to the well-rehearsed arguments concerning the causes of housing need in rural areas of England and Wales—in particular, the shortage of local authority accommodation and the rising prices of private housing. These arguments are reinforced by the structure of housing tenure in the study parishes, where a relative lack of local-authority housing is accompanied by a high level of owner-occupation (see Table 4.5). Individual parishes, however, showed significant variation from the overall pattern, with some, such as Ashleworth and Staunton, displaying far higher proportions of local-authority housing and others a disproportionate bias in favour of the owner-occupied sector. The proportion of private rented property is again variable, being higher in those parishes where local authority provision is poor and vice versa (with the exception of Pauntley, which has relatively low proportions of each).

The perception of need amongst those living in the study area was not as widespread in the case of housing as it had been in that of employment. Almost one-third of respondents (32.3 per cent) did, however, believe that there was a need for more housing within their parish. It was largely felt that this housing should be aimed at the less well off, especially the young, who could not afford present prices in the area and were unlikely to be given the option of renting from the local authority (at least not locally). Rather predictably, the perception of housing need varied between different social classes, with perception being lowest amongst the middle-class residents (particularly those most recently arrived in the parish). This low perception results, presumably, both from a failure to recognize or acknowledge the genuine needs of other sections of the population and from a desire to protect their own interests in terms of preventing house-building. In other words, their perception of housing need was very much tempered by a wish to preserve the village (physically and socially) as it is, and to control, very tightly, any new development.

Service Needs. In addition to housing and employment, the survey also sought to establish the needs of the local population in relation to the provision of other services, principally transport, retailing, and health services. The variation in personal circumstances and expectations amongst respondents, and the disparities in existing provision between different parishes, made the real extent of service deprivation very difficult to pin-point, and the identification of a common level of need amongst residents impossible. Respondents living in Staunton and Corse, for example, had access to the combined facilities of these parishes which included a primary school, a regular and reliable bus service to Gloucester, a shop and post office, a doctor's surgery and dispensary, and even a police house. In comparison, the only public services offered by Chaceley (other than postal and milk deliveries) were a village hall and a telephone box.

The measurement of need in the context of service provision is further compounded by the *adaptability* of many residents, which was of a much higher level than in the case of housing or employment. The steady decline in levels of services in rural areas generally has meant that many residents have been forced to adjust to infrequent transport provision and lengthy journeys to shops, doctors, schools, etc. This adaptability can, however, take many different forms. The middle-class young or middle-aged family may simply need to make more frequent journeys by private car, buying in bulk on shopping trips and planning social activities more carefully. For the elderly and low-paid, similar 'adaption' may involve long walks to surviving services, relying on neighbours or lifts, or simply accepting reduced choices and opportunities. In any event, adapting to service decline does not reduce the real need, it simply masks the perception of the need.

Because of the difficulties of evaluation, especially the variation between social groups, attempts to draw conclusions concerning general levels of service need within the parishes would be misleading. Such conclusions are best made in the context of the impact of specific decisions. One exception to this rule is, perhaps, transport. Many residents had strong views concerning local transport deprivation and the distribution of social need, specifying the 'elderly' as a sector of the population for whom transport was a particular problem and amongst whom need was felt to be greatest. Moreover, it was also recognized that, without transport facilities, the elderly were likely to be disadvantaged in a number of other respects, including shopping and even cashing pensions.

What this discussion of need in relation to services (and indeed to employment and housing) does clearly demonstrate is the variation that exists by social group. While perhaps not referring specifically to social class, respondents spoke frequently of the problems of the less well off (the other group to gain particular attention being the elderly). It was not possible, using the questionnaire, to decipher any spatial pattern in the occurrence of need—individuals and groups, rather than places, were consistently identified as the focus of need by respondents. This may lead us to question the strategic planners' categorization of rural areas, and their intention to use this categorization as a means of resource allocation. Clearly, however, planners are working within very firmly held expectations of their role, of which one major part is an adherence to spatially based policies. More important is the degree to which planners attempt to use allocative policy (even that constrained by the need to adhere to spatial criteria) to enforce socially progressive goals—the extent to which, for example, they promote low-cost housing or manually based employment.

The answers to these questions can only really be approached through a detailed consideration of individual policy decisions. The commitment of planners to addressing the problems of rural areas through broad strategic policy has been examined above. It is only through the local investigation of specific 'key' issues and decisions, however, that we can ascertain whether such commitment is reflected in the local implementation of policy. The final section of this chapter will turn, therefore, to an examination of selected 'key' issues. In this section, information is drawn not only from the questionnaire and written documentation referenced above, but also from a series of detailed interviews with policy-makers.

KEY ISSUES: POLICY AND IMPACT

Key Issue I: Local-Authority Housing in Staunton

Two separate housing issues were identified within the parish of Staunton; both are worth considering here, as both have a bearing on the existence of need, and demonstrate different aspects of the implementation of housing policy as discussed above. Staunton itself is one of the more accessible and better-serviced of the study parishes. Such qualities have caused it to be singled out in district plans as a potential area of development (particularly in the light of the relatively poor quality of the surrounding agricultural land and the proximity of the 'area of decline'). In line with its status as an H3 village, and with the consequent policy directing development to areas where basic levels of services already exist, a decision was made in the early 1970s to build an estate of forty local-authority houses in Staunton.

This decision, leading to what was to become the last real local-authority development in rural Gloucestershire, met with considerable opposition from both local decision-makers and residents, and would certainly not have gone ahead following local-government reorganization in 1974. As it was, the building began before this time and was completed in full by 1981. The main opponents to the development protested on the grounds of scale, arguing that local need did not warrant the building of an additional forty dwellings. The eventual acceptance of low-priority applicants for these houses was proof, so it was argued, of the absence of need on the scale catered for.

However, the use of local-authority waiting lists as a measure of housing need is fraught with problems. In the case of this development, as in many rural areas, need is only identifiable in relation to supply. Prospective tenants frequently place themselves on the waiting lists of urban areas where supply, and thus chances of allocation, are much greater. Nevertheless, it is pertinent to note that all the forty houses built as part of the Staunton programme had, at the time of survey, been filled, and a growing waiting list was emerging (eleven families in 1979 and nineteen in 1983). The perceived continuing need for new housing amongst respondents of the study parishes (including Staunton) is evidence that, for some sections of the population at least, the Staunton development was not over-ambitious.

Clearly, the impact of the housing development, just like the perception of need, varied between different sectors of the population: to some it provided the opportunity of living in a rural area (for many their 'home' area), while for others it simply constituted a threat to the traditional social and physical character of the village, as well as a refuge for some of the more 'undesirable elements' of society. On a wider level, many residents remarked on the 'spin-off' benefits from the council estate—notably the improvements in services, especially retail facilities. Again, however, these observations were more commonly made by the residents of the local-authority estate, and not by the owner-occupiers. Only 11 per cent of owner-occupiers recognized any positive benefits of the housing estate, and for most its construction had served to reinforce existing aspirations concerning conservation and to strengthen anti-development feelings.

Unfortunately, despite the declared 'spin-off' effects of the housing development, the intention of making Staunton a local centre (of which the housing estate was part) has not been reflected in any redistribution of public resources or real expansion of service provision. Consequently, while opportunities have been provided for limited numbers of working-class people to live in Staunton, the poor levels of services and employment have detracted from the quality of life of many who have chosen to do so. Planners appear to be caught in a 'catch 22' situation. Without substantial housing development of this kind, it would seem impossible to generate jobs and services, and yet there is no guarantee that these will automatically follow in the wake of new housing. The severe financial constraints imposed by central government dictate that rural communities are frequently dependent on the private sector for the most basic services. Even expanding villages like Staunton, however, fail to offer sufficient returns on investment.

Consideration of the second housing issue, discussed below, helps to place this earlier issue in perspective, and to shed greater light on the apparent inconsistencies between stated planning objectives and the implementation of policy decisions.

Key Issue II: Private Housing Development in Staunton

This second key issue concerns a proposal by a local firm of house-builders, Robert Hitchins Ltd., to develop a large private estate on the edge of the village. The issue was still unresolved at the time of the survey, despite complicated and lengthy negotiations between the house-builders, the District Council, and ultimately the secretary of state.

The fact that the decision-making process has been so drawn out in this particular case is indicative not only of the general lack of consensus concerning development within the countryside but also of the considerable power and resources (financial, technical, and legal) that have been displayed by the house-builders. The series of events which led to what has become, in the eyes of decision-makers, a very thorny local issue can be summarized as follows:

(i) An initial planning application was made by Robert Hitchins Ltd. for the building of 200 houses on the edge of Staunton. The proposal comprised two separate developments, one of 20.4 acres and the other of 12.5 acres, and was to include dwellings of different size, as well as shops, roads, and a primary school.

(ii) The proposal was rejected by the Forest of Dean District Council and, following an appeal by Hitchins, this decision was upheld by the secretary of state. The main objections to the proposal were that the scale of development would exceed local needs and, perhaps more importantly, would stretch the target of 250 set by the county (GCC, 1979) as the *total* number of new dwellings to be built in Gloucestershire for the period up to 1996. Hitchin's proposal would, it was felt, represent extreme concentration of development within the county, both spatially and temporally.

The Inspectors report in upholding the District Council's decision spoke of the 'possible injurious and adverse effects upon the existing community'. It did suggest, however, that development on the smaller of the two sites within Staunton might be acceptable. Such development would be more in keeping with the character of the existing village and would, it was suggested, consolidate development along the western side of the Gloucester–Ledbury (A417) road.

(iii) Hitchins challenged the decision to reject the appeal in the High Court. They won the case on the grounds that the secretary of state had failed to make clear the extact reasons for rejecting the proposal.

(iv) As the result of the High Court ruling, Hitchins appealed for a second time against the original decision by the District Council to reject the application. This time the house-builders asked that only development on the 12.5 acre site be taken into consideration—again, this development would be a mixed scheme, aimed at a wide market, and involve considerable 'planning gain' in the form of shops and a school. This time the focus of the debate was shifted slightly with the contention by Hitchins that the total allocation of land for housing development within the structure plan was inadequate to meet the long-term predictions of growth within the plan itself.

(v) In 1983 the appeal was rejected by the secretary of state for the second time, again with reference to the scale and environmental consequences of the proposal. At the time this research was completed Hitchins were about to embark on their second High Court case, and both sides appeared to be resigned to the fact that the issue was far from being resolved.

Since no final decision has been reached concerning this issue, its impact cannot as such be measured. The various arguments that have been rehearsed do, however, reflect the anticipated impact from each side. As mentioned, the decision-makers suggest that the implications of the proposed development would be harmful to the character of the village and surrounding area. This was a view echoed by those few residents (5 per cent) who commented on the issue, all of whom were middle-class owner-occupiers. Alternatively, the house-builders argue that there is a real need for the development (especially since it would provide a number of smaller, lower-priced houses), and that its impact would be important in assisting in the development of Staunton, helping to boost employment opportunities and service provision within the surrounding 'area of decline'.

Various internal inconsistencies in the decision-making process have arisen during the course of this application. First is the basic inconsistencey between the stated intention of developing the area in line with its H4 status and the strict anti-development stance of the district and county planning decisions. Secondly, while in the course of negotiation it appears that the district might be prepared to accept a scaled-down proposal for about 65 dwellings—indeed, this is provided for within existing district policy (Forest of Dean District Council, 1982)—the county remain firmly committed to a virtual ban on development. They stated during the appeal by Hitchins that they 'would not object to a cul-de-sac of say 10 houses' (Letter from DoE to Robert Hitchins Ltd., 27 September 1983), but would not sanction development of a larger scale. They argue that such a stance is not incompatible with the aims of addressing the problems of rural areas but is simply in keeping with the spirit of 'appropriate' growth and environmental protection within which these aims were established.

Both housing issues in Staunton have demonstrated the gulf that has arisen, on the side of decision-makers and that of residents, between the anti-development lobby and those who regard the development of villages as an important and necessary part of satisfying local need and ensuring the maintenance of thriving communities. While this may be a somewhat simplistic interpretation of the major interests within the rural housing market, it is nevertheless important that the consequences of the two rather extreme positions be addressed. Pressure for development in the more accessible parts of the countryside, together with rising house prices and a growing concern for the protection of the environment, is, moreover, likely to increase this polarity, as house-building and general development in rural areas become of major political significance.

Key issue III: Village Shop and Post Office in Upleadon

Both need and impact are more easily identified in the third 'key' issue, the provision of a small shop/post office in the village of Upleadon, not least because the opening of this service occurred just a few months before the start of the questionnaire survey and thus attracted much comment from respondents. Prior to the opening of this shop, the nearest retail and post office services were in the village of Newent, the previous shop in Upleadon having shut down twelve years before. Despite the relatively short distance to Newent (the trip taking approximately ten minutes by car), the lack of a shop in Upleadon was seen as an inconvenience to villagers and particularly to older residents, many of whom had been forced in the past to rely on lifts from friends and relatives in order to make the journey to Newent to cash their pensions.

The village shop was opened in 1983 by an old 'village family' returning to Upleadon. They first established, through a locally distributed questionnaire, that a need for such a shop existed and then proceeded to convert a house and two garages into suitable premises. As well as providing a conventional shop for the sale of everyday groceries and newspapers, the owners obtained recognition and training from the Post Office which also allowed them to open a post office service. But despite initial enthusiasm from residents and the sporadic use of both shop and post office by many, respondents in Upleadon tended to view the venture as a convenient saving of time, particularly in an emergency, rather than as an essential service or a real alternative to the retail facilities in Newent. High prices, as with many similar shops, tended to dissuade residents from using it on a regular basis, and indeed the major use appeared to be for the provision of Sunday newspapers. Even the elderly people questioned seemed to regard the trip to Newent to cash pensions as a welcomed trip out of the village rather than as a great hardship. They thus used the village service not regularly but as an *alternative* to Newent if they so needed it. The shop was not used very often by residents *outside* Upleadon.

With this level of use, the shop was unable to produce a viable profit, and the owners were forced to close after only fourteen months. The sale of the shop premises as 'granny flats'—for which demand and price is currently high—means that once again Upleadon is without a shop and post office. Clearly, the impact of this service was concentrated amongst too few residents to make it a viable, self-supporting venture. It could be argued that, since this is the case, then the service was not really required. The provision of Sunday newspapers for a handful of village residents and the cashing of the odd pension hardly constitute life and death issues. The high mobility of most residents, their increasing self-sufficiency, and their willingness to resort to self-help solutions has reduced the need for this type of local facility and lessened the impact of its demise. But for those residents who *did* rely on the shop, its disappearance was seen as a significant blow. Moreover, for others in the village not only is the convenience of a local facility lost but the *choice* of service is removed. Instead of choosing to make the journey into Newent, residents are now forced to do so; and while for the majority, as noted, this entails no real hardship, for some it does impose limitations and constraints.

This issue, the failure of the shop and the impact of its closure, is related to another major issue within the parish, namely the provision of a minibus service to Newent using a vehicle owned and operated by the County Council. This service, again, was introduced around the time of the survey and coincided with the opening of the shop. The minibus allowed residents to travel quickly and cheaply to Newent, and consequently reduced quite significantly the need for the shop in the village itself. It is misleading to consider the impact of the shop and its closure without reference to the minibus, since it was quite clearly the improved mobility (within the lifetime of the shop) which reduced the need for the shop and ensured its eventual demise. Whether the shop would have failed regardless of the minibus service is unknown, but given the high numbers of elderly people who make use of the minibus, it may perhaps be argued that without it the difficulties of travelling to Newent might have meant a far higher level of dependence on village facilities in general and the shop in particular.

Without this service, the ability of some residents, the elderly and carless, to remain in Upleadon and Pauntley would surely be questioned. It demonstrates both the overriding importance of transport to the lives of those living in rural areas and also the capacity of one facility fundamentally to alter the quality of life of those who are dependent upon it. One elderly resident, for example, concluded that, without the minibus to get her to the health centre in Newent, she would have to go by bus or ambulance to the hospital in Gloucester—a round trip which would take the whole day.

Key Issue IV: The Stage Bus Service

It is interesting to consider the minibus issue within the wider context of the overall quality of provision of public bus services in the area. It has been shown above that, in the face of declining service provision, the importance of transport to the lives of those living in villages is considerable. The changing access of residents in the case study parishes to local public transport thus constitutes a key issue in its own right.

This work was undertaken before the deregulation of the bus service which came about as a result of the 1985 Transport Act. It is therefore possible, and indeed probable, that, given the broad implications of deregulation, the quality of the bus services in the study parishes will have changed since the survey was undertaken (Bell and Cloke, 1989). It is worth recording the 'pre-regulation' changes and their impact, however, since they give an indication of the likely costs and benefits that will accompany further changes in service provision. In 1983 Gloucestershire County Council had for some time been exploring the possibilities of offering some of their established routes for private tender. Quite significant changes had occurred in the rural parts of the county as a result of the uptake of some routes by private operators, and such changes affected individual parishes very differently. In some parishes the changes had led to definite improvements in the overall quality of the service, while in others the reverse was the case. More detailed consideration of individual examples is required in order to understand the full impact of the changes taking place.

Despite the recognition by residents of the high incidence of need which could be identified in relation to public transport, respondents did display a remarkable ability to look on the positive side of current service changes. The perception of levels of need clearly, in *specific* instances, had been subject to a degree of adjustment in the face of falling expectations. Thus, while residents were aware of overall hardship and deprivation caused by declining transport facilities, their ability to adapt had made them more tolerant of their own situation. So impoverished had become the provision in some areas, and so low the expectations, that it was the positive impacts of any changes that were remarked upon rather than the negative ones.

The main issue as far as local bus services were concerned appeared to revolve around the takeover of routes formerly run by the Bristol Omnibus Company (BOC) by a firm of private operators, Swanbrooks. Residents expressed mixed feelings as to whether this takeover had resulted in an improved service. On balance, for most parishes, the changes seemed to have improved access to Gloucester but at the expense of maintaining the route to Ledbury. Residents spoke of the cheaper (a reduction from the £1.20 charged by BOC to 40p for a return journey to Gloucester) and more efficient services offered by Swanbrooks. Changes in the timing of the services, again, appeared to benefit some and disadvantage others; a number of elderly residents mentioned the fact that the rescheduling of services allowed them to get to the doctors in Staunton for 9.30 a.m., while others complained that the long wait for a return bus often led them to walk home.

While, in the sample overall, 75 per cent of residents felt that some improvement had occurred in the quality of the bus service, in particular parishes this was clearly not the case. In Redmarley, for example, the withdrawal of the Ledbury service had left the parish completely without public transport. Residents of Corse, although still served by a bus to Gloucester, had also felt the loss of the Ledbury route since this, they argued, had reduced their access to places such as Hereford and Worcester. Suggestions by Gloucester County Council in their 1983 Transport Plan (GCC, 1983) that the use of 'unconventional' services would be considered where particular hardship existed has not resulted in the development of any such initiatives other than the Upleadon minibus mentioned above, and considerable need, as demonstrated in the questionnaire survey and discussed earlier, still exists within the study parishes.

That residents perceived there to have been beneficial changes in the quality of the services indicates both their low expectations and the narrow time-span to which they refer. Certainly, the takeover by Swanbrooks of certain routes within the area had brought improvements over the situation immediately preceding the takeover—BOC had for some years been struggling to maintain a deteriorating service. But these improvements had been marginal, and had done really very little to stem the continuing decline in the total level of servicing. Routes were still being cut where they could not produce a large enough profit, and, while resources appear to have been pooled to support the still-popular services, this is of little comfort to those, like the residents of Redmarley, who have been left with no service at all.

The steady withdrawal of county operations and their replacement with privately run services will, it is anticipated, place further routes in jeopardy. With no obligation to maintain 'socially necessary' services, the private operators are in a position to axe all but the most money-spinning routes. The implications of such a situation for rural residents are likely to be serious. The solution in many rural areas has been the development of 'alternative' services to replace the reliance on the stage bus service. These are often favoured on rural routes as they are more flexible and generally cheaper to provide than conventional services. The Upleadon/Pauntley county-run minibus discussed above demonstrates the benefits that can be provided by unconventional transport services, and the need for such services that exists within the Gloucestershire study parishes. Unfortunately, the public provision of these alternative solutions tends to be limited, and, both generally and in Gloucestershire, they are increasingly becoming the province of self-help initiatives and voluntary groups. Such solutions, while extremely worthwhile in their own right, cannot provide a co-ordinated and comprehensive alternative to regular stage bus services, representing piecemeal responses to specific examples of need rather than viable widespread alternatives.

Key Issue V: A Doctors' Surgery in Staunton

The final 'key issue' to be considered in this chapter concerns a new doctors' surgery, built just before the survey period in Staunton. While the surgery did not represent a *new* service, since it was simply replacing the previous doctors' surgery, it is worth considering here since it constitutes one of the most crucial and well-used local services. The fact that the decision to build a new surgery had demonstrated a continuing commitment to the provision of medical facilities in the area was of great importance to residents, and prompted considerable comment. The new surgery, moreover, provided not only for doctors' consultation but also a dispensing service for prescriptions, a particularly valuable addition for those living in the remoter parishes and having no direct access to a chemist.

In considering this issue, it is important to know a little about how decisions concerning the siting of doctors' practices are made. At a broad level, decisions on the density of provision within an area are the responsibility of the Family Practitioner Committee (FPC). The FPC operate a categorization of districts based on an accepted average ratio of patients to doctors of around 2000 : 1. According to this ratio, areas are classified as either restricted, intermediate, open, or designated; the first two categories indicating a higher than average doctor–patient ratio and thus a well-serviced area, the latter denoting a lower than average ratio and hence a need for more doctors. The categorization, made totally on the basis of population density, takes no account of problems of remoteness and accessibility. Rural areas, where population densities tend to be low, appear in purely numerical terms to be well serviced. There is no consideration given, however, to the ability of patients to reach the service; so, despite a more favourable doctor–patient ratio, people living in rural areas may actually experience poorer access to doctors.

The precise location of a surgery within a designated 'area' is not specified by the FPC, but left to the doctor's own choice. While this choice may not be crucial in densely populated urban areas, where both provision and access are high, in rural areas it assumes a far greater importance. Ultimately, it is clear that the choice of Staunton as the site of the new surgery was based not so much on any careful analysis of relative levels of need within the locality but on a combination of predetermined thresholds, doctors' preferences, and historical factors. Financial resources were made available to the Staunton doctors by the Gloucestershire FPC, although, again, these did not entail any constraints regarding the siting of the service itself.

Like the issue of the local bus service, the impact of the new doctors' surgery had been variable throughout the parishes, and the perception of that impact was tempered by resident's low expectations and by relief that the service continued to exist. For those living in Staunton itself and the neighbouring parish of Corse, the provision of the surgery was quite clearly of great benefit; it was well used and highly regarded. The added facility of the dispensary was considered particularly beneficial. To residents of the other study parishes, the impact of the service was dependent upon their access to it, so that for those with a car the surgery represented a handy alternative to a trip to Gloucester or Newent, while for those dependent on public transport its inaccessibility made it of little benefit. Over 60 per cent of the elderly residents reported difficulty in reaching the surgery, and many who were able to get there remarked on the time constraints imposed by infrequent bus services or lifts from friends.

In attempting to overcome the problems of access, doctors from the Staunton practice showed themselves to be very willing to visit people in their homes and also to schedule appointments, where necessary, to fit in with bus timetables. Clearly, however, a situation in which patients' access to regular medical facilities is dependent on the adaptability of doctors and on the willingness of neighbours to provide lifts is not satisfactory. Even so, despite often awkward and time-consuming journeys, generally poor levels of servicing had persuaded the majority of residents to believe themselves fortunate in having access to health care. Few spoke of the ways in which through, for example, more sensitive planning of bus services their situations could be improved, preferring instead to dwell on the problems that would arise if even the Staunton service did not exist.

CONCLUSION

The examination of key issues has served to demonstrate the absence of a straightforward association between policy and impact in rural Gloucestershire. It has shown how the original intentions of policy-makers can be distorted by the different levels of state activity, and by the different agencies involved in the policy process and its implementation. The account of the preparation of the Gloucestershire structure plan has served to underline the disparity which may exist, firstly, between the planners' priorities and the published written policy document and, secondly, between the aims and interpretation of county and district decision-makers. The disparity itself indicates the in-adequacy of using written policy statements to analyse either the local manifestations of rural decision-making or its outcome.

The longitudinal examination of policy formulation and impact has also enabled the clarification of the role and importance of the central state. The direct influence in terms of the wording of the emphasis of policy was clearly demonstrated in the preparation of the structure plan; there were, however, signs of the continuing influence of the centre in the interpretation and implementation of policy at the *local* level. This was particularly obvious in relation to the financial controls exerted by the central state over the distribution of public resources, and the limitations on spending, within which local decision-makers were forced to operate. Thus the lack of central-state funds determined that, for example, whatever the priorities of local policy-makers, there would be no further development of local-authority housing. Financial directives are accompanied by ideological and legislative controls on behalf of the central state. The case of housing again provides a good example of the importance of central-state ideology for the direction of local policies, while bus deregulation demonstrates the role of legal controls in restricting the autonomy of local decision-makers and imposing the preferences of the centre.

The discussions of policy-making and outcome have also drawn attention to the problems of identifying and targeting need in rural areas. The growing polarization of rural society has helped to mask the problems of deprived groups in the countryside, while low expectations and the ability to 'make do' has further reduced the identification and awareness of need both by residents and by policy-makers. The Gloucestershire study has demonstrated the extent to which problems of hidden need have been reinforced by a lack of public resources available for the provision of rural services and employment. There is no guarantee that the intentions of county policy-makers can be translated into resource injection, even where such intentions are shared at the local level.

Where public resources are not forthcoming—and where the private sector shows no sign of stepping into the gap—planners and communities are beginning to turn to voluntary initiatives or some form of partnership scheme in order to meet existing need. In Gloucestershire the full potential offered by, in particular, the partnership schemes seemed, at the time of the research, not yet to have been explored. The Rural Action Group (RAG) represented, perhaps, the closest attempt to co-ordinate the limited resources of the local authorities with other public and private agencies and community groups. Interestingly, despite (or perhaps because of) the limited financial and decision-making powers at its disposal, the RAG did command considerable support from those committed to rural policies. It is likely that such groups are being seen as the only chance of addressing rural needs within the political and financial constraints of contemporary policy-making.

Finally, it is important to recognize the continuing power of 'environmental objectives' in the formulation and implementation of policies for rural areas. Structure plan policies and the intervention of the secretary of state indicate the degree to which the aims of conservation and those of encouraging rural prosperity are seen as mutually exclusive; and even where pro-development policies have been instigated at a county level, their implementation has been influenced by *local* concerns for environmental protection. The event to which a preference for preservation as opposed to development can be interpreted as a tendency, on behalf of policy-makers, to place self-interest before the interests of the community has been discussed above. In Gloucestershire there was certainly a feeling that, if not evident in the formal planning process, the motivation of the protection of private property was important in preventing the recognition of social need and the demand for housing. Clearly, the existence of such uncertainties seem further to confuse the relationship between policy and impact in rural areas, and to reinforce the view that an understanding of rural policy must be based, not simply on written statements, but on a detailed examination of the mechanisms of the policy process and of the motives of those involved in its formulation and implementation.

5

Inter-governmental Relations and Rural Policy: Some Examples

INTRODUCTION

The account in Chapter 4 of a very detailed study in one rural area of the UK—Gloucestershire—highlights many of the conceptual themes introduced in Chapters 1–3. In this one small area we see a localized policy arena where both élites and managers appear to exercise decision-making power. It is also important to recognize that key structural interests—landowners, housebuilding and development capitalists, and so on—are catered for in the resultant consensus option, even if during the policy-making process their cause remained in the gloomy areas of the back stage while the 'pro-rural' policy elements associated with Policy H4 took the limelight. Consequently, the exercise of elements of structuralist power can also be recognized in this example.

Beyond the localized policy arena, however, these carefully orchestrated plans were overpowered by the dominance of central government. Not only were the proposed structure plan policies emasculated by the central review process, but it also became clear that central-government decisions relating to public housing, education, transport, and so on were far more important than local decisions in determining or influencing change in rural areas of Gloucestershire. The suggestion arising from the Gloucestershire illustration is, therefore, that the degree to which the local state in rural areas is able to act on available discretion is greatly influenced, not only by the potential compliance of capital interests in the locality, but also by the balance of inter-governmental relations as dictated by the social relations which underpin the *central* state. Local states with jurisdictions over rural areas do not appear to be able or willing to promote radical local action against the tide of the fundamental functions and aims of the central state.

We acknowledge that the Gloucestershire study is not necessarily representative of 'rural' areas, and may in some ways be unique. Nevertheless, it can be used as a yardstick for further studies of local-state decisions and action in different nation-state and political economic contexts. In this chapter we make a modest contribution to the available illustrative material on the function and apparatus of rural local states in different settings. There follow four 'cameos' of the influence of inter-governmental relations on rural policies in different contexts. These are neither detailed nor exhaustive. They merely begin to indicate how studies of power and inter-governmental relations can provide information about the policy outcomes which affect rural areas. Together, they offer some further pointers to the importance of concepts of the state in understanding rural change and rural policy. At the end of the chapter, we offer a broader, international viewpoint on some of the themes which arise from these four examples.

ECONOMIC RESTRUCTURING AND A DOMINANT CENTRAL STATE: THE CASE OF RURAL NEW ZEALAND

Inter-governmental Relations

The framework for inter-governmental relations in New Zealand consists of a three-tier network of authorities. At the lowest level, the county authorities are charged with responsibility for the land-use activities of subdivision and zoning in their *district schemes*. Most rural counties exhibit a political structure which is both conservative and pro-agricultural, and the dominant mode of planning and policy at this level is that of control of development so as to maintain the *status quo* of agricultural prosperity. Local politicians tend to react against formal and direct local-state intervention in local economic and social affairs. Thus the planning function is rarely allocated sufficient budget or full-time professional staff, with the result that rural councils have little hope of sophisticated or ordered resource allocation (Cloke, 1986*b*). In practice, the amount of land tax (a significant element of the total budget in rural areas) which local authorities are able to collect is limited, and their attentions are thus focused on a limited range of functions, including water supply, waste disposal, and roads (Willis, 1988).

The 1977 Town and County Planning Act superimposed a formal tier of regional planning on to the existing local state in New Zealand. The intention was to establish a series of regional authorities who could forge agreements between national and local decision-makers, and then enforce these agreements to the extent of their being legally binding. The reality has been that regional planning has been hindered by powerful institutional constraints. First, as noted by Norwood (1981), different forms of regional authority were established. The Auckland Regional Authority (Rankin, 1979) was a special case with its own legislation, and represents the most comprehensive planning agency at the regional level. Otherwise, there were to be *regional councils* (for urban regions), which were to have their own separate staff and tax-raising capabilities, and *united councils* (for the rest of the country), composed of nominated representatives from existing local authorities, and lacking the power to appoint separate staff and raise taxes.

For rural regions, the united-council format meant considerable problems for rural planning. Housed in one of the existing local authorities, and relying on a financial levy from constituent counties, the united councils experienced tremendous internal frictions, borne of the essential conservatism and parochialism of local politicians. This hamstrung position is due partly to central government's refusal to grant initial powers and finances for independent regional authorities, and partly to its unwillingness to grant subsequent devolvement of bureaucratic power, and financial resources, unless the united councils can prove themselves to be administratively competent. Yet the competence of the united councils is depressed by the lack of power, finance, and co-operation from central government, so a form of vicious circle operating against the united councils has developed.

Thus most decision-making powers over rural areas are retained at the central-state level. Moran (1989) has stressed that agencies of central government—especially the Ministry of Agriculture and Fisheries and the Ministry of Works and Development, along with a host of other resource-based and *ad hoc* agencies—have been most influential in planning and policy-making for rural New Zealand.

Central-State Policy Changes

In a position where central-state policies are the dominant influence over the planning of rural change, any radical alterations to those central policies can render the local state helpless in mitigating the impacts of change in rural localities. Since the election of David Lange's Labour government in 1984, a series of rapid and radical policy changes has occurred. Under the guidance of Finance Minister Roger Douglas, a package of new right financial policies was introduced (dubbed 'Rogernomics' after the Reaganomics equivalent) which included:

removal of wage and price controls;
liberalization of the financial sector;
floating of the New Zealand dollar;
reduction of import tariffs;
removal of import controls;
alterations to the tax system;
reductions in public expenditure;
removal of agricultural subsidies;
restructuring of the state sector into several corporations which were to be run along private sector lines (corporatization).

A full account of these changes can be found in Boston and Holland, 1987, Bollard and Buckle, 1987, Collins, 1987, and McKinley, 1987, and an assessment of the impact of deregulation on rural sectors is provided by Cloke, 1989*a*. Although rural areas are directly affected by all the different policy strands of the package, two changes are particularly important. First, the removal of agricultural subsidies has placed a number of farmers— particularly the younger, heavily indebted farmers and those farming in depressed regions—at risk, leading to a knock-on effect in many agricultural service communities. Although the impact of this policy change will take a few years to work its way through, the new market-orientated approach will almost certainly lead to a significant number of farmers leaving the land. Secondly, corporatization has led to immediate job losses in many rural areas. The new Forestry Corporation announced lay-offs in a number of rural towns, and this has been exacerbated by the Department of Conservation's reluctance to permit forestry development in some key marginal regions. The new Coal Corporation has similarly created significant redundancies in order to slim to its new 'private sector-style' specifications.

Much of the burden of the restructuring of New Zealand's economy, therefore, has been borne by the rural regions. Indeed,

Britton and Perry (1987: 56), reporting on an assessment of New Zealand's regions by the Ministry of Works and Development, paint a bleak picture:

The MWD review concluded that there was 'no obvious prospect' for early recovery in the peripheral regions—a large chunk of the country comprising the West Coast, Wanganui, Aorangi (South Canterbury), Wairarapa, East Cape and Southand. The disturbing question left unanswered in the report was how the residents of these regions could be encouraged to accept a permanently reduced level of economic activity.

Fig. 5.1 gives an impression of these peripheral regions. An indication of the nature of the rural state in New Zealand is given by examining the ability of planners and policy-makers in one of these regions—the West Coast—to respond to the centrally sponsored trends associated with economic restructuring.

The Local-State Response

The West Coast of South Island, New Zealand is remote both in terms of distance and because it is separated from the urban centres of the east coast by the main Alpine range, and from the urban centres of the North Island by the Cook Strait. Agricultural production is dominated by dairying, but the land quality is often poor, and significant areas have only recently been developed for farming. The major industries are resource-based, particularly involving agriculture and forestry product processing, coalmining, and tourism. More recently, gold prospecting has become important again, with a rise in world gold prices.

The West Coast has its United Council, based in Greymouth, and the regional planning scheme was approved in 1982 (West Coast United Council, 1982). This scheme is prefaced by a detailed statement of objectives which, although couched in the typically independent style for which West Coasters are known in New Zealand, clearly raises considerable expectations for the role of the local state (in this case the regional and local authorities and other agencies at these scales) to regulate change on behalf of the residents of the region:

Objective 1. The overall objective of the West Coast Regional Planning Scheme shall be to safeguard the interests, promote the

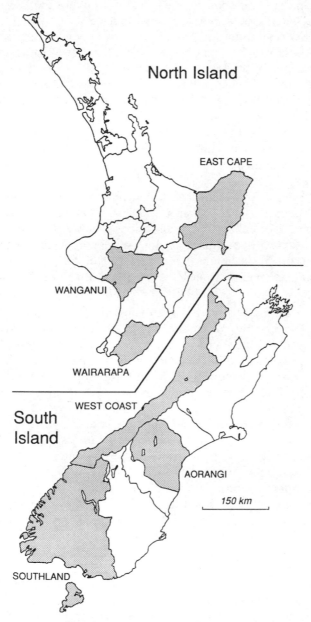

North Island

EAST CAPE

WANGANUI

WAIRARAPA

WEST COAST

South
Island

AORANGI

150 km

SOUTHLAND

FIG. 5.1. Peripheral Regions in New Zealand

unity and provide opportunities for the people of the West Coast as residents of the region and New Zealand.

In order to attain the overall objective, policies for the West Coast Regional Planning Scheme shall be chosen to achieve the best balance of the following objectives:

Objective 2. To make it possible for all those who wish to live in the West Coast region to do so; to make it unnecessary for families and social groups to disperse unwillingly.

Objective 3. To recognize that the region, its communities, and its inhabitants have a right to retain their own identity and have a say in determining their own future; to make it possible to exercise this right.

Objective 4. To safeguard the personal freedoms and initiatives of the people of the region, recognizing that personal freedoms and initiatives involve basic obligations to society.

Objective 5. To extend to the residents of the region the benefits of advancements in civilization. The West Coast Regional Planning Scheme shall facilitate the provision of the following:

(a) Opportunity for gainful employment; opportunity to pursue the art, craft, trade, or profession of one's choice.

(b) A standard of living commensurate with the endeavours of the region's people.

(c) Housing suited to the needs of the people.

(d) Improving standards of health through preventative, educational, and curative measures; access to health and welfare services.

(e) Access to education and technical knowledge.

(f) Access to commercial and professional services.

(g) Access to cultural, recreational, and religious facilities.

(h) Availability of mutual support for welfare, recreation, cultural activities, and social interaction.

(i) Availability of support in times of disaster or difficulty.

(j) Security for people to retain and enjoy the results of their efforts, and to have confidence in the future of the region.

(k) Minimized hazards of injury, accident, and crime, including hazards from natural causes.

(l) Access to other parts of New Zealand and the planet.

(m) A physical environment planned and conserved to serve the needs of present and future generations.

Objective 6. To make it possible for West Coast residents to meet the following obligations to society, the region, and the country:

(a) To support themselves and their dependents through gainful employment.
(b) To support one another in times of difficulty or disaster.
(c) To ensure their activities will not impose unnecessary burdens on the community or individuals, whether at present or in the future.
(d) To be wise and prudent in the use of resources whether natural or man made; to ensure existing assets are not used wastefully or allowed to run down unnecessarily.
(e) To ensure demands made on the environment will not be inconsistent with achieving regional objectives in the longer term.
(f) To contribute to the material and aesthetic well-being of the region and the nation.

The economic restructuring policies of the Lange government have hit the West Coast hard. Young (1986: 13) highlights the impact of redundancies due to corporatization in parts of the region: 'in Greymouth, another forest-dependent economy, unemployment was already running at 9% before the Coal Corporation declared its redundancies in March. It now stands at 10.6%. In addition to lay-offs in the coal and forestry sectors, the new Department of Conservation introduced policies of 'locking up' some of the main areas of forestry, thus inducing a further downward spiral in forest-related industries in the region.

In December 1986 the West Coast United Council wrote an open letter to the prime minister, following an emergency council meeting to discuss the crisis in the region:

This crisis arises from the actions of your Government, which are collectively and systematically removing the usable resource base from this region, dismantling the public service, planning, and professional infrastructure of the West Coast, destroying the ability of this Council to exercise its statutory responsibilities . . . and denying the right of the people of the West Coast to have their needs considered by your Government because their number is small.

The letter highlighted a number of important issues, including:

(i) *Hospitals*: the West Coast region is discriminated against by the policy of population-based funding of hospitals rather than seeking to achieve equity of access to hospitals wherever people live.

(ii) *Forestry*: the United Council had been seeking to protect the local forestry industry against the conservation agencies based outside the region. Central-government decisions to allocate forest lands either to production or protection reduced the productive forest area in the West Coast from 13 per cent to 5 per cent of the region, with consequences for the viability of the local forestry industry, the need for labour, and the ability to collect local taxes.

(iii) *Conservation interests*: the central government had made public statements to the effect that, because the West Coast represented only 1 per cent of New Zealand's population and only one parliamentary constituency, it could not withstand the pressure from national single-interest groups to make decisions on the West Coast to satisfy those groups and disregard the views of local people who are most affected by those decisions.

(iv) *Job losses*: the restructuring of government departments (corporatization) led to redundancies in the coal and forest industries of the West Coast.

(v) *Harbours*: the government had withdrawn grants to the Greymouth Harbour Board and had divested the administration of the Port of Westport.

The United Council admitted that these policies were not intentionally discriminatory. Rather, it recognized that national policies were being implemented in a sectoral manner without a realization of the cumulative impacts on regions such as the West Coast. However, it insisted that the only way of overcoming unintentional discrimination was to strengthen West Coast regional and local government, perhaps involving a restructuring with a strong regional-policy core, and regional-government corporations running regional commercial functions.

The case of the West Coast, where only 11 per cent of resources are controlled by private enterprise and the remaining 89 per cent are determined in the capital, Wellington, by public-sector agencies, may be an unrepresentative one. Nevertheless, it does highlight a number of aspects of the state and its impacts in rural areas. Power in New Zealand is highly centralized. It is difficult to imagine how local pluralistic power, as expressed through local-state agencies, could counteract central-state intentions and interests, even though the West Coast is a Labour constituency dealing with a Labour government. Certainly, the plea for greater regional control over state-owned resources has fallen on deaf ears, even though New Zealand's regional planning legislation provides for binding agreements between government agencies and regional councils once regional plans have been agreed. The situation of centralization provides a fertile breeding ground for the exercise of élitist and managerialist power at the centre. Equally, the recent trends towards deregulation and corporatization have been seen by some as a precursor of wholesale privatization. Such changes may point to the exercise of structural power by dominant capital and class fractions.

So far as concepts of the local state are concerned, Cockburn's idea of a local mirroring of central proclivities towards the creation of flourishing environments for capital accumulation are not borne out here. The local state in the West Coast may be emaciated, but it is no puppet, being concerned more with labour than capital in its political pronouncements. In some ways, Saunders's dualism between central issues of production and local focus on consumption can be read into the West Coast example, although some consumption decisions (for example relating to health) seem also to fall outside the sphere of influence of the local state. Predominantly, then, it appears that local social relations are the significant determinant of the local state. Internal conflicts between social and economic groups inevitably occur in the region, but the greatest turbulence arises betwen the imposition of external decisions on the region, and the reception of these decisions by the rather independent and place-related West Coasters. The low level of private-sector involvement in the area permits, in this particular case, a conflict between local labour and central-state capital.

A SMALL AND CONSTRAINED LOCAL 'STATE': COUNTY GOVERNMENT AND PLANNING IN CANADA

Any account of state activities in rural Canada should acknowledge the diversity inherent in Canadian society. As Lapping (1956: 6) suggests:

Though it may appear homogeneous to outside observers, Canadian society is divided along all manner of ethnic, historical, geographic, and economic cleavages—French/English, native/European, East/West, North/South, old/new Canadians (recent immigrants), rich/poor, urban/ rural, male/female, old/young.

A short description of federal provincial–municipal relations in the context of the state and rural Canada will inevitably gloss over these important stratifications, of which 'rural' is only one of many potential foci. Nevertheless, Canada offers an example of a federal state where power is divided between the national centre, the provincial centres, and the localities. As such, the nature and identity of the local state with jurisdiction over rural areas is subject to two tiers of central relations, in contrast perhaps to the centrality of state affairs to be found, for example, in New Zealand.

Central–Local Relations?

Detailed accounts of the governmental framework covering rural Canada can be found in Hodge (1988) and Bryant (1989). Briefly, the provincial governments tend jealously to guard the major resource management functions of the state, but they do look to the federal government for advice and finance in certain spheres of rural intervention. For example, Lapping and Fuller (1985) discuss the responsibilities delegated to the federal government for promoting rural development. A series of national programmes in the 1970s and 1980s have addressed first the problems of rural poverty, rural community life, and the family farm, and later the regional disparities of industrialization and urbanization. These programmes have been enacted on a cost-sharing basis with provincial governments, and may be illustrated by the outcomes of the Agricultural and Rural Development Act (ARDA) which targeted the problems of rural poverty.

The ARDA programmes established normative indicators of socio-economic disadvantage in rural areas, and offered provincial governments some resources to allow farm rationalization, the transfer of marginal land from agriculture to forestry, and in general the promotion of larger-scale and highly capitalized rural enterprises. Later, the ARDA schemes sought to relocate rural people to places where jobs were available, and, paradoxically, to promote local economic development through the training of local development officers and with the aid of full local public participation. This trend towards community-level development was reversed in the late 1970s, though, as one-off, single-sector development projects became the norm of ARDA programmes again. In these programmes the central federal state was characterized by a 'preoccupation with economic criteria and quantitative objectives of development' and a 'technocratic approach to planning' (Lapping and Fuller, 1985: 116). Further: 'Legitimization was not seen as deriving from the people but from the bureaucracies and institutions in place which assumed authority for rural Canada (p. 117).

In these circumstances the provincial state has a key political role in inter-governmental relations. It can delegate downwards to local authorities, and it can invite participation from federal government by way of invoking programmes such as ARDA. It can therefore be viewed as the political fulcrum of planning policy and practice in Canada (Hodge, 1985). Provincial governments create policies in particular functional arenas (for example, pollution, agricultural land conservation, and transport) and exert considerable control over local planning policies dealing with land-use and development controls, subdivisions, public participation, and so on. Although local authorities have responsibility for these policies, they lack the political strength and financial capacity to tackle rural problems. With a tax base stemming almost entirely from taxes on real estate, most are heavily reliant upon provincial subsidies, and are therefore subject to the strings attached to these subsidies. In these crude terms, then, the local state may again be viewed as small-scale, and dependent on central power for the operation of much of its policy apparatus.

These interrelations are illustrated by Smit *et al.* (1984) in their discussion of non-farm residential development in rural areas on the fringe of urban centres in Ontario. Three levels of policy and action are encountered:

(i) *The federal level.* Despite expressions of general concern, the federal Canadian government has issued few policies relevant to non-farm residential development: it has no authority with respect to provincial land; and its policies tend to be sectoral in nature, thus treating housing, for example, as a discrete national phenomenon, and not being able to cope with a widely scattered and indistinctly defined problem in the rural–urban fringe. The federal government's influence on good-quality agricultural land,

and federal–provincial co-operation on these issues, is governed by a recognition of provincial political control over land under their jurisdiction.

(ii) *The provincial level*. Each province has derived a series of major land-use planning statistics (the Ontario Planning Act is an example). In so doing, local autonomy and power have been commensurately reduced as provincial governments have tightened planning controls. The Ontario Act (introduced in 1946 but subsequently much amended) claimed for the provincial state the rights and responsibilities connected with approving local land-use decisions. A new Planning Act in 1983 attempted to introduce greater local accountability and autonomy, but 'though the new Act does achieve this end, the predominance of the Provincial interest, and conformity to provincial aims, still exists' (Smit *et al.*, 1984: 73).

(iii) *The local level*. In each of the ten provinces, legislation exists permitting those rural communities which have been incorporated as municipalities (lower-order local authorities) to carry out local land-use planning. In Ontario, for example, there are three main planning functions which are delegated to local authorities.

local planning administration (although this in turn may be undertaken by upper-tier authorities such as counties at the request of the local community);
official plans, which are not mandatory but *are* necessary for municipalities to qualify for the delegation of ministerial powers;
land-use control, through the implementation of zoning by-laws.

This impression of strong local accountability, and of the local state being able to influence the pace and scale of development within its jurisdiction, is perhaps illusory. The assumption that lower-tier local-state agencies have the professional capacity and political power to maintain these planning functions is questioned by Hodge (1988: 182):

Rural communities are small and the job of making planning policy and implementing it usually falls to a few hard-pressed officials. Small municipalities frequently have administrative staffs of less than five people . . . . Rarely does one find a planner on staff in communities less than 15,000 in population. This has often led to a disdain of planning edicts from the province: Planning Acts may be disregarded and plans, where they exist, may be ignored. Lastly, large numbers of rural communities are not eligible in any case to undertake land-use planning because they are not incorporated [as municipalities].

Local political control is also severely hampered by relations with other strata of the state. Upper-tier local states often assume responsibilities for planning administration in cases where municipalities have insufficient resources to do the job themselves. Official plans must be submitted to the provincial government for approval, and local plans must therefore conform to the provincial interest. Even local land-use controls are subject to appeal at provincial level, and must themselves conform to official plans and, ultimately, to the provincial interest. These inter-governmental relations exert significant constraints on the activities of the local state in the planning arena.

What Can the Local State Achieve?

Again, all we can do in the context of this chapter is to present cameos of the nature and effectiveness of the local state; but some impressions of the capacity for local action may be gained from a brief study of planning in one county—Huron County in southern Ontario (Fig. 5.2). Huron has a population of around 60,000 and consists of twenty-six municipalities. Its planning board, consisting of five professional planners, carries out most of the local-state planning functions in the area, and the political concerns of locally elected representatives to the county reflect the location on the eastern fringe of Lake Huron. These political concerns are reflected in the statement of five broad problem areas defined in the official Plan (Huron County Planning Board, 1978: 31):

(i) Of the 45 miles of Lake Huron shoreline, 53 per cent has been used for sporadic, ribbon, cottage development. Public access to the beach areas is limited or non-existent in certain areas.

(ii) The provision of public recreation and open space lands is an issue which extends to a region which is substantially larger than that of Huron County.

(iii) Public agencies such as the Ministry of Natural Resources and the conservation authorities may play a reduced role in the provision of lands in public ownership for recreation and open-space purposes.

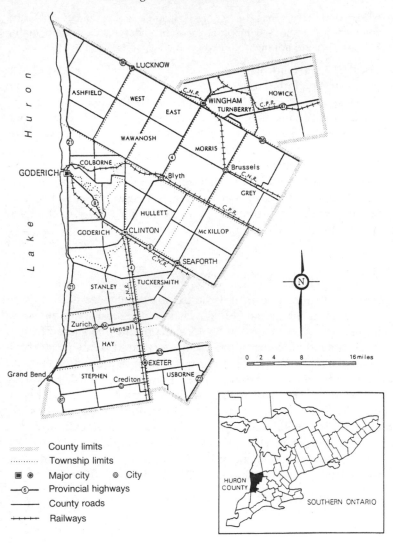

FIG. 5.2. Huron County, Southern Ontario, Canada

(iv) The present jurisdictions of the conservation authorities do not include all the lake front, an area where they are needed.

(v) Over 3,000 acres of Class I–III recreational lands which have a high to moderately high capability for recreation use exist at present in the County.

The political desire for action on local conservation issues is matched by a need for controlled growth in economic and housing development, so as to increase the local tax base and to further local business interests.

The function of planning in Huron County includes economic development and energy co-ordination as well as land-use planning. However, the bulk of activity is in the land-use planning arena, at least partly because the Ontario Planning Act is very much orientated towards land-use. The implementation of land-use planning policies has had clear social implications in Huron County, and the turbulence between conservation, development for the affluent, and the housing problems experienced by disadvantaged groups is an interesting one.

In the past, planning in Huron County has been dominated by traditional use of zoning and subdivision regulations. Zoning by-laws were set up to ensure that new housing should be of a certain minimum size and frontage, and thereby led to the development of expensive properties. Such by-laws were underpinned by a desire to maintain and enhance local tax bases. It can be suggested that these regulations discriminated against less affluent family groups, as did the widespread use of single family residential zones, which prevented occupancy by more than one family and thereby outlawed renting, lodging, or house-sharing—all mechanisms by which lower-income groups might have gained access to the housing market.

By the mid 1970s there had developed something of a housing crisis, with a boom in house and land prices in the area. If the local state had been dominated solely by powerful and affluent local class groups, then this crisis would not necessarily have provoked a response. As it was, the social relations in Huron County were more complex: a growing proportion of elderly citizens, including retired farmers, were of influence in the locality, as were local entrepreneurs who required a pliable, working-class labour pool in order to achieve their goals of production and accumulation. These groups therefore exerted pressure through the local state for changes in the planning/housing balance. Planners were required to examine their regulations to find ways of reducing minimum frontages and house and lot sizes. In the event, even with changes to local regulations, any schemes to house specific groups of the local community could only be implemented with help from the provincial government. For example, senior-citizen housing schemes were established, with the provincial government paying the building costs, and then receiving rent from the occupants according to their income. Such schemes faltered after only a few years because the financial policies of the province began to reflect the political wish to restrict public expenditure. Instead, provincial politicians encouraged local service clubs (such as the Lions Clubs) to raise funds for senior-citizen housing projects. The service clubs would then charge full rent and the province would pay rent allowances to the occupants according to income. Not only did the voluntary sector find it difficult to raise the initial investment costs involved, but the scale of demand for accommodation in rural areas is small, such that even schemes of 15–50 units do not necessarily fill up fast. The builder, whether in the private or voluntary sector, does not therefore get a full and immediate return on investment. Without public-sector investment, therefore, such special schemes are unlikely to be attractive.

Other schemes incorporating financial inputs from the provincial government have been similarly emasculated by the trend towards public-expenditure restrictions. Co-operative housing schemes, whereby the government purchases land, establishes the infra- structure, and then sells lots to self-build community groups, and government-assisted purchases of existing housing stock have both faltered in the 1980s. Huron County planners are able to make few responses to this ebb and flow of central-state intervention. Schemes for particular municipalities to buy land, subdivide it, and sell it cheaply to retired farmers, for example, have been exemplary in principle but very difficult to fund in practice.

Although it would be unwise to suggest that Huron County in any way represents the local state in rural Canada, this brief illustration does indicate the dominance of central–local relations in the context of a federation of provinces. In some ways the struggle for 'local' autonomy might be seen as having been successful at a *provincial* level, in that the province has achieved distinctive areas of political action which are *in* but not *of* the national social relations which underlie federal power. In terms of scale and function, however, the provinces represent to rural Canada, a part of the *central state*, alongside the more centralized federal level of government. A two-tier central state seems to have violated the smaller local tiers of government, both in terms of the functions and responsibilities they carry out and in terms of the discretion and autonomy available to them. While it is certainly the case that local social relations will influence the political objectives of the local state (within the shifting emphasis of housing policies in Huron County), it appears that the power to enact such objectives is largely dependent on central-government financial aid, unless the objectives concerned merely reflect the direction of market-orientated change, in which case little intervention is required.

RURAL PLANNING IN A HEAVILY URBANIZED STATE: THE CASE OF THE NETHERLANDS

The Netherlands provides a very interesting example of the organization of central–local relations in rural areas. The very high relative density of the population throughout almost the whole country presents unique problems in terms of the planning of rural areas, particularly in relation to the location of urban growth. Problems of settlement expansion are compounded by other demands on rural land, notably from the highly intensive system of agriculture and from recreational uses. Conflicts between different types of land-use appear to be reflected at all levels of policy-making, exerting a strong influence on central and local decisions and helping to shape the nature of inter-agency relations.

It is not only the nature and intensity of rural planning problems which makes the Netherlands an interesting focus for attention in this context. A strong academic tradition in rural geography and the analysis of rural planning issues has emerged in the Netherlands which has incorporated strong links with planning orthodoxies in Britain. Comparative planning approaches have examined the similarities which exist between the two countries, relating both to the characteristics of rural areas and to the principles of rural planning policy (Clark *et al.*, 1984). In general, Dutch rural studies have suffered, like those in Britain (see Chapter 1), from a reluctance to develop theoretical perspectives or to explore specific issues within a broader state–society context. Thus a recent conference on world rural sociology (Bologna, 1988) saw some Dutch contributors debating the existence of a rural–urban dichotomy with little or no evidence of progression beyond the ideas of the 1960s (Constandse, 1988). These conceptual orthodoxies are reflected in governmental research relating to rural areas in the Netherlands, which remains very largely empirical and orientated towards the examination of physical planning problems. Issues surrounding the allocation of resources amongst different social groups or the distribution of power within society appear poorly developed within Dutch rural geography and planning, while class-based analyses as a whole are not widely supported.

Rural Geography of the Netherlands

It is clearly important, before examining the relationship between the central and local states in Dutch rural planning, to grasp something of the characteristics of the rural areas themselves and of the nature of population change in these areas. De Smidt (1986) identifies three principal geographical areas of the rural Netherlands:

(i) A semi-periphery in the northern and south-western regions. This is the most sparsely populated area of the Netherlands and suffers from problems of accessibility. The area is characterized by vast tracts of agricultural land, and consequently its future as a region is seen to lie largely at the mercy of EEC agricultural policy as initiated from Brussels (De Smidt, 1986). In terms of settlement planning, regional policy for the area has maintained a process of rationalization aimed at reducing problems of accessibility by adopting a key village approach to service distribution.

(ii) An area of small farms and much higher population density in the southern and eastern regions. Conflicts between agriculture and the environment represent the principal focus for rural planning in this area, and policies are consequently heavily influenced by national and regional objectives. The strong dependence on agriculture has created problems of rural unemployment as capital replaces labour on even the small, family-based farms.

(iii) The region known as the Green Heart in the central Netherlands. This is a highly accessible rural area, close to the major centres of population, and has been very profoundly influenced by suburbanization processes and by recreational demands from city dwellers. The intensification of dairy farming has also placed considerable pressure on land resources and had far reaching effects on the environment.

Each of these rural areas has experienced very different levels of population change over the past 25–30 years. Like Britain and other industrialized countries, the Netherlands as a whole has seen rapid deconcentration of the city population—predominantly within the rural areas surrounding the urban centres and to the eastern and southern regions (see Fig. 5.3). Migration into the peri-urban regions was particularly strong between the early 1960s and late 1970s. Since this time, however, growth has slowed

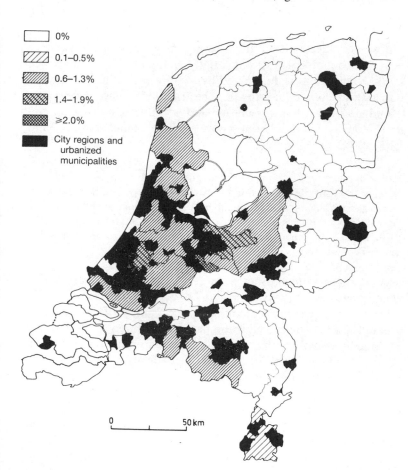

FIG. 5.3. Annual Average Population Growth in the Netherlands, 1976–1981
Source: Atzema and Dijkstra, 1986: 50

considerably, with evidence of some reurbanization during the 1980s (Atzema and Dijkstra, 1986). De Smidt (1986) suggests, that with an increasingly elderly national population a reduction in the willingness of both people and economic activities to move too far away from their existing locations will see a fostering of urban renewal and a further slowing down both in the rate of suburban-ization and in the growth of more peripheral rural areas of the country.

The State and Planning for Rural Areas

Much fuller accounts of these issues may be found elsewhere (e.g. Groenendijk, 1988); but, briefly, national-level, rural policy in the Netherlands is dominated by a concern for the control and direction of population growth. The traditional view in physical-planning terms is that population and activities should be spread more equally over the country as a whole. Thus, Atzema and Dijkstra (1986: 45) argue:

National Policy . . . is aimed at affecting spatial changes in order to minimise the prospective conflicts between spatial claims. The state, by means of mapping out objectives and making use of instruments to realise these objectives, directs structural change in peri-urban rural areas. In the 1970s one could see a growing governmental concern in population changes of settlements in peri-urban regions.

The Dutch government was, at this time, committed to protecting what some authors (Atzema and Dijkstra, 1986; Groot, 1972) refer to as 'liveability'—essentially, the *quality* of life in rural areas. The rapid suburbanization process appeared to be having a profoundly negative effect on both the environmental and social quality of life in rural areas, as well as diverting much-needed investment from the cities. In response to the problems of suburbanization, the central government implemented a system of zoning for rural land in peri-urban areas (see the Report on Rural Areas, 1977, and the Urbanization Report, 1976, quoted in Atzema and Dijkstra, 1986). This zoning, based primarily on landscape quality, advocates either the incorporation of urban functions with agriculture and 'national' land-uses or their separa-tion. The basic aim of such policies, however, was to restrict the increase in population growth in the accessible rural areas (especially that from urban migration), and to direct development back into the cities. In the more peripheral areas, growth centres, identified by regional authorities, were selected into which growth was to be channelled.

In the context of this chapter, the objectives and details of Dutch central-state policies for rural areas are less important than the administrative and political structures, and the power relationships through which these policies are implemented. One key question in this context, therefore, is the extent to which local levels of governmental policy-making operate autonomously of central-state control. To what extent can regional and provincial levels determine their own policy objectives and implement local strategies? Alternatively, how far are national directives imposed upon local policy-makers? Clearly, we do not have the space here to suggest answers to such questions in anything other than a very sketchy form. Nevertheless, it is possible to make a number of general observations about the Dutch policy-making system and its implementation in rural areas which add to the information about how local states in rural areas of different nations compare.

In discussing policies for the restriction of population growth in peri-urban areas, Atzema and Dijkstra (1986) identify the goals of national policy (as described above) and the extent to which these goals are adopted by the provincial authorities in the formulation of their regional plans. On the one hand, they argue that national objectives are adopted by the regions, and, indeed, that the regions are expected to follow this line, with the national directives being presented as 'essential political statements'.

On the other hand, they suggest that

there are no coercive measures to prevent these directives being neglected because there is no direct hierarchical structure between national spatial plans and those of the province. [Thus] if the state wants its physical planning policy to be carried out it must convince governments at a lower level by well-founded arguments, it cannot enforce measures. (p. 48)

Their arguments support the view, then, that regional policies maintain a considerable degree of independence from national government. It would seem, however, in the case of broad issues of population growth and control, that the local-state authorities retain a strong political allegiance to the central state. Further research is needed to ascertain the actual basis of that allegiance—

whether it is founded, for example, on a financial dependence which would, in reality, give the local state very little real autonomy from the centre, or whether it is more accurately an indication of shared objectives for rural policies and people.

Further light may be shed on this question by looking at the work of municipal governments. At the local level, policy-making in the Netherlands is still directed towards issues of land-use and the management of physical space. There is thus bound to be a high degree of overlap between national and even international objectives and the priorities of regional policy. The municipalities, however, are concerned to a large extent with issues of consumption relating to the socio-economic problems of rural communities, and with service provision. It is perhaps at this level that conflict between the local and central states would be most obvious, and the dependency of municipalities more significant, in determining the direction and effectiveness of local-level policy for rural areas.

A view shared by a number of Dutch academics (see Groenendijk, 1984; 1988; De Bakker and Piersma, 1986; De Boer and Groenendijk, 1986) is that municipal authorities exert considerable influence on settlement planning in rural areas. This influence is particularly strong in terms of the distribution and location of housing and public services. The firm reliance on policies of resource concentration by rural municipalities into larger settlements is, however, again in accordance with national and regional spatial planning. Conflict is avoided through the management of the dependence that exists between the different levels of policy-making, and as a consequence the powers of the municipalities are extended. But it is, again, difficult to ascertain how far the illusion of independence and power rests on a firm understanding that prevents or minimizes any challenge to the central state. Certainly the research quoted above would seem to indicate that local government is permitted a significant degree of independence in the direction of settlement policy, for example, in deciding on growth centres within the municipality. But the research in question has not been designed specifically to address the issue of central–local relations, and consequently the role of financial dependence or political affiliation has not been tackled.

The problems of using secondary analysis for the examination and analysis of issues as complex as the relative autonomy of local and regional government are painfully evident. Direct, cross-national comparisons would make little sense in the light of such inadequacies. A number of worthwhile issues do arise, however, in the context of this discussion of Dutch rural policy. Firstly, rural planning in the Netherlands is clearly dominated by physical and spatial issues which derive, primarily, from the very high density of the population, and which cast doubt on the description of any region or municipality as peripheral or remote. The centrality of these issues appears to minimize the opportunity for conflict between the aims of central and local government in the formulation of policy. Secondly, a commitment to the concept of 'liveability' (albeit mainly in relation to the control of population growth) helps to bridge the gap between the national and local state, by incorporating national as well as local government within the arena of public consumption. Finally, the fact that the housing market is largely government-controlled provides the state with a 'great opportunity to implement its own spatial planning policy' (Van Ginkel, 1986: 64) and further minimizes the chance for either local/central or public/private conflicts.

A CENTRALIZED POLITICAL ECONOMY AND LOCAL RURAL CHANGE: THE CASE OF HUNGARY

A final illustration of central–local state relations and their impact on policies for rural areas relates to the situation in Hungary. Clearly, Hungary provides a very different case, in terms both of the development of rural settlements and of the organization of the decision-making process, from those developed capitalist nations already discussed. Its inclusion here is partly a response to those differences, but also in recognition of the fact that, despite the very different principles of national political organization, many of the tensions concerning the relative autonomy of local government *vis-à-vis* the centre, noted in relation to other examples, appear to be an influential force in policy-making in rural Hungary. The basic dependency of the locality on the central state, articulated most clearly through financial control, is again apparent as a key factor in the formulation and implementation to rural policy.

Analysis of rural development and of policy-making itself, in Hungary, is hampered by a lack of recent (translated) research. There are signs, however, of a growing interest in and commitment to rural research within Hungary, especially in relation to structural changes taking place within the rural economy (e.g. Polgàr, 1988; Répássy, 1988) and to the development of the rural community (Fogarasi, 1988; Juhasz, 1988). Cross-national comparisons are being made (Enyedi and Veldman, 1986), providing important introductions to the processes operating within rural Hungary, and to the intensity and direction of major socio-economic changes within these areas. Again, while comment here must be brief, a few key observations will be used to generate useful insights into the policy-making process as it affects rural communities and, at a very basic level, the degree of autonomy afforded to local decision-making agencies.

Rural Development in Hungary

While direct comparisons are very difficult, settlement development within rural Hungary appears to be at a very different stage to that noted in other cases. Growth, both in population and economic capacity, has been restricted mainly to the peri-urban areas. Remoter rural areas have demonstrated continuing stagnation, with declining levels of population and little or no industrial investment. The historical legacy of the war has been held partly to blame for the particularly sparse and declining populations of settlements on the Great Hungarian Plain. The rural areas surrounding major towns and cities, however, have experienced rapid growth during the 1970s. Industrial expansion, involving in particular branch plants, led to population growth outside the main centre and encouraged the revitalization of declining rural communities. In general, as Lackó (1986) observes, rural Hungary in the 1960s and 1970s was characterized by intensive differentiation, with some villages growing rapidly and some declining rapidly.

Where industrial expansion and population growth did occur in rural parts of Hungary, it was not as the result of carefully constructed rural development policies, initiated with concern for the economic and social well-being of rural communities, but rather in response to the availability of cheap labour. While regional planning in the 1960s acknowledged the need to equalize regional differentiation in the economy, such recognition was not manifested in policies to facilitate the spread of industry. It was national industrial processes, the creation of branch plants in sites where pools of readily available labour existed, together with general economic conditions within Hungary that were largely responsible for the diffusion of industry into the smaller towns and villages (Table 5.1 indicates very broadly the changing ratio of agricultural to industrial jobs in Hungarian villages during the period 1960–80). Thus, as Kárpáti (1986: 129) points out, the establishment of industry outside the main urban centres in fact 'brought no fundamental change in the direction of the accumulation of handicaps, or in the territorial distribution of power-relations in the sphere of production'. Rather, it simply reinforced the existing settlement differentiation.

Moreover because industrial expansion was mainly in the form of branch plants, the jobs created for rural people were not necessarily secure. Factories were developed in old buildings using out-of-date machinery, and were consequently often short-lived. Levels of pay for workers were poor, and conditions generally compared unfavourably to those existing within urban-based industries. Few national resources were put into the development of infrastructure in the rural areas because, as Kárpáti (1986: 129) again argues, the national powers which control these industries have 'little interest in the communal development of villages'.

In terms of recent industrial development within rural Hungary, then, the centre has clearly imposed its dominance and left little opportunity for local independent action. The extent to which this stance is echoed in attitudes towards more general economic and social progress is more difficult to identify. Lackó (1986) and Kárpáti both indicate a commitment by the Hungarian government to addressing the problems of spatial and social inequalities, and

Table 5.1. Industrial Jobs as a Proportion of All Jobs in Hungarian Villages, 1960–1980

	1960 (%)	1970 (%)	1980 (%)
Agriculture	69.2	53.7	43.8
Industry and construction industry	19.7	26.2	28.2
Others	11.1	20.1	28.0

Source: Barta, 1986: 39.

an awareness of the need to look beyond short-term programmes in the elimination of such inequalities. Both authors acknowledge, however, that a lack of theoretical and analytical research restricts our understanding of the precise relationship between different levels of policy-makers—or, indeed, between the settlements themselves.

In describing the main trends and objectives of Hungarian settlement policy, Lackó (1986: 33) suggests that, following the dynamic expansion of. industry (as described above), there is a need to move into a second stage that will concentrate on local settlement development. Such a phase would necessitate 'all those who are affected by consequences of decisions [taking] part, directly or indirectly, in the decision making', and would, by definition, involve the decentralization of decisions and a growth in local democracy. Until now, while the Hungarian government has, it is suggested (Kárpáti, 1986) taken various steps designed to encourage local initiatives, the 'maldistribution of the central economic and development funds' has still, crucially, prevented the growth of community power and local autonomy.

Clearly, then as in examples from other parts of the world, a real commitment to improving the quality of life for rural residents and the satisfaction of local people (Juhasz, 1988) is seen to lie in the extension of powers to the local level. Whether in the development of industry or in the provision of housing, the assumption is that the local community is in a far better position to determine existing need and formulate the most appropriate policies for meeting that need. In Hungary, greater local autonomy is seen as essential if less developed rural areas are to prevent the siphoning off of resources by the urban centre which will ensure their social and economic decline. Such autonomy is also important to limit the social selectivity of migration within the more prosperous rural regions.

But a recognition of the need for greater local independence is, once again, almost meaningless in the face of continuing rigid financial control from the centre. Past development strategies in Hungary have, whether directly, through the limiting of resources, or indirectly, through the encouragement of national economic processes, ensured and reinforced such control. And while aspirations for future policies stipulate an enhanced role for regional and local interests, such a role, involving, for example, the formation of local initiatives, is still dependent on the handing down of resources from the centre and, indeed, on the generation of those resources by major industrial interests.

THE STATE AND CHANGING GOVERNMENTAL RELATIONS: RURAL POLICIES IN A CHANGING WORLD

A recent international review of policies and plans for rural people (Cloke, 1988) posed the question of whether rural areas in developed nations were experiencing similar problems. Although variations in scale, administrative structure, and political dominance have to be taken into account, the answer to the question turned out to be yes; and in particular three categories of common problem emerged.

Problems Connected with Old Resource Regions

In the main, rural areas tend to be synonymous with previously important but now declining resources, and are therefore character-ized by symptoms of contemporary under-development. Often the extreme symptoms amount to rural deprivation, and in some larger nations whole regions are affected by deprivation because of their economic, political, and geographical marginality. Elsewhere, deprivation is interspersed with rural regeneration, characterized not only by the wealth of adventitious inmigrants but also by the shift of ex-urban economic enterprises. These generalizations are illustrated above in the cases of the West Coast in New Zealand— a marginal, deprived region—and the heavily urbanized rural areas of the Netherlands. Whether wholesale or dispersed, deprivation is experienced by key groups:

the remnants of the former agricultural economy;
the *nouveaux pauvres* who have consciously decided to live in the rural environment but also do not have wealth or income to overcome prevailing disadvantage;
elderly components of all social groups (including the formerly adventitious);
racial minority groups;
the unemployed or underemployed in old resource regions;
rural women who lack mobility.

Clearly, the existence of these deprived groups within rural populations would pose important policy decisions to local and central states were pluralist power assumed to be functioning in the nations and sub-nations concerned.

Capital Restructuring and State Intervention

The second group of common problems experienced in rural areas arose from the complex interactions between the restructuring of capital and the changing nature of state intervention in market-led processes. Old resource regions have not just been left to decline. Capital restructuring resulting in decline has attracted policies of alleviation from the state, and capital restructuring resulting in rejuvenation has also been linked with state intervention through different forms of economic enticement. In agriculture, for example, restructuring in terms of substituting capital for labour has been inextricably entwined within state agricultural policies, usually involving heavy subsidy. In recent times there has been pressure on governments to reduce or remove such subsidies. These pressures reflect both the internationalization of political power and capital and the internecine conflicts which can emerge between different sections of capital where state support of one is disadvantageous to others through higher taxes, inflation, and interest rates. The combination of fluctuating world prices and the uncertainty of state support has resulted in declining food prices, problems for young and indebted farmers, and downstream impacts in rural communities.

The capital–state interaction in a growth mode is perhaps best illustrated by the case of manufacturing industry. In many parts of the developed world there has been an urban-to-rural shift in manufacturing activity, usually with the state being actively involved in promoting rural industrialization. But the advantages of rural areas to incoming capitalists include the availability of a low-wage, non-unionized workforce, and new employment attracted on these grounds may serve to extend the persistent problems of low incomes in rural areas.

Service Delivery

The third set of rural problems again relates to state policy, but in this case in the context of providing adequate levels of services to the small, dispersed, rural population. In the past, service policies were underpinned by notions of equality, egalitarianism, and strategic necessity. More recently, governments have demonstrated a propensity to transfer public-sector responsibilities, such as that for service delivery, to the private sector, following strategies of deregulation and privatization. Again, the nature and extent of state intervention may contribute to specific problems occurring widely in rural areas of the Western world.

POLICY FOR RURAL AREAS

Many of these commonly experienced problems reflect the conceptual expectations discussed in Chapter 1. Certainly they do cast doubt on the view that policy acts as a response to problems, since so often the policy 'response' appears to be an integral part of the reproduced problem. In this light it is very interesting to note the commonalities which are emerging in state policies for rural areas throughout the developed world. Some of these commonalities are clearly evident in the four cases presented earlier in this chapter: the dominance of centralized policy decision; the inability of local rural communities to achieve policy goals without reliance on devolved power and finance from central or provisional governments; the ability of central-state agencies to dictate both the perception of what rural problems are and the agenda for the alleviation of these problems; and so on. Three broad categories of common policy are briefly discussed here.

Top-Down Centralized Policies

Rural policy is dominated by decisions made at the central level, and by resultant actions which are to a large extent imposed on the locality with relatively little discretion to alter policies to suit local circumstances. These top-down policies tend to be sectoral in nature, dealing, for example, with agriculture rather than with an integrated view of rural areas. Agricultural policy is the dominant example because in most states it is the principal sectoral policy. Whereas other economic sectors have undergone capital restruc-turing with only indirect support from the state, agricultural capital has consistently received major direct subsidies. Moreover, these subsidies have become entrenched within the power relations of the state and have proved difficult to adjust, particularly with the internationalization of political power, notably within the EEC. Resistance to policy restructuring has also been ineffective because of the powerful internal political lobby enjoyed by agricultural interests. In turn, central-state agriculture departments have taken a lead in promoting the well-being of the rural sector, even though that sector is by no means homogeneous and the political lobby is dominated by the farmers who are more highly capitalized and operate on a larger scale. In this way, rural welfare has become agricultural welfare, with the state acting in support of the needs of the dominant sectors of agricultural capital. This edifice of state support has already been broken down by the Lange government in New Zealand (Cloke, 1989*b*); and with agricultural power seemingly on the wane, and other sections of capital rebelling against the costs of state-subsidized regulation of agriculture, it seems likely that changes (albeit slow changes) to agricultural policy will occur elsewhere.

Another top-down sectoral policy which has had impacts in rural areas is regional policy. Governments have been active in promoting industrial growth in marginal areas through various economic incentives, and in some cases these marginal areas overlap with rural areas, and so regional policy might be seen as rural policy. The political momentum for regional policy, however, has come from the perceived need for government action in old industrial areas, rather than for any equivalent action to respond to the needs of the *rural* economy. Thus top-down policy has been formulated for non-rural interests, as a response (as the case of Hungary clearly demonstrates) to the demands of capital—for example, for cheap labour or more space. The spin-off effects for rural populations help legitimize regional policies, although such effects are not generally a central objective.

There are regional-policy exceptions to this state of affairs. Agencies such as those in the Tennessee Valley and Appalachians in the USA, and the Highlands and Islands and Mid-Wales in the UK, have been established in response to the challenges of largely rural regions. Even here, however, development policy activities have tended to be located in the major urban centres, and the differential impacts of rural deprivation are often untouched by policy initiatives. The only significant example of specific regional planning at the localized rural scale has occurred in France (Clout,

1984; 1988) where so-called rural-action zones and rural-renovation zones have been established. Even in this case, however, the zones tend to represent a series of specific élite areas rather than a comprehensive programme of regional-policy initiatives in all rural regions of the country. In many Western states, moreover, there has been a significant decline in commitment to regional policy, particularly in the face of a boom in private-sector-led development in more accessible areas (e.g. the 'green heart' of the Netherlands or the south-eastern region of England). Any benefits, intended or unintended, accruing to rural people as a result of regional policy have similarly taken a downturn.

In the past there has been something of a commitment by central states to the maintenance of basic levels of welfare and public services in rural areas. Such a commitment has generally overridden economic criteria which dictate that the provision of services such as health, education, and transport is more expensive within sparsely populated localities. Subsidies have ensured a standardization of prices and allowed public facilities to be provided at realistic rates. The current policies of new right governments have brought changes to these top-down, welfare-orientated policies, however, the ideological beliefs of such governments favouring a move towards market-orientated decision-making, not only in the provision of basic public services but also in the planning of private-sector services. Under such conditions, the needs of rural people fall foul of the demands of the market, attracting a much lower priority within the newly privatized delivery systems than they did in the previously regulated systems.

Middle-Level Policies

Top-down policies appear to have been increasingly dominant over recent years in most developed nations. The middle-ground policies formulated by local governments with jurisdiction over rural areas have, by contrast, been relatively uncontentious and largely unidirectional. Middle-level policies have in the main focused on the designation of rural growth centres whose role is to act as service centres, and as points of intervening opportunity at which flows of outmigration might be interrupted. Growth centre policies have been linked with an economic necessity to rationalize settlement patterns. As public-sector services have been increasingly constrained by central restrictions on public expenditure, as private-sector decision-makers have sought economies of scale in their investments, and as planners have bowed to the sheer pragmatic benefits of resource concentration, the growth centre or 'key settlement' strategy has become almost irresistible. However, this policy of 'convenience' has clear distributional impacts, particularly amongst disadvantaged residents of rural places which are not selected for growth. Here, there is a direct link between planning restrictions and social recomposition, favouring gentrification and the new middle classes who are able to take advantages of these locations under market-led conditions.

Bottom-Up Responses

With a dominant centralized policy-making procedure, and an often compliant local state pursuing middle-ground policies of convenience, the scope for bottom-up community action appears strong if pluralist frameworks of power are to be acknowledged. Indeed, there has been a strong trend towards the incorporation of local community action into the mainstream of social and welfare policy in many developed nations. Does this mean, then, that the state recognizes the virtues of local democracy and the need to engender community cohesion through collective activity? Or is the turn towards governmental acknowledgement of the need for self-help merely a cop-out, in view of the increasing inability or unwillingness of public-sector agencies to deal with problems relating to the social and economic viability of rural communities? These issues are discussed in detail in Chapter 6, but we would suggest that, while in some cases community action can act as a useful supplementing apparatus for rural-welfare provision, there is often a mismatch between those communities which are able to help themselves and those communities who are most in need of help. Essentially, these trends towards greater acknowledgement of self-help should be seen in the wider context of the inexorable rolling back of the welfare state by contemporary new right governments.

RURAL POLICY AS STATE FUNCTION

Judging both from the examples presented in this chapter and from wider evidence of rural change in developed nations, the response to the economic crisis of the late 1970s and 1980s has been a significant reorganization of power and political administration in a majority of nation-states. Mostly, increasingly power has accrued to the centre, thus weakening the discretionary powers of the local state (such as they were) and emasculating the potential for responsive planning and policy-making at the regional and local levels. Paradoxically, this centralization of power has occurred during a period which has been loudly pronounced by government as an era of decentralization of responsibility. The increasing gap between power and responsibility is crucial in the understanding of this paradox. Even where some power has been decentralized, and where local agencies have been given more opportunity to act in response to rural problems (as, for example, in France), the ability of local agencies to exploit these opportunities has been hampered by the lack of financial resources with which to implement discretionary schemes. Thus, whether power within nations has been openly centralized or apparently decentralized, the result has been a similarly reduced capacity for local agencies to engage in financially and administratively autonomous local planning.

There is a clear indication from the four cameos included here that this reduction in local-state capacity has been to the detriment of welfare-based policy in rural areas. Central states appear, to varying degrees, to acknowledge the particular problems that occur in rural localities (in, for example, the declared concern for 'liveability' within Dutch rural strategic policy). Any manifestation of these concerns, however, has increasingly been overridden by broad structural processes which dictate the movement of capital and the distribution of resources, and by a political ideology which consistently subordinates social to economic aims. The removal, moreover, of many functions out of the area of public-sector control into the private sector further reduces the capacity of either local or central states to implement welfare-based policy.

Claims that the anti-intervention and anti-planning ideologies espoused by new right governments have led to increased 'freedom' for either local rural states or, indeed, rural populations are patently untenable. Such stances simply create an environment in which the private sector can flourish. 'Freedom' is consequently afforded to, for example, the private developer or large farmer, generally at the expense of the already disadvantaged classes within rural society. As the examples presented here show, a common response to the lack of public resources for rural areas is the involvement of community groups in the development of self-help or voluntary initiatives. This expression of individual 'freedom' helps to legitimize central-state and private-sector policies in the eyes of right-wing governments, but provides no comprehensive or consistent alternative to public services or welfare approaches.

Rural policies, therefore are being fashioned as part of crucial and far-reaching changes to the interrelationships between different levels of government and between the state sector and the private-capital sector. Their analysis should incorporate (as has been made obvious by the examples included above) broad tendencies in the political/ideological shift of central government, not only in Britain but in the developed world in general. The implications of these changes penetrate beyond the formal policy process into the arena of democracy and political participation. The evidence presented clearly leads us to question pluralist concepts concerning the distribution of power and the role of the public in decision-making. It is to this crucial area that we now turn.

6

Public Participation in Rural Planning

INTRODUCTION

The analysis of decision-making has largely focused so far on the 'professional' arena. Links have been drawn between social need and inequality, and between the actions of decision-takers from both the public and the private sectors. The intention in this chapter is to look beyond the role of the professional in the policy-making process and to consider the contribution of rural residents to the formulation and implementation of policy for rural areas. The chapter explores the extent to which those living in rural communities can exert influence over either the construction or outcome of policy, and questions the notion of the 'ordinary' member of the public as a passive and helpless recipient of resource allocation decisions. The analysis embraces not only theoretical but also practical perspectives in examining both the potential for participation and specific examples of public involvement in decision-making and service provision.

Chapter 2 examined in some depth the different theoretical perspectives through which the role of the state can be analysed and assessed. Such perspectives, as has been shown, vary in terms of their conceptualization of the power relations between state and society; and much of the discussion of pressure groups and participation has not only been placed within a conceptual framework of power relation, but has also served to reinforce the use of particular constructs of power.

A brief summary of the contemporary analysis of pressure groups and power relations serves to emphasize the importance of these concepts. At a fundamental level, the conceptualization of pressure has centred on aspects of pluralism and corporatism. As Ball and Millard (1986: 2) point out:

the major tenet of pluralism is that political power is fragmented and dispersed. Decisions are seen as the outcome of a complex process of group interaction and bargaining. The political system permits and even encourages people to organise so as to further their demands as members of groups.

Pluralism appears to be important both as an empirically derived description of what actually happens and as a rather rosy statement of intent regarding what ought to be a proper framework of power relations. On the one hand, a range of commentators have observed pluralism as a significant aspect of political and social life. For example, Hugh Thorburn's work on pluralism in Canada led to the conclusion that 'Whereas pre-war democratic societies tended to be dominated by a clearly identifiable elite . . . modern societies have been visible elites, but an obvious and busy interest group system in constant interaction with government' (Thorburn, 1080: 151); while Ralph Miliband's Marxist thesis on power (1973a: 131) concedes:

Democratic and pluralist theory could not have gained the degree of ascendancy which it enjoys in advanced capitalist countries if it had not at least been based on one plainly accurate observation about them, namely that they permit and even encourage a multitude of groups and associations to organise openly and freely and to compete with each other for the advancement of such purposes as their members may wish.

On the other hand, there is a suspicion that pluralism is more apparent than real. Access to power is not equally available to all classes and interests. There is inequality between pressure groups, and this is seen by pluralist thinkers to be 'unavoidable within free society' (Coxall, 1986: 168). Perhaps, then, power within a seemingly free society is not as 'free' as is commonly perceived. Perhaps it is the notion of pluralism rather than the actual achievement of it which is most important in understanding the distribution of power in contemporary society. Coxall himself hints at this when he attempts to answer the question of whether pressure groups exert too much power:

The claim that pressure groups exert excessive influence is therefore 'not proven'. This does not mean that the sum of sectional interests may be identified with the national interest in any specific instance. What may in a broader sense be claimed to be in the national interest is the system of pluralism itself. For bargaining between *important* groups is a more democratic and potentially effective way to conduct politics than a simple command–obedience relationship between parliament and the rest. (p. 166; our italics)

Pluralism is thus reduced to the power of 'important groups', which in turn may be a legitimation for wider structural or élite interests.

Clearly, powerful interest groups have been seen to influence policy-making, and here the notion of corporatism becomes important. The work of Schmitter and Lahmbruch (1979), Cawson (1978), Smith (1979), and others has developed into a conceptualization of how key functional groups (often representing capital and labour) have been directly integrated into the governmental policy-making apparatus. The benefits of partnership are mutual. The favoured groups attain access to decision-making, and monopoly status as representatives of their area of interest. Governments benefit apparently from the expertise of the groups concerned, but perhaps more importantly attempt either to exercise control of these interests through partnership or to legitimize the incorporation of these particular interests through seemingly participatory partnership (depending on how you look at it). In Britain, for example, the period between the early 1960s and 1979 has been characterized as a period of corporate economic management between government, business, and unions, whereas during the post-1979, Thatcher era these sectional groups have lost much of their corporate influence in public policy-making.

Both pluralism and corporatism have been the subject of substantial mutual critique, which is summarized thus by Ball and Millard (1986: 284–5):

Much of politics is indeed less adversarial than the pluralist approach implies, and there has been a blurring of the state–society distinction as social structures such as unions or business or farming groups assume certain administrative functions traditionally ascribed to the state. However, the development of routine procedures for consultation is not sufficient for 'corporatism' nor necessarily incompatible with pluralism.

Perhaps more powerful are the critiques which emanate from élitist and structuralist concepts of power relations. Élitism stresses the biased use of powerful state apparatus for the benefit of key political and economic sections of society. Structuralism also suggests a centralization of power, reflected in the interaction of socio-economic structures, class and capital, and political machinery. Both concepts argue against the view of diffuse power offered by pluralism, and both seek to explain the apparent corporatist phenomenon in terms of the centralization of power, rather than as the successful operation of a system of participation and pressure groups within a pluralist framework.

What purpose, then, does public involvement in policy-making serve? Is it simply tolerated as a means of legitimizing state action, or is it to be seen as an integral and necessary part of the policy process? The purpose of this chapter is not to present a detailed critique of the various interpretations of public participation as offered by different theoretical perspectives. It is important, however, that any discussion of the role and potential of public involvement and voluntary approaches stems from a basic understanding of such differences. Analysis must recognize that conclusions concerning the purpose and contribution of public participation at all levels within the decision-making process are wide open to debate according to how one interprets state–society relations.

OPPORTUNITIES FOR PUBLIC PARTICIPATION

The National Context

Taken at its broadest level, the entire political system of Britain is based on the principle of public participation. Democracy demands that, ultimately, political decisions rest in the hands of the people as expressed through elected representatives. In voting for these political representatives, all electors have the opportunity to influence decision-making and to participate in the process of government. This opportunity exists at both the national level, in the election of members of parliament, and at the local level, in the election of local councillors. Classic liberal theory sees these representatives as the means of communication within a democratic system, between the decision-makers, those in power, and the community.

The democratic content of decision-making could, therefore, be said to hinge on the principle of representation. When this principle itself is analysed, however, flaws are evident, and the ability of representative democracy to reflect the wishes of the electorate must be questioned. McLennan (1984) identifies two areas of contention concerning the relationship between democracy and representation: the type of representative and the nature of the constituency. The first of these addresses the distinction between notions of trusteeship and delegation. Should the elected representative simply be responsive to the electorate—taking their interests into account but ultimately being trusted to apply

independent judgement—or should they be more clearly accountable to the interests of the constituents? The second major area of
contention embraces the distinction between territorial and
functional representation, and challenges the system of voting as a
means of selecting representatives. Should representatives be
chosen according to geographical boundaries or in recognition of
the differing interests of members of society? The centrality of
these complex issues to the question of public participation within
the democratic process cannot be denied.

Recognition of the many problems surrounding representation
in the political, especially parliamentary, system leads inevitably
to the consideration of more direct means of public participation.
Direct or participatory democracy has been seen as one 'alternative'
(Darke and Walker, 1977) whereby the electorate take part in all
major or specified decisions. That such a system could be
organized on any equitable basis, at least at the national scale, is,
however, highly dubious and in many ways quite impracticable.
Direct participation is seen to occur, therefore, only in the context
of single, specified issues, for example, nuclear disarmament or
women's rights. Its status is that of 'extra-parliamentary' activity,
and it is seen by many (especially those on the right of the political
spectrum) as running *counter* to the aims of democracy.

While the principle of representation is fundamental to the
nature of participation, there are clearly elements of the structure
and framework of government which influence the ability of
individuals and groups to take part in the decision-making process.
The fact that key government departments, such as the Foreign
Office and the Treasury, are not fully accountable to the
Commons or even to the Cabinet, for example, is indicative of the
relative weakness of parliamentary power over areas of state
activity, and must beg questions of public accountability. Equally
important is the issue of access to information and the willingness
of those in power to inform the public about their actions. A
considerable degree of autonomy exists, for example, amongst the
security services and police, and—particularly under the present
Conservative administration in Britain—there seems to be a
growing desire to protect that autonomy from scrutiny by
members of the public. Another critical area of secrecy and
misinformation is that relating to environmental issues (Goldsmith
and Hildyard, 1986). In general, as McLennan (1984: 248) writes,

'Britain lags behind other capitalist democracies such as Sweden and the USA, in upholding democratic rights of access to information and state accountability.' It should again be stressed that these issues, and the accompanying interpretation of, for example, the powers vested in individuals (or 'representatives') within government, are closely tied to specific perspectives on the operation of the state, its control by élites, and its autonomy *vis-à-vis* the electorate.

This very brief discussion of public participation as embraced in the principle and operation of democracy at the national scale has illustrated the wide-ranging potential of the debate. A number of texts provide a far greater insight into the complexities of the subject than is permitted here (e.g. McLennan *et al.*, 1984; Boddy and Fudge, 1984; Ball and Millard, 1986). But while the centrality of national channels and broad principles of participation are acknowledged, the analysis of participation in the context of local administration is perhaps more central to this book's focus on the potential for a rural state. Consequently, the remainder of this section will concentrate on the nature of public participation in local (specifically rural) decision-making both within the framework of local government and beyond the machinery of formal decision-making.

The Local Context

Opportunities for public participation in local-level decision-making include both passive involvement through representation and more direct involvement in response to planned participation exercises. The first of these, participation in the formal machinery of government through the election of local councillors, embraces many of the problems raised already in relation to the principle of representation within national and local democracy. While, theoretically, local councillors may be expected to be less remote than MPs, and therefore more responsive to the needs and demands of the electorate, in reality their ability to represent the wishes of the public is still open to considerable debate. The machinery of decision-making at the local level, with its close and continued adhesion to party politics, places a tight rein on the autonomy of local councillors, and means that, in some instances, they are forced into acting directly *against* the immediate interests of the electorate. In addition, local councillors themselves may reinforce the appearance of remoteness, with wider public involvement in the decision-making process being firmly resisted as a possible threat to their jealously guarded 'professional' authority.

A crucial element in relation to representation at the local level is the right of practically all individuals to stand for election (the only exception being people under twenty-one). The workings of local policy-making and administration also include provision, via the 1972 Local Government Act, for the co-operation of members of the general public on to specific local-authority committees and working parties (Darke and Walker, 1977). And yet, as we discuss below, such opportunities, even if widely available, cannot realistically be seen as feasible for the majority of the electorate. Furthermore, they neither circumvent the real problems of representation nor offer the public in general greater *direct* access to the decision-making process.

Public participation in the context of local-state activity cannot be analysed without at least a passing reference to the wider operation of central–local relations and the former's dependence thereon. With the expansion, in the early 1970s, of local-government functions came the need for much greater public participation in the decision-making process. Concessions in, for example, the previously mentioned Local Government Act of 1972 were introduced, but not, it may be argued, with any real commitment on behalf of central government to the devolution of power. Only in the area of planning were any attempts made formally to increase the potential input of the public, and even here serious constraints applied. Commonly, attempts to increase public participation were put into practice with no real change to established procedures, such as in the appointment of 'public-relations' officers. More recently, the withdrawal of local-government functions by the central state, together with the curtailing of local autonomy through the imposition of financial, administrative, and legislative control (Saunders, 1984*a*; Duncan and Goodwin, 1985) has further reduced the opportunity for, and effectiveness of, public participation at this level.

One final aspect of the opportunities for public participation through representation in rural areas is the network of Parish Councils, which have long been seen as the mouthpiece of local opinion in rural areas and a valuable instrument of community representation. Their perceived importance has increased markedly since local-government reorganization and the demise of Rural District Councils in favour of larger districts, often including urban centres. Indeed, the actual powers of the Parish Councils were extended in the 1972 Local Government Act, when they were given the right to spend the 'parish rate' as they chose. This Act also formalized the Parish Council's right of consultation on local planning applications.

In terms of representational capacity, the Parish Council has the advantage of being highly accessible to the local electorate. It is, theoretically, in touch with local issues and well informed as to needs and problems within the community. Parish Councils' exclusive dependence on voluntary, 'non-professional' officers, however, means that they vary enormously both in commitment and effectiveness, and in terms of their capacity adequately to represent the major view. As discussed in following sections, the Parish Councils' organization, together with their history and tradition, renders them open to domination by élites and, in such instances, far from effective as a representative body (e.g. Buchanan, 1982). This variation in effectiveness may be important in terms of the comparative roles of Parish Councils, and yet such variation takes place only within certain strictly defined limits. Ultimately the direct power commanded by even the most dynamic and active Parish Councils can, at best, be described as restricted. The opportunity is provided for the Parish Council to represent the views of the community (or at least one section of it) at certain stages within the decision-making process— the obvious example being in the preparation of the county structure plan—but no guarantee or requirement states that these views must then be incorporated into policy.

Many would argue, therefore, that the Parish Council is simply another mechanism by which the central state deludes the public that its views are being represented in local government and decision-making (McLaughlin, 1987). Moreover, in providing this concession to local opinion, the state essentially fragments collective interests and dissipates any threat of group political action. Another body of opinion suggests, however, that the Parish Council constitutes a mechanism of public political representation whose ultimate effectiveness is out of all proportion to its role in the formal administrative process (Perks, 1977; Warmsley,

1982). For while the Parish Council rarely challenges the authority of either the central or the local state, its ability to raise public awareness and act as a catalyst for independent group activity should not be underestimated. Clearly, much depends here on the interpretation of self-help and voluntary action. If such activities are seen as a major challenge to established power at the local level, they may be assumed to confer on Parish Councils an essential role in public participation. But as a calculated and controlled dissemination of local-state responsibilities, the encouragement of such action can attribute only an advisory or organizational role to the Parish Council, and a minor stake in public representation in decision-making.

In addition to participation through representation, there exist some limited opportunities for *direct* public involvement in decision-making. Individuals can participate as members of pressure groups, for example, or through community action (Marsh, 1983; Smith *et al.*, 1985). The status of such groups is frequently difficult to establish. In some instances, examples of 'extra-parliamentary' activity, in bypassing the channels of representation, is seen to run counter to the principles of democracy, and is thus feared by those in established positions of power. It can be argued that often, however, pressure groups are simply attempting to extend democracy, and that their efforts to organize outside the formal decision-making process only indicate frustration concerning the effectiveness of involvement through representation. Too many different types of pressure group exist for generalizations concerning their role and efficacy to be very helpful. It should, however, be noted that pressure groups do carry considerable potential for public participation. Such potential is frequently lost in the dependence on single-issue campaigns and on fluctuating levels of public support. Possibly the most relevant aspect of community action to consider in the context of this study is its potential and real links with voluntary and self-help initiatives in rural areas. These links will be explored below (see 'Self-Help: The Voluntary Response' below).

Participation in the Planning Process

Perhaps the most important perceived opportunity for direct public participation in decision-making is that embodied within the statutory requirements of the planning system itself, chiefly concerning the preparation of structure and local plans and the submission of planning applications. It has been argued that the fact that planning alone incorporates these arrangements for citizen involvement places an 'unreasonable burden' on the operation of planning departments (Darke and Walker, 1977). More significantly, it has the effect of constraining public participation within strictly defined parameters. Participation as a consequence becomes marginal, and is transformed into an *activity* contained within planning rather than being a *process* running through decision-making.

The main watershed in the history of public participation in planning is generally considered to be the setting up of the Skeffington Committee in 1968 and the subsequent publication in July 1969 of its report, *People and Planning*. The main purpose of the Committee was to 'consider and report on the best methods, including publicity, of securing the participation of the public at the formative stage in the making of development plans for their area' (Committee on Public Participation in Planning, 1969, para. 1). The Town and Country Planning Act of the previous year (1968) had advocated greater involvement by the public in the new two-tier plan system, and it was largely in response to this perceived need that the Skeffington Committee was set up. Hitherto, public consultation had been very much at the discretion of the individual local planning authority, and depended greatly on the commitment of the planners to informing the public and involving them in decision-making (Fagence, 1977).

The main recommendations of the Skeffington Committee hinged on what it saw to be the major defect of the planning system, its failure to communicate. Thus the report was largely about ways of making the public better acquainted with planning procedures (Cox, 1976). It stressed the need for increased exchange of information between the public and the planners, advocating to this end that 'community forums' be established. While such recommendations were considered to be a step forward in terms of public involvement in the planning process, they were hardly innovative, expressing to a large extent 'conventional democratic processes and formalities' (Fagence, 1977: 265). They avoided issues of cost, time, and expertise—the practicalities of public participation—simply providing, as they saw it, a *means* of involvement. 'Community forums' went on further than the setting up of exhibitions and displays which, while valuable as a means of education, could do very little to encourage public participation.

The Skeffington Committee rather gave themselves away when they asserted that with good publicity and active 'community relations', people should be able to study, discuss and present their views on a particular local plan within six weeks of first being informed. Could they have proposed such a brief time if they had seen the main task as anything other than the mobilisation of consensus?   (Cox, 1976: 191–2)

   The spirit of the Skeffington Committee's recommendations was incorporated into post-1968 planning legislation in the form of both the 1971 Town and Country Planning Act and the 1972 Town and Country Planning (Amendment) Act. The new system of structure and local plans embodied a greater commitment to public consultation, and also included specific statutory requirements that all objection to structure plans were to be considered by the secretary of state. There was also a shift, within the structure plan system, away from 'formalised, legalistic inquiry into objections . . . (towards) . . . intensive but formal discussion by participants who are interested but not necessarily objectors' (Cox, 1976: 194). While such moves were clearly a considerable improvement on what had gone on before, they nevertheless still relied greatly on the discretion of individual planning authorities as to the *means* of incorporating public participation into decision-making. More importantly, particularly within the current political climate, final powers remain very firmly within the hands of the secretary of state. Thus, while the mechanisms arguably exist for effective public involvement within the formal planning process, such mechanisms are open to considerable misuse.

POTENTIAL FOR PUBLIC PARTICIPATION

In considering the concept of public participation, and documenting the range of opportunities which exist for public involvement in the decision-making process, we have touched on some of the limitations inherent in the current system (noting, for example, the problems surrounding the notion of representation). We now have to look more closely at these limitations so as to consider, at a rather less abstract theoretical level, the potential offered by recognized opportunities for public participation. Particular attention will be extended to problems surrounding non-participation, and to the ways in which the organization and operation of public participation as an element of the planning system excludes, by its very nature, certain groups within society.

Serious doubts have already been expressed concerning representational democracy and the opportunities it provides for public input into decision-making. These doubts extend not only to the principle of representation but also to the mechanisms of its operation. At a national level, the electoral system can be viewed as inherently unfair. The geographical organization of constitutency boundaries, together with the 'first past the post' system, often results in significant differences between the proportion of parliamentary seats held by any one party and its overall share of the vote. These discrepancies give rise, periodically, to calls for reform of the system and a move towards proportional representation (for example, following the 1983 general election in Britain, when the Liberal/SDP Alliance gained a considerable proportion of the total votes cast but very few seats). It is not the intention here to enter into a lengthy debate on the pros and cons of proportional representation. It is mentioned here simply to illustrate that, while democratic in theory, the electoral system can be manipulated to allow the general public a greater or lesser degree of choice.

Evidence from voting trends suggests that there is a decline in the numbers of people getting involved in the political process, both in Britain and in other Western democratic countries. Figures quoted by McLennan (1984) point to an increase in those failing to vote in general elections in the UK (as many as 25 per cent of the electorate did not vote in the 1979 general election), and a mirroring of this pattern in the USA. This trend is reinforced in Britain at the local level, with less than half those eligible actually voting in local elections. As a result, elections are increasingly dependent on national party political decisions, rather than being about local needs and local issues. Local elections may be seen as little more than opinion polls, and thus severely limited as a democratic mechanism (Darke and Walker, 1977). Electoral behaviour demonstrates a growing sense of public alienation and remoteness, from the political power base, and from those responsible for resource allocation. This alienation is frequently reinforced as activities and decisions are ascribed a degree of complexity and mystique designed to limit their accessibility. Whether this process takes place consciously or unconsciously is impossible to ascertain at the general level. It does, however, certainly help to protect the positions of those in command of authority, ensuring that the majority of the public only become involved in the decision-making process over 'life or death' issues.

Feelings of remoteness and alienation also influence formal participation in the planning process, and lead to an apparent apathy amongst members of the public. A number of authors (e.g. Lowe and Goyder, 1983; Marsh, 1983; Warmsley, 1982) have attempted to study closely and explain this apathy, particularly in relation to the actual mechanisms for participation. One of the main conclusions of these and similar studies is that the way in which public participation exercises are organized and implemented is as much to blame for the lack of public response, as are the issues themselves, or the real interests and concerns of individuals and groups within society.

By virtue of the way in which it is carried out and publicized, participation in planning demands a relatively high level of education. Planning itself is regarded as essentially a technical activity, which cannot easily be understood by the 'ordinary' member of the public who is not familiar with the decision-making process. Language and terminology help to exclude those without the appropriate background and confidence, and ensure that participation is left largely to the more articulate, assertive, and educated sections of society, more often than not the middle classes (Blowers, 1980; Hoggart, 1984). Moreover, participation generally requires a significant commitment in terms of time and money, and, again, these resources are much more likely to be at the disposal of the middle rather than the working class.

Clearly, the form of participation is highly influential in terms of stimulating public involvement. 'One-off' public meetings (the most frequently employed method of 'participation'), or highly formal inquiries, favour the aware, the confident, and the articulate. Such methods also perpetuate the idea that public participation is an event and not a continuous activity, and that it exists for interested parties to express their opinion on certain issues rather than as a means of keeping the public informed and stimulating debate. Instead of acting as a two-way, continuous exchange of ideas and information, public participation in the planning process frequently deteriorates into an isolated, self-contained formality, rather like a gift bestowed by the planning authority on uninterested and undeserving communities. Ambrose (1986: 74) writes: 'public participation . . . is an almost meaningless phrase, or one with misleading connotations . . . . consultation procedures often seem to have the effect of absorbing, rather than transmitting, local opinion about developments.'

Not suprisingly, public participation in planning is becoming increasingly dominated by interest groups as distinct from individuals (Blowers, 1980). The need for high levels of technical expertise, and the availability of considerable resources in the form of time and money, means that it is much more realistic and rewarding for the interests of the individual to be represented through community action or pressure groups, especially where such interests are highly controversial and likely to conflict with those of powerful economic and/or political bodies. It is important to reiterate here the role that interest groups can play in facilitating public involvement in the decision-making process. Interest groups will almost certainly add credibility to individual causes; frequently they contain within their ranks members with greater expertise on a specific issue than exists amongst the so-called experts from the planning departments (Lowe and Goyder, 1983). The larger interest groups benefit from direct and sometimes informal contact with key political actors (at both a national and a local level) and consequently have vastly superior access to information. Finally, a major strength but also a weakness of interest groups is their orientation towards single issues, in that many are formed simply to address one specific local issue. Thus, while they can pursue individual causes with considerable skill, their role in helping to promote the interests of broader groups, and in sustaining support for those interests, is not so well developed. Indeed, part of their success depends on their remaining aligned with particular issues rather than with the wider needs of sections of society.

Public involvement in the planning process, then, is very closely tied to the means and form of participation, requiring an understanding of the way in which the system works and a familiarity with established procedures and techniques. Non-participation, however, cannot simply be attributed to the lack of such skills or knowledge. In addition, it may be a conscious decision relating to the perceived worth to individuals of involvement. In order to participate, in other words, the individual must recognize the likelihood of some benefit (to him or herself) resulting from his or her actions, and this brings us back again to the handling of public-participation exercises by decision-makers. If the public is poorly informed concerning either its statutory rights to participate or the issues themselves, it is unlikely to believe in its own capacity for influencing decisions, and will thus be disinclined to take part in the public-participation process (Buller and Hoggart, 1986).

As Warmsley (1982: 47) contends: 'frequently members of the public develop the belief that the planning authority is not interested in their views, that it has a more cynical purpose for inviting public participation, and therefore that public participation is a futile activity.' But just as public participation should not be regarded as a 'one-off' event, so the outcome of citizen involvement must be assessed in the light of long-term effects rather than immediate results. While the motives for individual (and group) involvement will probably relate directly to one specific issue (Napier and Maurer, 1978)—the environmental implications of a town bypass, for example—and thus 'success' will be dependent on the outcome of that issue, it can be argued that the process by which information is exchanged between decision-makers and the public, through which debate is stimulated and compromise found, is as important as the issue itself. If outcomes of public participation are seen in terms only of the redistribution of power, then most of the changes towards citizen involvement in decision-making must be dismissed out of hand (Darke and Walker, 1977). If, however, value is placed on the raising of public awareness and the stimulating of political debate that public participation can allow, then a rather different view of its role may be appropriate.

In summary, the above discussion has criticized the existing mechanisms for public participation in decision-making as being both inadequate and ineffective. It is not only the machinery for incorporating public opinion within the system, relying as it does on the ability of individuals to understand and get involved in complicated and time-consuming procedures, but also the commitment of government and policy-makers that is at fault. Present opportunities for public participation are often overridden by large-scale business and economic interests—a trend which is likely to become increasingly marked with the privatization of services and the reduction in 'public accountability'. One notable example is water privatization, and the transfer of massive assets, in the shape of land and capital, to private water companies. This transfer will necessarily reduce public participation in decisions concerning the use of, for example, land owned by water authorities—with serious implications for issues of environmental quality and access in rural areas. The concentration of public participation within *planning* procedures also helps to limit its effectiveness, ensuring that many issues remain outside the scope of such participation. The current attack on planning powers from the central state (in, for example, the growing involvement of the secretary of state in the planning appeal system) has served to reduce further the opportunities for public participation in decision-making.

PUBLIC PARTICIPATION IN RURAL COMMUNITIES

Discussion in the first part of this chapter has been couched in fairly general terms. With the exception of comments made concerning the role of parish councils, observations on the nature of opportunities for, and constraints on, public participation can be applied equally to urban and rural society. Problems regarding access to information, means of participation, and value of involvement, for example, characterize public participation in all localities. Having said this, however, there are various qualities associated with rural communities which, it may be argued (e.g. Hoggart and Buller, 1987; Mormont, 1985), exert a highly specific and unique influence over the nature and direction of participation in these communities. The following section will elaborate upon these qualities, and on their particular contribution to public participation in the decision-making process.

Scale and Structure of the Rural Community

The scale of communities in rural areas itself exerts an important and often far-reaching influence on the nature of public participation, especially on the level of citizen involvement. It can be argued, therefore, that issues of planning and resource allocation are of much more immediate concern to the community as a whole than they might be in larger, more 'anonymous' towns and cities (Perks, 1977; Hoggart and Buller, 1987). For example, the implication of school closures are generally more localized in rural than in urban areas, due partly to the lack of choice offered within such localities. The need for, and benefits of, public participation in rural areas is much more evident to the individual, and thus possibly encourages greater involvement. Such arguments could, however, be applied with similar justification to distinct community areas or groups within large urban areas, where the issue of local choice may not be as applicable but where the strength of local impact may be just as relevant. Perhaps more important in the rural context is the role and influence of 'community spirit'— again, not a quality that exists exclusively in rural areas but one, it is argued below, that, because of its particular place within the rural ideology, makes a distinct contribution to rural life, and through this to community involvement in decision-making.

The point has already been made (see Chapter 1) that one of the most enduring 'qualities' of rural society in Britain is a sense of community spirit. Whether founded in fiction or reality, the perceived association between tight-knit, caring communities and village society has constituted one of the most powerful formative influences in both traditional and contemporary rural social and economic relations (see Newby *et al.*, 1978; Strathern, 1984). In terms of public participation, this rural ideology has helped to promote a cohesiveness amongst rural residents which might otherwise be lacking. Hoggart and Buller (1987) suggest that such cohesiveness helps to overcome the 'free-rider' problem—the belief that participation is unnecessary by the majority as the minority will carry the burden of responsibility. In addition, this cohesiveness may encourage participation through obligation, in that a strong sense of local identity and attachment to a community may inspire residents to get involved in decisions of resource allocation even if they themselves may not be directly or immediately affected. Feelings of local or community identity are particularly important in relation to the generation of a specific form of participation not as yet considered, that of self-help or voluntary initiatives, which form the subject of the final section of this chapter.

The relationship between the internal dynamics of rural communities and public participation has been profoundly influenced by changes in the social structure of rural areas (see Chapter 1). Levels of public involvement and awareness and, perhaps more importantly, the issues around which participation has been mobilized have been influenced by new frictions and new interests within rural society and by new attitudes towards rural space (Mormont, 1985). The influx of middle-class residents into many rural areas has at one level acted as an important stimulus for public participation, providing communities not only with much-needed resource in terms of expertise, time, and money but also with a new group of educated and articulate residents, often with an understanding of citizen rights and local political structures. Their own expectations concerning rural society, and a consequent strong resistence to change in any shape or form, means that these 'new residents' frequently become important actors in the initiation and organization of local public participation. On another level, however, the new residents may have a less desirable effect on rural participation, at least as far as the interests of other classes are concerned. The particular set of interests and ambitions they bring with them may conflict with those of long-standing, especially (although not exclusively) working-class residents.

In order to understand the contradictions this may imply for public participation, it is necessary to refer back to the major structural changes occurring in rural areas. These changes, which include the broadening of rural markets, the diversification of the rural economy, and the development of communications, have had profound implications for 'both the economic status and symbolic status of rural space' (Mormont, 1985: 561). The countryside in areas of high pressure (as opposed to areas of population decline) is increasingly seen as an object of privatized consumption to which access is dependent on individual wealth. In addition, it continues to act as a site of major infrastructural undertakings (motorways, airports) and primary industrial development (mineral extraction, power stations, etc.). The emerging set of conflicts have quite profound implications for rural participation and social struggle:

From now on, if what could be termed a rural question exists it no longer concerns issues of agriculture or of a particular aspect of living conditions in a rural environment, but questions concerning the specific functions of rural space and the type of development to encourage in it. (Mormont, 1985: 562)

At the community level, the dominant interests of the new middle-class residents—the preservation of the environment and the protection of property values—can lead to conflicts *within* public participation. Issues concerning collective consumption, such as the closure of the village school or the withdrawal of a bus service, may excite collective action inspired by 'community' feeling, as noted above; but it may be that, by virtue of their superior access to resources, the middle classes fail to recognize the problems which exist for other groups. Buchanan (1982) recounts the failure of members of Suffolk County Council and other village representatives to recognize problems of unemployment and social need in rural Suffolk. More significantly, where arguments concerning development and service provision conflict with environmental objectives, it is the latter which is more likely to draw support from the middle classes (Little, 1984; Buller and Lowe, 1982).

Clearly, generalizations of this kind concerning the nature and direction of middle-class decision-making are dangerous, and require careful scrutiny in the context of specific communities. Yet clearly, while the increase in middle-class involvement in public participation in rural areas may yield certain benefits in struggles over issues of collective consumption, not all sections of society share the same interests. Consequently, conflicts may arise over the issues around which people choose to organize and, more specifically, middle-class support for environmental concerns may dominate public-participation exercises. We now move on to investigate more closely the role of environmental groups in decision-making in rural areas, and to examine their significance in the wider operation of public participation in rural decision-making.

Environmental Groups and Public Participation

In considering the role and importance of environmental groups in public participation, it is helpful to distinguish between the very well-established national groups with long-term objectives and the local, often community-based, action groups concerned with single issues and short-term political processes. The two are clearly related, and share fundamental values in that both are sustained by and draw strength from the environmental movement (Lowe and Goyder, 1983) and both have benefited in terms of support by the recent 'greening' of public opinion (Porritt, 1984; Sandbach, 1980). But very considerable differences exist between the two types of group as regards organizational structure, access to information and resources, and basic position within the political decision-making framework of the country. While much of the discussion presented here relates to the organization and operation of *local* environmental groups, it is important to place such groups in context by considering the role and status of the national bodies and, in doing so, to look very briefly at the underlying philosophy of the environmental movement itself.

A concern for the environment is not a recent phenomenon (e.g. Smith *et al.*, 1985; Buller and Hoggart, 1986), and consequently many of the best-known environment groups and conservation societies are relatively long-standing. The National Trust, for example, was established in 1895, the Royal Society for the Protection of Birds (RSPB) in 1889, and the Ramblers' Association in 1935. Victorian environmentalism, however, existed largely amongst intellectuals as a reaction to economic liberalism (Lowe and Goyder, 1983), and this was reflected in group membership which tended to be highly élitist, drawing support from leading figures in cultural and political life. It was not until the middle of this century that the environmental movement achieved a much broader patronage, with groups attracting membership from a far wider social base. Lowe and Goyder (1983) draw attention to periods of sudden growth within the environmental movement, with the most recent taking place in the early 1970s and being shared by most advanced capitalist countries. They identify connections between these periods of growth and stages of national economic expansion, suggesting that heightened environmental awareness follows sharp economic and industrial growth as people reassess 'non-material values'.

In addition to periods of sudden growth, environmental groups have enjoyed, over the last two to three decades, a steady and quite considerable expansion in support. Membership of such groups has been estimated as something in the region of 2½–3 million (Lowe and Goyder, 1983), which means that the environmental movement is now larger than any trade union or political party. Moreover, the degree of passive support which exists for environmental protection and preservation is enormous, and suggests a much wider and more general sympathy than even group membership indicates. A frequently voiced comment on the membership of environmental groups, however, is that it is very significantly biased in favour of the middle classes. Passive support, it is estimated, may be more ubiquitous, but actual group membership has been shown to be concentrated amongst white-collar and professional people. Most evidence for this exists at the local level (Buller, 1983), although some data have been collected to demonstrate the middle-class bias of national as well as local environmental groups (Cotgrove, 1982; Lowe, 1977; Lowe *et al.*, 1986). Such evidence illustrates, moreover, that even the more 'radical' environmental groups (for example, Friends of the Earth), exhibit a 'solidly middle-class' membership (Lowe *et al.*, 1986). This middle-class bias in the membership of conservation and environmental groups does not necessarily mean that the environment is predominantly a middle-class concern. It simply reflects the dominent characteristic of all voluntary organizations, namely that 'they tend to be formed and supported mainly by the middle class' (Lowe *et al.*, 1986: 117).

The key question regarding the role and importance of environmental groups is whether such evident popular support is in fact reflected in the political influence they command. The large range of national environmental interest groups (Lowe *et al.*, (1986) suggest something over fifty) and the diversity of concern which they cover makes them an important resource in terms of knowledge and expertise, to which MPs, policy-makers, and the media commonly turn. While often severely limited financially, the professionalism and commitment of the work-force of such groups, together with the patronage of public personalities or members of royalty, helps to extend both their political influence and their public standing. Government departments frequently draw on the expertise of established groups such as the Council for the Protection of Rural England (CPRE), using them for consultative purposes over specific policy issues.

Beyond their valuable technical advice, the role of national environmental groups in the political process is somewhat debatable. As Lowe *et al.*, (1986: 121) point out, even the seemingly powerful bodies such as the National Trust or the CPRE 'are not of central importance to the effective performance of government or the economy'. Perhaps more importantly, they lack political or economic sanctions, and are concerned, essentially, with issues of consumption rather than production. Thus, where access to important areas of public policy-making *is* permitted, the environmental groups are still unable to generate sufficient political muscle to challenge dominant economic concerns. The organzational structure of the environmental movement as a whole provides an additional barrier to political influence. Because so many groups have overlapping interests, rivalry and competition may exist not only for funding but also for public support. An inevitable lack of co-ordination between the groups helps to dissipate any political influence they may secure through public concern, and reduces their credibility within decision-making circles (for example, in negotiations concerning the passing of the Wildlife and Countryside Act in 1981).

Considerable time could be devoted at this point to discussing the precise role of different environmental interest groups, and to providing examples of their involvement in political decision-making. Of greater relevance to the central themes of this chapter, however, is the analysis of the organization and influence of *local* environmental groups and their role as vehicles for public participation in decision-making. As noted above, environmental interests play a major role in local-level rural politics, with the protection of the landscape and the enhancement of private property prices being one of the major concerns of many rural dwellers, especially the most recently arrived. In almost all of southern and central England, the premium placed on 'a house in the country' and the emergence of the countryside as a 'positional good' (Newby, 1980; Punter, 1982) both sustains and is reflected in battles over environmental conservation. Such battles indicate more than simply a desire to protect the landscape from residential and industrial development. They draw very deeply on the meaning of the countryside and its place within the national culture. As Bouquet and Winter (1987) assert, the dominant values espoused by the rural way of life include privacy and protection of private property, and environmental protectionism represents one focus for the expression of such values.

The extent of the formal environmental movement at the local level in rural areas is very difficult to gauge. Tentative estimates are provided by, for example, Philip Lowe; but the proliferation of small-scale 'amenity societies' or village conservation groups, and the tendency for groups to combine in response to individual campaigns, means that it is impossible to calculate their actual number at any one time. Many of the characteristics of local environmental groups mirror those of the national bodies, in that they are dominated by the middle classes and frequently retain within their membership significant technical expertise and under-standing. A high proportion of membership tends to be of retirement age (Lowe and Goyder, 1983) and generally shows considerable dedication and commitment to the cause (whether this be conservation and the environment in general or specific local issues). The nature of their involvement in local political action and decision-making is generally 'responsible' and 'reason-able', and as a result their activities remain largely within institutional frameworks and rarely transcend legal boundaries.

The relationship between local environmental groups and planners is often very good. Contact between the two is not necessarily based on conflict—the planners may make regular use of technical expertise from within the environmental groups, for example. In turn the groups may assume a disinterested approach, showing a concern simply with 'good' planning and design rather than fighting on behalf of specific sections of the community. More generally, the values upheld by the environmental groups are frequently those which appeal to the planners themselves—'legislation and public opinion have made conservation a legitimate concern of local government' (Lowe and Goyder, 1983: 95)—and consequently they have become enshrined within the official policies of many local authorities. At the same time, it may be argued, the incorporation of the views and expertise of environ-mental interest groups within formal and informal planning procedures serves a useful purpose for the planning system itself. Such groups form an important focus for public participation, and their involvement demonstrates the good intentions of the planners but at the same time reduces the likelihood of serious confrontation on other, more emotive, distributional issues. As Buller and Hoggart (1986: 147) write, 'conservation and enhance-ment of environmental quality is believed to be for the collective good', and the willingness of planners to listen to the views of environmental campaigners is taken as a sign of their concern for the rural community as a whole.

While the importance of conservation as a major political issue in rural areas (and one on which the public holds very strong views) continues to grow, the battles are increasingly being fought at the level of planners versus the central state (Pye-Smith and Rose, 1984). The actions of local environmental groups, while certainly not irrelevant, serve rather to reinforce and legitimize local planning policy than to direct national political decisions. An over-concentration on environmental issues within public participation at the local level can, moreover, be detrimental to the recognition of other aspects of concern and other areas of need within the rural community. In such instances environmental groups, being identifiable, accessible, and law-abiding representatives of 'the public', can become surrogates for lay interests in general, consulted by planners on a range of issues *beyond* simply environmental concerns, thus reinforcing the view that the benefits of conservation are distributed equally throughout the rural community.

The role of environmental groups in public participation, then, is a significant one—not only in relation to the specific aims of rural conservation and landscape protection, but also in terms of the influence exerted on broader aspects of decision-making and on the participation process itself. In establishing 'the environment' as a legitimate focus for public involvement in the planning process, and one with which all social sectors share a common concern, environmental groups have effectively secured middle-class control within public participation. Contrary to popular interpretation, environmental interests do incorporate distributional consequences. Such consequences are particularly profound in rural areas, where, as pointed out earlier, the environment has increasingly become an 'object' of consumption. Hence the use of environmental groups as a vehicle for public involvement in planning simply reinforces these distributional consequences, and ensures that other interests are less likely to be represented. The growing number of battles that are currently being fought, particularly in southern England, over the development of rural land, moreover, together with the changing policies towards the use of agricultural land, is likely to result in a strengthening of the hold of both national and local environmental groups on public participation in rural areas.

Other Areas of Public Participation in Rural Communities

Environmental groups aside, probably the highest incidence of direct public involvement in policy-making in rural communities is found in relation to single-issue campaigns concerning, for example, the withdrawal of public services and the closure of facilities. Numerous examples from all over rural Britain could be cited here as evidence of the very hard-fought and protracted battles that have been staged (e.g. Forsythe, 1984; Moseley, 1985). Earlier it was suggested that changes in the class structure of many rural areas have hindered the recognition of some of the problems faced by the more deprived classes within rural society and hence the representation of these groups in local politics. As far as local campaigns over specific cases of service loss are concerned, however, there is often considerable unity of purpose amongst social groups; battles to save local schools or prevent village shop closure are frequently supported by a very wide social base and cut across political affiliation.

The involvement of middle-class groups in struggles over local consumption issues is particularly pertinent to the discussion of community-based participation. In defending threats against collective consumption and the provision of public services, certain sections of the middle class are seen as acting contrary to wider political allegiance. Rural areas have traditionally been strongly conservative in terms of political outlook. But while the majority of residents may be confirmed Tory voters, their involvement in community politics generally opposes the rationalization of services and the trend towards greater centralization which have become major tenets of Conservative party policy. In rural areas, the ideology of community and the image of self-supporting villages does much to stimulate middle-class defence of local facilities as well as participation in community campaigns. Such well-placed allegiance does, however, have a tendency to evaporate when struggles turn to the issue of local housing provision or industrial development, and it appears that threats to private property largely, although not exclusively, inspire more predictable responses and divisions of loyalty.

It is not possible to generalize as to the degree of success achieved by community-based campaigns in rural areas. If success is defined, for example, by the protection of a service from closure or the preservation of an existing facility in its traditional form, then examples of success are probably neither prolific or long-lasting. The lack of autonomy afforded to the local state as the arena of struggles over consumption issues ensures that, however sympathetic it may appear, it holds little power over the financial and political demands of the central state. The chances of completely overturning government directives on, say, school closure are, therefore, very slight. But such direct success is not the only object of community-based campaigns. Very often 'partial' success, in the form of service reorganization or re-distribution, may be claimed. Successes on this basis may constitute very thinly disguised delaying techniques, or simply alternative means of reduction, but they can also signal positive achievements for rural communities and the participants in local campaigns.

Lastly, it should be noted that local public participation over issues such as the withdrawal of bus services or village shop closure can also serve in itself to reinforce community and collective action and to bring residents together. While such unity rarely develops into any form of major political directives from within the community, it can establish a group of 'concerned residents' in relation to individual issues which may be helpful in stimulating alternative responses: fired with enthusiasm and with a sense of shared experience, groups 'failing' in their initial demands may feel inspired to find their own solutions to service closure. Self-help or voluntary initiatives may be seen by such groups as the only alternative to their ability to succeed in political struggles.

SELF-HELP: THE VOLUNTARY RESPONSE

In the final section of this chapter, we turn to a discussion of the voluntary sector in the context of public participation. Voluntary responses, and self-help initiatives in particular, may be interpreted as evidence both of close public involvement in the decision-making process and/or of dissatisfaction with existing (or non-existent) policy prescriptions. These responses have been seen variously as positive attempts to find alternative solutions to problems of under-resourcing within an established planning framework (e.g. Moseley, 1985; Rogers, 1987) or, more negatively, as 'last-resort' tactics in response to an impotent and ineffective rural planning system (e.g. McLaughlin, 1987). What is clear is that, while voluntary approaches may exhibit common character- istics in terms of organization and purpose, their relationship with the formal planning process and their role as vehicles for public participation varies enormously with individual schemes. Overall, their profile appears to be increasing markedly, such that they can no longer be rapidly dismissed as tangential to the more formal planning process, but must be scrutinized as an integral part of that process.

Although by no means peculiar to rural areas, voluntary approaches have become very firmly associated with rural communities. Again, the whole concept of self-help is closely allied to the traditional image of the rural community with its firmly entrenched networks of internal support and caring. The historical evolution of village society in which individuals depended either on the personal patronage of the 'lord of the manor' or on the help of neighbours and kin, has worked to reinforce the ideology of self-help; and, while social relations within rural communities have moved very significantly away from this traditional model, certain social practices have remained preserved within the dominant imagery associated with rural life. It is not only the imagery of self-sustaining close-knit communities which is found so attractive, and which reinforces the contemporary ethos of voluntary approaches, however. Rural residents, particularly the newly arrived, take a pride in their perceived independence. The fact that the state fails to provide them with certain services and facilities may not be seen so much as a hardship but as a positive attraction, and their necesssary involvement in the provision of their own services becomes simply a clearer indication of the uniqueness and 'innocence' of rural life. More importantly, it may also be regarded as a resistance to imposed change from 'outside' the community.

It is evident that attitudes towards voluntary action and the willingness of individuals to become involved in self-help schemes varies amongst different groups of rural residents; and such variation says much about the current nature and characteristics of voluntary action. As with other aspects of public participation, self-help schemes in the planning sphere tend to be dominated by the middle classes. In fact, for many of the same reasons—superior access to resources, familiarity with decision-making processes, and a knowledge of likely channels of support and advice—middle-class residents are frequently the initiators or the main actors within voluntary responses. This middle-class domination of voluntary action is to some degree contradictory, since it is the middle classes who are least vulnerable to the withdrawal and contraction of rural services. The motivation behind their involvement in self-help schemes relates, in many instances, more closely to the desire to preserve the village as a 'living entity' and to sustain the ability of the rural community to reproduce itself than to any real need for a particular service function. The retention of services is seen as vital to the preservation of village character and to the maintenance of a 'balanced community'. While the middle classes may not require the continuation of the village shop or school for practical purposes, such facilities are important components of the traditional images associated with rural life, and for that reason are worth preserving.

Participation in voluntary action is biased not only by class but also by gender. Generally, women are involved to a far greater extent than men in self-help, particularly in relation to community-based caring activities (Stebbing, 1984). Current right-wing political ideology, in which 'the family' is seen as the most important basis of all social relations, has helped to reinforce women's domestic role, at the same time emphasizing their supposedly 'natural' caring skills and duties. It has been argued elsewhere that pressures on women to conform to the expectations of this domestic role are especially high in rural areas (Little, 1988) due to a lack of public services and to the dominant *rural* ideology which sees women at the centre of the home and as the 'linchpin' of the rural community (Davidoff *et al.*, 1976). Voluntary activity is frequently seen as an extension of this role, as women are often forced, through the absence of alternatives, to organize their own child care facilities or transport services in order to carry out their domestic work. More broadly, the expectations of women's responsibilities within the wider rural community emphasizes and promotes their key role within the voluntary sector.

As far as their practical organization and operation is concerned, self-help schemes in rural areas take a great variety of forms. At one end of the range are the small-scale, highly amateur concerns such as the countless 'community' shops in which informal groups of residents act as wholesalers and distributors, buying in quantities of groceries for local sale on a non-profit-making basis. Alternatively, schemes may be run along more professional lines, relying less on sporadic interest and more on more permanent and organized commitment. Many transport schemes tend towards such levels of organization, due to the need for formal timetabling and, very often, considerable financial outlay on behalf of 'volunteers'. A major criticism of self-help schemes is that they are frequently short-lived. The initial enthusiasm of volunteers may be quickly lost—especially where schemes encounter teething troubles or fail to elicit the kind of support originally anticipated. Smaller, less formal schemes are particularly vulnerable, since they tend to rely on fewer volunteers and operate, very often, on a weak financial footing.

As well as ranging in size, formality, and durability, self-help schemes also vary significantly in terms of their relationship with the formal planning process. Clearly, the standing of individual schemes *vis-à-vis* planning policy can be pertinent not only to the success of such schemes but also, more broadly, to the status of voluntary action. As resources for the financing of public services in rural areas become more and more restricted, policy-makers are obliged to consider alternative methods and types of provision. One such alternative is to go into partnership with the voluntary sector—essentially, to incorporate self-help schemes within the parameters of public-sector policy-making. This can be done by making financial resources or staff and administrative expertise (or both) available to residents involved in voluntary activity to initiate and sustain 'essential' schemes.

Examples of this type of co-operation and co-ordination can be found in most counties. In Gloucestershire, the Local Authority operates a scheme through the county surveyor's department in which grants are made available to village groups wishing to set up voluntary transport projects. Such grants are discretionary, and dependent on clear evidence of commitment and knowledge from the volunteers. While important to those schemes that have made use of them, the grants are, it seems, not effective as a means of stimulating action, and such schemes rely ultimately on initiation from the village level. Few attempts have been made to advertise their existence, and the scheme appears to represent a half-hearted response by the local authority to 'inevitable' service closure rather than a positive attempt to replace and re-establish necessary transport routes. Links between public-sector agencies and voluntary groups can also be made via recognized bodies such as the Women's Institute. In Gloucestershire, a scheme for transporting elderly people to hospital operates in a number of parishes in Tewkesbury District – the scheme is staffed by the WI but financed by the District.

On a more formal basis, Parish Councils and Rural Community Councils (RCCs) provide recognized lines of communication between public and voluntary sectors. RCCs in particular see themselves as initiators as well as facilitators of voluntary action (Rogers, 1987), capable of playing a major part in organizing public responses to social need and service decline. Their role, like that of voluntary action in general, is perceived to be of growing importance in relation to formal service provision, and their profile is consequently much enhanced. There is a danger, however, in attributing too great a value to the work of RCCs in this respect. While supported at the county level by enthusiastic, hard-working, and often very well-qualified staff (Standing Council for Rural Community Councils, 1984) in terms of resources, the RCCs can provide little real help either through the direct provision of services or through assistance to voluntary groups. Their role is largely advisory and their power very limited in the face of central-government policy decisions.

This aside, voluntary action has found significant support from within the central state. Not only does the whole ethos of voluntarism appeal to current right-wing philosophy regarding private enterprise and the independence of the individual, but it also locates responsibility for service functions very firmly within the community, thus absolving state obligation. Ultimately, the collusion of the local state and the community in the provision of voluntary services can be recognized as contradictory to the good of both sectors. Joint action serves to legitimize voluntary action as a normal part of service provision, but it also weakens the position of the local state in relation to the power of the centre. As voluntary activity becomes more and more acceptable, so the necessity of the local state becomes increasingly questionable. Clearly, this places the community—the volunteers—in a highly vulnerable position, removing the buffer of public responsibility and accountability at the local level.

The issue of self-help, like many of those raised in this chapter, demands far more detailed attention than can be devoted to it here. This chapter has discussed self-help simply as another form of public participation within decision-making. It is important, however, for the wider study of rural planning that the role of voluntary action in rural areas be fully appreciated not only in the context of resource allocation and service provision at the community level but also in relation to the changing responsibilities of policy-making agencies. The relationship between public, private, and voluntary sectors is of fundamental importance to the future of decision-making in rural communities. Within this relationship the role and scope of public participation, whether direct, in the form of self-help schemes, or indirect, as part of the formal planning process (in, for example, attendance at public inquiries), cannot be overlooked.

This chapter has touched on the wide range of issues of relevance to public participation. While many of these have been of a general nature, the particular rural dimension of such issues has been emphasized in, for example, the study of environmental groups and the workings of the parish council. Discussions surrounding the role of self-help have demonstrated the need to look at both the direction *and* the mechanisms of public participation. The changing priorities of rural residents, particularly in relation to environmental objectives, are clearly important in determining the issues around which people choose to mobilize and the likely direction of public participation. Such changes will exert an important influence on, for example, community representation and local politics. But in terms of the relationship with formal decision-making procedures, the analysis of public participation needs also to consider the mechanism through which it operates, for such mechanisms are largely responsible for the real potential for change. Planned public-participation exercises are, in the way they are constructed and implemented, carefully controlled by the central state, and even the role of *ad hoc* interest groups is frequently manipulated to serve the dominant interests.

In overall terms, the issue of participation presents a conundrum for those seeking to analyse the ability of rural people to influence local decision-making. On the one hand, local voluntary action has clear benefits *per se* relating to community cohesiveness, and a potential for responding sensitively to local need. The advice proffered from umbrella organizations such as Action with Communities in Rural England (ACRE) has been invaluable in making local volunteers aware of the possibilities for achieving these benefits. On the other hand, when seen in the context of policy-making in an inter-governmental and class framework, such local participation is merely a minor nibbling at the edges of rural change. Some will see the promotion of community self-help as an evasive tactic by government, and as a legitimation of policies to withdraw public-sector services and faculties from rural areas. Even the self-help organizations themselves have tended to be colonized by particular class groups representing the dominant social relations of the locality. As such, local 'participation' becomes a useful surrogate for local élites and dominant classes, and the outcomes of élite and structural power are given the gloss of supposed pluralism. Even the local managers can get in on this act, sometimes using local participation as the justification for promoting their own preferred policy options. Thus managerialist power can also be 'protected' by supposed pluralism. The conundrum is that, while these legitimations appear to be an essential part of the exercise of local power, limited pluralism does seem also to exist, in that participation groups do appear to achieve some of their objectives on some occasions. The cutting of this knot may have to be done with the sword of *scale*. Although local benefits do accrue, any prospect of using local participation over a wide scale to act on behalf of the interests of deprived classes in rural areas appears illusory. This rather pessimistic conclusion takes us straight back into the realm of power, and constraints on action, to which we return as a concluding comment to the book.

7

Conclusions

The question posed by the title of this book is in some senses unanswerable. To ask 'Is there a rural state?' is to contemplate just the same definitional quagmire that has enveloped those attempting to conceptualize 'rural'. The question is perhaps best seen, not as an end in itself, but as a means of introducing concepts of state power and activity to the analysis of rural economy and society. This book has attempted to demonstrate how any discussion as to whether there is anything distinctive about the local state in 'rural' areas must be prefaced by an understanding of the context of state activity, and the role of this activity *vis-à-vis* capital and class change. In doing so we have stressed the importance of political-economy perspectives (Chapter 1), the relevance of concepts of the state and of power relations (Chapter 2), and the links between policy, implementation, and outcome in rural change (Chapter 3). From there we have gone on to assess both the limits to state activity and to citizen participation (Chapter 6) in localities recognized as rural, drawing examples from our work in Gloucestershire (Chapter 4) and, more broadly, from other international contexts (Chapter 5).

Any idea of distinctive local states in different locality types will be bound up with the interdependence of scale, territoriality, and the state. There has been a continuing discourse on these issues (Johnston, 1982; Giddens, 1985; Mann, 1986), as a result of which the state has been viewed, at least in part, in terms of the territory of its jurisdiction.

This idea can be taken to opposite extremes. Agnew (1987) suggests that the locality should be the primary scale of political analysis, arguing that people are socialized in specific places and acquire political identities in specific places. Although he acknowledges that national and local scales are interdependent, his emphasis on local political identity could lead to a view of particular localities as being of an unchanging political character. For example, rural areas in Britain might be seen as perpetually

Conservative, because of the socialization and political culture of the localities concerned.

An opposite emphasis has emerged from proponents of a world-economy perspective on power. Here, nation-states might be viewed as having less power than they seem to have, because their role is simply one of mediation within a world economy dominated by international capital. Taylor (1985), for example, characterizes the nation-state as *ideology* and the locality as *experience*. Once again, if taken to a logical extreme, this type of characterization diminishes any notion of power in the central state, and particularly in the local state.

According to their own frame of reference, each of these opposite extremes is supportable. Localities are important in the understanding of place and politics. The power inherent in international capital is a dominant force for change. Yet each is flawed by its lack of a full appreciation of the interrelationships between scales. Political identities may be constructed at the local level, but the issues on most local political agendas tend to be formed at the national and international levels. Conversely, to characterize central and local states as mere ideology and experience is to ignore the evidence (some of which has been presented in this book) that varying degrees of autonomy and discretion are available to, and are exercised by, the institutions of the state at national and local levels.

Those localities which we recognize as 'rural', then, should be viewed as part of the territory of the central and local state. In some ways, territoriality might be seen as partially definitive of the nature of the state, but we must exercise great care here in our use of the notion of territoriality. The traditional orthodoxy in rural studies is to obscure the concept of territory by referring instead to characteristics of land-use and environment. Thus territory may be delineated by factors of rurality—extensive land-use, countryside, low population densities, and so on. But territory is the product of far more complex social, economic, and political relations. Yes, the rural environment does influence these relations, but it is not the causal factor in the derivation, or changing nature, of territory. Local territories, therefore, should rather be viewed as composites of social relations and political economy, although the exact boundaries of state territories are obviously described by administrative division, which often includes a potentially random factor.

'Rural' territory, therefore, is being defined by the changing nature of state and social relations in the localities concerned. State and social relations cannot themselves be defined by any causal factor of rurality.

The rural state, then, is a somewhat artificial notion which merely attempts to address fundamental questions of state and society in particular localities whose 'rurality' may be a matter of historic economic and social structures rather than contemporary ones. This does not diminish the importance of political economic studies in these areas. Indeed, it is precisely because the progress made in studying 'urban' localities (equally difficult to define and categorize) has not been mirrored in 'rural' localities that we still need to emphasize and explore the benefit of these approaches in the context of rural studies. Equally, the changing social relations which are occurring in rural areas represent an interesting, important, and, in some cases, distinctive illustration of class conflict born of social recomposition, which in turn is driven by economic restructuring. The increasing dominance of service classes in some rural parts of southern England is an example of this (see Chapter 1). In that the local state is, at least in part, characterized by dominant local social relations (according to the concept proposed by Duncan and Goodwin outlined in Chapter 2), some of the distinctive characteristics of particular class fractions—their aspirations, their attempts to construct their own culture and environment according to their own designs, and so on—will be evident in the activities of the local state through the colonization by these class fractions of local political leadership roles. The state will not reflect rurality as we have traditionally defined it; but it will reflect the dominant social relations which have developed in localities where particular rural characteristics have prevailed in the past or continue to apply in the present.

THE NATURE OF CONSTRAINT

The analysis of the form, function, and apparatus of the state, and the interpretation in this context of policy and change occurring in rural areas, permits us to focus on the nature and extent of *constraints* on state action. A clear understanding of such constraints is a fundamental prerequisite for any evaluation of the ability of planning and policy to achieve particular goals: the prerogative and willingness of the state to respond to changes and/ or conflicts; the likelihood that consistent bias will be generated towards some interests and classes and against others; and the available discretion at central and local levels within which different local power relations operate.

In a very simple form, the notion of constraints to emerge in this book can be likened to a funnel, with wider scope for action in the top-down arena of the central state, and a significant narrowing of discretion—and therefore strengthening of constraint—in the arena of the locality. We are thereby accepting that the engine of change in late capitalist nations is that of the drive towards enhanced capital accumulation by international corporate capital. Different fractions of capital will compete with each other, and therefore precise locations of dominant power will be changeable as competition and conflict result in dynamic constructs of capital dominance. Thus the power of agricultural capital seems to be at present being usurped, at least in part, by other capital fractions— particularly connected with finance and commerce—in many nations. Nevertheless, despite this dynamism, capitalism survives and thrives on long-standing structures of ownership, exchange, and class conflict which serve to reproduce its power.

We also accept that the form and function of the state reflect both the power of dominant capital interests and the importance of maintaining the basic structures of capitalism. The state, then, is committed to the role of initiating policy which facilitates the reproduction of suitable environments for accumulation. It is also concerned to service other requirements of capital and class élites, particularly in their desire to design their own environmental consumption and cultural conditions.

Given these assumptions, the central state is subject to considerable and definitive constraints on action. The power being exercised through state institutions of government, administration, judiciary, and policing effects a fundamental bias in the direction and derivation of state activity. It is at this point that many of the state's apparent objectives for rural areas become apparent. Yet the available evidence suggests to us that the state cannot be viewed merely as a puppet of capital interests. Its role is much more than that of parasite or neo-government. In terms of constraint on policy and action, there remains at the central-state level some considerable autonomy and discretion.

Of course, the foregoing assumptions suggest that the state acts within an 'art of the possible', prescribed by dominant capital and élite classes, but in *relative* terms the funnel of constraint remains wide. This available autonomy is exploited by governments within the state. This distinction between state and government is of crucial importance. What appear to be radical changes in direction by different governments fired by different ideologies occur within the constraints imposed by capital and class power in the longer-term form of the state.

As our attention moves from the central state to the local state, the constraints on action and reaction become more firmly prescribed, and the political economic 'art of the possible' permits less autonomy and less discretion than in the central arena. Not only are the structures and requirements of internationally dominant capital and nationally dominant class pressing in on the local scale, but action in the locality is also constrained by the relationship between central and local states, and between the governments working within them. The function and apparatus of the local state is heavily prescribed by the centre. Such discretion as exists is additionally constrained by a local 'art of the possible' deriving from a particular configuration of local social relations.

Duncan and Goodwin's work on the local state, stressing these dominant local social relations, provides a useful approach to local power (see Chapter 2). It does not completely refute Cockburn's idea of a local state which, like its central counterpart, exists simply to further the interests of capital. Indeed, wider capital interests than these *are* served locally, but the mechanism by which they are served appears to be the constraints which are handed down from the centre. Thus, if local social relations favour capital élites and classes, then there is a double measure of favour for capital structures and class élites—emanating from both central constraint and local political input. If local social relations are in opposition to capital interests (such as was the case, for example, with the metropolitan authorities in the early 1980s), their discretion for radical action will be constrained by the boundaries set by the centre. If these limits are transgressed, then the expectation is that further financial or legislative controls will be imposed to restore 'proper order'. In the case of the metropolitan counties, these further controls consisted of abolition legislation. In the more localized case of the Gloucestershire structure plan

(Chapter 4), all that was required was the use of the power of veto available to the secretary of state for environment within central government.

Although this is a crude representation of constraint, the idea of a funnelling of power describes the increasing restraints on action from the central to the local levels, and also stresses the 'pouring through' of power from the condensates of capital and social relations beyond the central state. The influence and requirement of capital are thus experienced at all levels of policy and planning.

Give this overall view of constraint and power, what factors *do* influence the discretion which is available to governments? At the central level, where quite radical swings of policy are possible within the 'art of the possible' set by the form of the state, governments will have several concerns. A structuralist analysis would suggest that the scope for consumption-orientated policies depends on the degree of legitimation required to pursue production-orientated policies in support of capital interests. The more obvious and socially painful the policies related to production, the greater the legitimation required by way of public-sector provision of health, education, and other social benefits. This relationship between consumption and production policies has not been evident in the last decade in Britain, where policies to promote economic restructuring have led to high rates of unemployment, yet there have been concomitant attacks on benefit systems and a rolling back of the welfare state.

Central governments, then, appear to be interested in more than just legitimation, important though this is. They are, for example, interested in being voted back into office, and so may seek to appease the majority of their constituents while ignoring the claims of the deprived and disadvantaged classes which represent a minority of the total. Also important in this context is government response to pressure groups. If interest groups can persuade government that a particular policy change will either benefit particular supporting classes of the political party involved or will help to maintain the electoral support of the required majority, then there is opportunity for discretion to be exercised. If, on the other hand, the concerns presented by pressure groups do not fulfil these criteria, then there is less likelihood that action will ensue, however worthy the cause. Two other factors are also important here in understanding action in the context of governmental autonomy and discretion. The first is the exercise of managerial power, both by public servants and by professions—each with potentially key positions in policy networks. The second is ideology, which is often used glibly as an explanation for the derivation of particular policies, but which often works in tandem with more pragmatic reasons, some of which are discussed above. The overriding influence on government policy, however, is the form of the state in which it is set, which dictates that policies in support of capital accumulation are pursued, with these other interests being important but secondary. It should be stressed that the needs of capital may vary—for instance, from policies of regulation at one point to policies of deregulation at another; from vast direct state investment in resource industries in one round of restructuring to privatization of that investment in another. These variations have been well documented by social scientists. What we have done less well, and what is therefore a priority for future research, is to conceptualize the mechanisms through which dominant capital informs government of its needs—through its own pressure groups such as the Confederation of British Industry, through the instrument of political and economic élites, through a political sensing of 'the mood' of capital, or through a manipulation of political ideology. There has been little emphasis on these mechanisms from the perspective of rural change.

The mediation potential for government at the local level is set within narrower confines, but nevertheless should not be ignored as an arena for action. Again, we would reject the idea of the local state being a mere puppet, responding either to the string-pulling of the centre or to the directives of wider capital and class power. Local decisions can be important, but in rural areas they are unlikely to be radical. The balance of central–local power relations is usually towards the centre (although France may be an exception to this), and so decision-making in the locality is likely to be constrained both by a legislative power of veto held by the centre and by public-expenditure restrictions imposed by the centre. Within these boundaries, the influence of dominant local social relations will prevail, with pressure group activities again being important if the demands being made are politically functional. The Gloucestershire study also shows that local government represents a fruitful arena for managerial power through agenda-setting and decision orchestration by local-government officers. Moreover, such power is not always used in the (postulated) implicitly self-interested direction. The 'pro-rural' policies being promoted in Gloucestershire (Chapter 4) were in support of deprived classes, and political support from Conservative party councillors was achieved both by substituting the idea of deprived 'places' for deprived 'people' and by appealing to latent sentiments of paternalism and beneficence.

Despite the potential for policy manipulation by political and managerial élites, the constraints imposed by the centre on the locality are both restrictive and (seemingly) getting tougher. All the attempts to formulate a positive policy for rural areas in Gloucestershire came to little because of central government's power to veto the policy, and because local agencies had insufficient power and resources to promote positive action without the blessing of the relevant central agencies. Indeed, the biggest challenge to central government by local rural political groups in Britain in the late 1980s has been the very sectional opposition to what are perceived as over-lax central-government restrictions on development in villages. Far from being a protest against prevailing dominant social relations, this represents a colonization of the 'common good' by locally dominant classes seeking to establish *their* local environment according to *their* design.

Given these constraints, it should not be surprising that policy and planning intervention on behalf of rural deprived classes have been minimal and somewhat token in the latter years of post-war Britain. Local action has taken place, sponsored by the development planning system, by voluntary action, and as part of the wider establishment of the welfare state; but the balance of political interest—itself constrained by capital and class interest—has been against radical action in rural localities.

THE PROSPECT FOR RADICAL CHANGE

A political economic analysis of constraint on policy and planning for rural areas tends to produce gloomy and pessimistic conclusions. A tight funnelling of constraint is envisaged, within which the potential for action either barely exists, or (more probably) is not exploited by political leaders in central and local government. To end the analysis at this point would represent an acceptance of conceptual determinism of the most dangerous kind: capital always gets its way; élite classes always dominate; working classes will never gain access to power; sectional self-interest will prevail forever.

What, then, are the prospects for changes in the balance of power relations and the constraints which follow? We live in a decade of fatalism in Britain. Marshall *et al.* (1988) mimic the analysis of Lukes (1984) in this matter:

Ordinary people are now convinced that there is no alternative to the morality of the acquisitive society; that Britain's seemingly intractable economic problems are quite beyond human control; that social inequalities are therefore unalterable. As a result they have settled down in a mood of quiet disillusionment to seek their private satisfactions and pursue conflicting sectional demands. (Marshall *et al.*, 1988: 2)

To go beyond this fatalism we have to ask key questions relating to the concepts of power and constraint. Is it possible to foresee radical policy changes within the current balance of constraint? Do these constraints—the various 'arts of the possible' described above—shift, and if so how are these shifts brought about? In other words, are we restricted to thinking of radical governmental change within the state, or is the nature of the state itself evolving, bringing with it changes in the constraints on action? These questions are too large to be answered here, but we would offer some observations which might lay something of a foundation for future debate by rural researchers and theorists.

The first point to raise is that we have already witnessed radical policy changes in Britain in the 1980s. The Thatcher government, for various reasons, has succeeded in altering the previous orthodoxies without any real opposition from society. A mix of rampant new right ideology and remarkably astute political pragmatism has dominated a divided political opposition and avoided any prolonged and repeated class protest, while at the same time introducing major policy shifts directly favouring the private sector and the power of central government over its local counterpart. This government's policies to dismantle the ethic and practice of public-sector intervention have been just as radical as the policies in previous years to establish a public sector involvement in welfare, service provision, and industry.

Effectively, the Conservative party in Britain has undergone an internal shift in power relations. The formerly dominant landowner-based Tories, with their inherent attachment to 'caring Conservatism' preventing some of the more radical policies of support for ruling classes and attack on working classes, have now been discarded as 'wet' and replaced by new right Tories with no such scruples. This shift within the Conservative party mirrors a shift in wider social relations, with those capital fractions relating to finance, commerce, and service sectors increasingly able to compete successfully against the previously dominant sections associated with primary and secondary industries. Existing structures have been exploited by newly dominant capital sections, and new instrumental élites have also emerged.

It is our view that these changes go beyond the notion of radical governmental change within the state, and denote an evolution of the state itself, at least as far as the constraints imposed on government action are concerned. The changing nature of dominant capital has led to changing requirements from the state–society relationship. What is demanded now are markets free from government regulation, lower taxation, monetarist policies favouring high interest rates, low inflation, and low public expenditure. After all, who gains from high interest rates? Who loses from reduced public expenditure? Economic restructuring in the 1980s has made demands upon the state–society relationship which could only be fulfilled by reducing the priority given to discretionary policies of legitimation in the welfare and social-service sectors. Thus the policies of the Thatcher government have transgressed what in the 1970s would have been thought to be the art of the possible at central-state level.

The political wizardry involved in this radical decade, even taking account of an ineffective political opposition, has been to strengthen the control of central government over other participatory agencies (particularly local government) while at the same time reducing state control through privatization and deregulation. The ability of the local state to contest these policy changes has thereby been restricted, while the allegiance to market economics (the inefficiencies of which have in the past led to class and community opposition) has grown stronger.

The policy shifts in rural Britain reflect these changes in intergovernmental and public–private-sector relations. Many rural areas have become the chosen residential environments of newly dominant classes. They in turn have colonized local political leadership, and used available discretion to fight against new housing development so as to preserve both their investment and their cultural model-building exercise (a kind of Lego service class community). Formerly dominant farmer/landowner classes are being displaced in some areas, or have themselves become more business-orientated such that they sit relatively comfortable alongside the new 'town Tories'.

These changing social relations are also reflected in central-government policies. The corporatist power of agricultural capital seems to be waning in the face of conflict with other capital sections over the vast state resources which are directed into the agricultural sector through subsidies. It seems clear that if Britain were an independent nation state, more radical policies to deregulate agricultural support systems would have been implemented. Only the entanglement of membership of the EEC has restricted policy change in this area. Nevertheless, agricultural areas remain part of the Conservative constituency, and so central government has found it necessary to present small-scale policy initiatives such as the ALURE package (Cloke and McLaughlin, 1989) as a token state response to the need for agricultural diversification, despite the fact that agriculture-related populations do not now represent a majority in any of these constituencies.

On the other hand, the construction and finance capital involved in the house-building industry are a very important political constituency for the Conservatives, as well as playing a significant role in the wider relations beteen state, society, and capital. There has therefore been a tendency to introduce a more flexible approach to the control of housing development (see Blunden and Curry, 1988, for an up-to-date account), including a greater use of central-government prerogative to overturn decisions by local authorities to refuse planning permission for development. Here again the conjuring act may be seen in action, with government seeking to appease on the one hand its middle-class voting constituency, by standing firm against any incursions into green belt areas and by 'greening' its policies for countryside conservation, and on the other hand its development capital constituency, by ensuring that sufficient building land is released for capital accumulation in this sector.

This juggling of interest is becoming increasingly difficult.

Already there are clear signs of middle-class opposition to central-government policies for housing development, and it may be that the first real conflict between rural local government and Conservative central government will arise over this issue. It should be noted, however, that such conflict is more a function of intra-class struggle for dominance within the ruling party than inter-class struggle for power.

Other policies in the 1980s have been more directly related to inter-class conflict. The privatization of public services, the shrinkage in the welfare state, and the increasing refusal by the state to intervene to provide housing and job opportunities for deprived classes have served to increase the gap between the rich and the poor in line with other changes in society. Current rounds of economic restructuring and social recomposition appear to require that the needs of the disadvantaged be sacrificed in order to pander to the self-interest of a voting majority which is itself necessary to sustain support for sweeping policies of privatization and deregulation. Thus legitimation of support for capital and class interests via the provision of broad-scale public welfare is replaced by appeasement of individual self-interest.

If these radical changes can occur in one political direction, is it not possible to foresee an equal and opposite shift by a future socialist government? Could it not be that the constraints imposed by the state–society relationship could be stretched by a reallocation of societal resources favouring the disadvantaged classes, and that the state could evolve back in the direction of communal welfare? Again, these are big questions which cannot be fully answered here, but we would warn against any simplistic view of political relations in the state. Future rounds of restructuring and recomposition may well require a more sensitive and welfare-orientated approach to surplus labour, to women, to the elderly, and so on. Although it is sometimes difficult to think in these terms, Thatcherism is only a short-term, if radical, phase in the historical materialism of state–society relations. The north–south divide may well be diluted (witness the 'surprising' counter-urbanization of the 1970s); technological change may well dictate shifts in our current spatial and social orthodoxies.

In the short term, however, the political processes which might achieve these altered states are difficult to predict, particularly so far as rural constituencies are concerned. The Labour party has in the past seen no reason to give priority to rural areas, instead remaining urban-orientated. In any case, the Labour movement is having to turn increasingly to different fractions of the middle class for a support base. By so doing, it becomes saddled with the attitudes of these fractions to rural issues, and therefore becomes embroiled in issues of conservation and development which obscure the plight of deprived classes. Such a shift will also involve an increasing emphasis on issues of consumption. The possibility of centre-party involvement in any future government does little to alter this prognosis. So it may be at the level of the local state, diluted though its powers are, that some rural localities (outside the service class domination of the south of England) may experience some pressure for local action to increase access to resources in rural society. Such action will only become important if some of the constraints on the local state are lifted, and this is difficult to foresee at present.

Faced with the question 'What can be done now for deprived classes?', and faced with the conclusion that radical political change is difficult to foresee in the short term, we can only turn to the idea of change at the individual level, and to the idea of individuals turning to collective social involvement. Is the life-style of an acquisitive society inevitable? Is the pursuit of private satisfactions and sectional demands unalterable? Or can we perceive a situation wherein class divisions may be set aside in pursuit of good, care, selflessness, community, and altruism? We see some small signs of this situation in the co-operative movement, the peace movement, the willingness of individuals to volunteer to care for others, some beliefs within the major political parties, and in some radical and non-establishment elements of the church. Growth in the importance and influence of these and other movements may be our most practical initial goal in seeking to secure a better state for rural areas.

Bibliography

Abercrombie, N., and Urry, J. (1983). *Capital, Labour and the Middle Classes*. London: Allen & Unwin.

Abrams, P. (1978). 'Towns and Economic Growth: Some Theories and Problems', in P. Abrams and E. A. Wrigley (eds.), *Towns in Society*. Cambridge: Cambridge University Press.

Agnew, J. (1987). *Place and Politics*. London: Unwin Hyman.

Alexander, A. (1982). *The Politics of Local Government in the United Kingdom*. London: Longman.

Alterman, R. (1982). 'Implementation Analysis in Urban and Regional Planning', in P. Healey *et al.* (eds.), *Planning Theory Prospects for the 1980s*. Oxford: Pergamon.

Ambrose, P. (1974). *The Quiet Revolution*. London: Chatto & Windus.

—— (1986). *Whatever Happened to Planning?* London: Methuen.

Anderson, J. E. (1975). *Public Policy Making*. London: Nelson.

Association of County Councils (1979). *Rural Deprivation*. London: ACC.

Atzema, O. A. L. C., and Dijkstra, T. B. M. (1986). 'National Policy and Settlements in Peri-urban Regions', in Enyedi and Veldman.

Austin, D. M. (1983). 'The Political Economy of Human Services', *Policy and Politics*, 11, 343–59.

Bachrach, P., and Baratz, M. S. (1970). *Power and Poverty*. New York: Oxford University Press.

Baker, R. J. S. (1972). *Administrative Theory and Public Administration*. London: Hutchinson.

Ball, A., and Millard, F. (1986). *Pressure Politics in Industrial Societies*. London: Macmillan.

Banister, D. J. (1980). *Transport Mobility and Deprivation in Inter-Urban Areas*. Farnborough, Hants: Saxon House.

—— (1983). 'Transport and Accessibility', in M. Pacione (ed.), *Progress in Rural Geography*. London: Croom Helm.

—— *et al.* (1985). 'Deregulating the Bus Industry in Britain', *Transport Review*, 5, 99–142.

Barlow, J. (1984). 'Landowners, Property Ownership and the Rural Locality', Department of Urban and Regional Studies, University of Sussex, Working Paper 41, Brighton.

—— (1986). 'Landowners, Property Ownership and the Rural Locality', *International Journal of Urban and Regional Research*, 3, 309–29.

Barrett, S. (1980). 'Perspectives on Implementation', paper presented to the Social Science Research Council Central–Local Government Relationships Conference, Birmingham.

Barrett, S. and Fudge, C. (eds.) (1981). *Policy and Action: Essays on the Implementation of Public Policy*. London: Methuen.

—— and Hill, M. (1984). 'Policy, Bargaining and Structure in Implementation Theory: Towards an Integrated Perspective', *Policy and Politics*, 12, 219–40.

Barta, G. (1986). 'Rural Industry in Hungary', in Enyedi and Veldman.

Bartlett (1980). *Proceedings of the First Bartlett Summer School*. Bartlett School of Architecture and Planning, University College London.

Beer, S. H. (1965). *Modern British Politics*. London: Faber & Faber.

Bell, P. (1986). 'The Implementation of Planning and Resource Agency Policies in Rural Areas', unpublished Ph.D. thesis, Department of Geography, Saint David's University College, Lampeter.

Bell, P., and Cloke, P. (1988). *Bus Deregulation in the Powys/Clwyd Study Area: A Final Report*. Crowthorne: Transport and Road Research Laboratory.

—— and —— (1989). 'The Changing Relationship between the Private and Public Sectors: Privatisation and Rural Britain', *Journal of Rural Studies*, 5–13.

Berkshire County Council (1980). *Central Berkshire Structure Plan: Approved Written Statement*. Reading: Berkshire County Council.

Blacksell, M., and Gilg, A. (1981). *The Countryside: Planning and Change*. London: Allen & Unwin.

Blowers, A. (1980). *The Limits of Power*. Oxford: Pergamon.

—— (1987). 'Transition or Transformation? Environmental Policy under Thatcher', *Public Administration*, 65, 277–94.

Blunden, J., and Curry, N. (eds.) (1988). *A Future for the Countryside?* Oxford: Blackwell.

Boddy, M. (1983). 'Central–Local Relations: Theory and Practice', *Political Geography Quarterly*, 2, 119–38.

—— and Fudge, C. (eds.) (1984). *Local Socialism?* London: Macmillan.

Bollard, A., and Buckle, R. (eds.) (1987). *Economic Liberalisation in New Zealand*. Wellington, NZ: Allen & Unwin.

Boston, J., and Holland, M. (eds.) (1987). *The Fourth Labour Government*. Auckland, NZ: Oxford University Press.

Bottomore, T. B. (1966). *Elites and Society*, Harmondsworth, Middx.: Penguin.

Bouquet, M., and Winter, M. (eds.) (1987). *Who from their Labours Rest? Conflict and Practice in Rural Tourism*. Aldershot, Hants.: Gower.

Bracken, I. (1982). 'Problems and Issues in Structure Plan Review and Alteration', *The Planner*, 68, 12–15.

Bradley, T. (1983). 'Segregation and Marginality in Local Labour

Markets', paper presented at a conference of the Rural Economy and Society Study Group, University of Keele, Sept.

—— and Lowe, P. (eds.) (1984). *Locality and Rurality: Economy and Society in Rural Regions.* Norwich: Geo Books.

Bradshaw, J. (1972). 'The Concept of Social Need', *New Society*, 30 Mar.

Brindley, T., Rydin, Y., and Stoker, G. (1989). *Remaking Planning: The Politics of Urban Change In The Thatcher Years.* London: Unwin Hyman.

Britton, S., and Perry, M. (1987). 'The Burden of Change', *New Zealand Listener*, 27 June.

Broadbent, T. A. (1979). *Options for Planning: A Discussion Document.* London: Centre for Environmental Studies.

Bruton, M. J. (1983). 'Local Plans, Local Planning and Development Plan Schemes in England 1974–1982', *Town Planning Review*, 54, 4–23.

Bryant, C. (1989). 'Rural Land-Use Planning in Canada', in P. J. Cloke (ed.), *Rural Land-Use Planning in Developed Nations.* London: Unwin Hyman.

Buchanan, S. (1982). 'Power and Planning in Rural Areas: Preparation of the Suffolk County Structure Plan', in M. J. Moseley (ed.), *Power, Planning and People in Rural East Anglia.* Norwich: Centre for East Anglian Studies, University of East Anglia.

Buller, H. (1983). 'Amenity, Societies and Landscape Conservation', unpublished Ph. D. thesis, University of London, King's College.

—— and Hoggart, K. (1986). 'Nondecision-Making and Community Power: Residential Development Control in Rural Areas', *Progress in Planning*, 21, 131–203.

—— and Lowe, P. (1982). 'Politics and Class in Rural Preservation', in M. Moseley (ed.), *Power, Planning and People in Rural East Anglia.* Norwich: Centre for East Anglian Studies, University of East Anglia.

Byrne, T. (1983). *Local Government in Britain*, 2nd edn. Harmondsworth, Middx.: Penguin.

Cambridgeshire County Council (1980). *Country Structure Plan: Approved Written Statement*, Cambridge: CCC.

Castells, M. (1977). *The Urban Question: A Marxist Approach.* London: Edward Arnold.

—— (1978). *City, Class and Power.* London: Macmillan.

Catanese, A. J. (1984). *The Politics of Planning and Development.* Beverly Hills, Calif.: Sage.

Cawson, A. (1978). 'Pluralism, Corporatism and the Role of the State', *Government and Opposition*, 13, 178–98.

—— (1982). *Corporatism and Welfare.* London: Heinemann.

—— and Saunders, P. (1983). 'Corporatism, Competitive Politics and

Class Struggle', in R. King (ed.), *Capital and Politics*. London: Routledge & Kegan Paul.

Champion, A. (1987). 'Population Deconcentration in Britain 1971–84', Department of Geography, University of Newcastle upon Tyne, Seminar Paper 49.

Champion, A. G. (1981). 'Population Trends in Rural Britain', *Population Trends*, 26. London: HMSO.

Cherry, G. (1978). 'Rural Planning: Contemporary Problems and Future Policies', 4th Norman Wall Memorial Lecture, Midlands New Town Society.

Clark, D. (1980). *Rural Housing in East Hampshire*. London: National Council for Voluntary Organisations.

—— (1982) 'Social Planning in Rural Areas', *Town and Country Planning*, 51/9, 248–9.

Clark, G. (1980). *Housing and Planning in the Countryside*. London: Research Studies Press/Wiley.

Clark, G. and Dear, M. (1984). *State Apparatus: Structures and Language of Legitimacy*. London: Allen & Unwin.

—— Groenendijk, J., and Thissen, F. (1984). *The Changing Countryside*. Norwich: Geo Books.

Clavel, P., Forester, J., and Goldsmith, W. W. (eds.) (1980). *Urban and Regional Planning in an Age of Austerity*. Elmsford, NY: Pergamon.

Clegg, S., and Dunkerley, D. (1980). *Organisation, Class and Control*. London: Routledge & Kegan Paul.

Cloke, P. J. (1979). *Key Settlements in Rural Areas*. London: Methuen.

—— (1980). 'New Emphases for Applied Rural Geography', *Progress in Human Geography*, 4, 182–217.

—— (1983). *An Introduction to Rural Settlement Planning*. London: Methuen.

—— (ed.) (1985). *Wheels Within Wales*. Lampeter: Centre for Rural Transport, Saint David's University College.

—— (1986a). 'Implementation, Intergovernmental Relations and Rural Studies: A Review', *Journal of Rural Studies*, 2, 245–53.

—— (1986b). 'Observations on Policies for Rural Communities in New Zealand', *New Zealand Geographer*, 42, 2–10.

—— (ed.) (1987). *Rural Planning: Policy into Action?* London: Harper & Row.

—— (ed.) (1988). *Policies and Plans for Rural People: an International Perspective*. London: Unwin Hyman.

—— (1989a). 'Rural Geography and Political Economy', in R. Peet and N. Thrift (eds.), *New Models in Geography*. London: Unwin Hyman.

—— (1989b). 'State Deregulation and New Zealand's Agricultural Sector', *Sociologia Ruralis*, 29, 34–48.

—— and Hanrahan, P. J. (1984). 'Policy and Implementation in Rural Planning', *Geoforum*, 15, 261–9.

—— and Little, J. K. (1984). 'Social Profiles of Ten Case Study Parishes', Saint David's University College, Lampeter, Rural Implementation Project Working Paper 2.

—— and —— (1986*a*). 'Implementation and County Structure Plan Policies for Rural Areas', *Planning Perspectives*, 1, 257–77.

—— and —— (1986*b*). 'The Implementation of Rural Policies: A Survey of County Planning Authorities', *Town Planning Review*, 57, 265–84.

—— and —— (1987*a*). 'Officer–Member Relations in County-Level Policy-Making for Rural Areas: The Case of the Gloucestershire Structure Plan', *Public Administration*, 65/1, 25–43.

—— and —— (1987*b*). 'Rural Policies in the Gloucestershire Structure Plan: 1, A Study of Motives and Mechanisms', *Environment and Planning A*, 19, 959–81.

—— and —— (1987*c*). 'Rural Policies in the Gloucestershire Structure Plan: 2, Implementation and the County–District Relationship', *Environment and Planning A*, 19, 1027–50.

—— and —— (1987*d*). 'The Impact of Decision-Making on Rural Communities: An Example from Gloucestershire', *Applied Geography*, 7, 55–77.

—— and —— (1987*e*). 'Class Distribution and Locality in Rural Areas: An Example from Gloucestershire', *Geoforum*, 18/4, 403–13.

—— and McLaughlin, B. (1989). 'Crossroads or Blind Alley? The Politics of the ALURE Proposals in the UK', *Land Use Policy*, 6, 235–48.

—— and Moseley, M. (1989). 'Rural Geography in Britain', in P. Lowe (ed.), *Franco-British Rural Studies*. London: Bellhaven Press.

—— and Shaw, D. P. (1983). 'Rural Settlement Policies in Structure Plans', *Town Planning Review*, 54, 338–54.

—— and Thrift, N. J. (1987). 'Intra-class Conflict in Rural Areas', *Journal of Rural Studies*, 3 321–34.

Clout, H. (1984). *A Rural Policy for the EEC?* London: Methuen.

—— (1988). 'France', in P. J. Cloke (ed.), *Policies and Plans For Rural People*. London: Unwin Hyman.

Cockburn, C. (1977). *The Local State: Management of Cities and People*. London: Pluto Press.

Cohen, A. (ed.) (1982). *Belonging, Identity and Social Organisation in British Rural Cultures*. Manchester: Manchester University Press.

Collins, S. (1987). *Rogernomics: Is There a Better Way?* Wellington, NZ: Pitman.

Committee on Public Participation in Planning (1969). *People in Planning (The Skeffington Report)*. London: HMSO.

Connell, J. (1978). *The End of Tradition: Country Life in Central Surrey*. London: Routledge & Kegan Paul.

Constandse, A. (1988). 'Rural–Urban Relations on New Land', paper presented at the 7th World Congress for Rural Sociology, Bologna.
Cooke, P. (1983). *Theories of Planning and Spatial Development*. London: Hutchinson.
Cotgrove, S. (1982). *Catastrophe or Cornucopia?* Chichester: Wiley.
Cox, G., Lowe, P., and Winter, M. (1986). 'From State Direction to Self Regulation: The Historical Development of Corporatism in British Agriculture', *Policy and Politics*, 14, 475–90.
Cox, H. (1976). *Cities: The Public Dimension*. Harmondsworth: Penguin.
Coxall, W. N. (1986). *Parties and Pressure Groups*. 2nd edn., London: Longman.
Cumbria County Council and Lake District Special Planning Board (1980). *Cumbria and Lake District Joint Structure Plan: Written Statement*. Carlisle: CCC.
Dahl, R. A. (1961). *Who Governs?* New Haven, Conn.: Yale University Press.
Daniels, S. (1982). 'Landscape, Art and Visual Ideology', paper presented to the Geography and Humanities Study Group, Institute of British Geographers Annual Conference, Southampton.
Darke, R., and Walker, R. (eds.) (1977). *Local Government and the Public*. London: Leonard Hill.
Davidoff, L., L'Espérence, J., and Newby, H. (1976). 'Landscape with Figures', in J. Mitchell and A. Oakley (eds.), *The Rights and Wrongs of Women*. Harmondsworth: Penguin.
Davidson, J., and Wibberley, G. (1977). *Planning and the Rural Environment*. Oxford: Pergamon.
Davies, C. J. (1986). 'The Changing Roles of Officers and Members', *Local Government Studies*, 12, 12–19.
Dearlove, J. (1979). *The Reorganization of British Local Government*. Cambridge: Cambridge University Press.
De Bakker, D., and Piersma, A. (1986). 'Theory and Practice in Rural Settlement Planning: An Example of the Province of Friesland', in Enyedi and Veldman.
De Boer, T. F., and Groenendijk, J. G. (1986). 'Local Government and Small Villages in Peripheral Rural Areas: A Study of Municipal Policy-Making', in Enyedi and Veldman.
Dench, S. (1984). 'Youth Opportunities in Rural Wales: The Impact of a National Training Scheme in a Rural Environment', paper presented to the Rural Study Group, Institute of British Geographers Annual Conference, Durham.
Department of the Environment (1981). *Housing Conditions Survey*. London: HMSO.
Derbyshire County Council (1977). *County Structure Plan: Report of Survey*. Matlock: DCC.

De Smidt, M. (1986). 'Changes of Urban and Rural Areas in the Netherlands', in Enyedi and Veldman.

Devon County Council (1979). *County Structure Plan: Written Statement*. Exeter: DCC.

Dickens, P., Duncan, S., Goodwin, M., and Gray, F. (1985). *Housing: States and Localities*. London: Methuen.

Duncan, S., and Goodwin, M. (1982*a*). 'The Local State and Restructuring Social Relations', *International Journal of Urban and Regional Research*, 6, 157–86.

—— and —— (1982*b*). 'The Local State: Functionalism, Autonomy and Class Relations in Cockburn and Saunders', *Political Geography Quarterly*, 1, 77–96.

—— and —— (1985). 'The Local State and Local Economic Policy: Why the Fuss?', *Policy and Politics*, 13, 227–53.

—— and —— (1988). *The Local State and Uneven Development*. Cambridge: Polity Press.

Duncan, S. S. (1986). 'What is Locality?' Working Paper in Urban and Regional Studies, 51. Brighton: University of Sussex.

Dunleavy, P. (1980). *Urban Political Analysis: The Politics of Collective Consumption*. London: Macmillan.

—— (1984). 'The Limits to Local Government', in Boddy and Fudge.

—— (1986). 'Explaining the Privatisation Boom', *Public Administration*, 61, 13–34.

—— and Husbands, C. (1985). *British Democracy at the Crossroads*. London: Allen & Unwin.

—— and O'Leary, B. (1987). *Theories of the State: The Politics of Liberal Democracy*. London: Macmillan.

Dunn, M., Rawson, M., and Rogers, A. (1981). *Rural Housing: Competition and Choice*. London: Allen & Unwin.

Dunsire, A. (1978). *The Execution Process,* vol. ii: Control in a Bureaucracy. Oxford: Martin Robertson.

Elson, M. (1986). *Green Belts*. London: Heinemann.

Enyedi, G., and Veldman, J. (eds.) (1986). *Rural Development Issues in Industrialised Countries*. Pécs, Hungary: Centre for Regional Studies.

Fagence, M. (1977). *Citizen Participation in Planning*. Urban and Regional Planning Series, vol. xix, Oxford: Pergamon.

Flynn, A. (1986). 'Political Ideology: The Case of the Housing Act 1980', in P. Lowe, T. Bradley, and S. Wright (eds.), *Deprivation and Welfare in Rural Areas*. Norwich: Geo Books.

Flynn, R. (1981). 'Managing Consensus: Strategies and Rationales in Policy-Making', in M. Harloe (ed.), *New Perspectives in Urban Change and Conflict*. London: Heinemann.

Fogarasi, G. (1988). 'New Organisational Forms in Hungarian Rural

Settlements', paper presented at the 7th World Congress for Rural Sociology, Bologna.

Forest of Dean District Council (1982). *A Rural Settlement Strategy for the Forest of Dean*. Cinderford: Forest of Dean District Council.

Forsythe, D. (1984). 'The Social Effects of Primary School Closure', in Bradley and Lowe.

Fothergill, S., and Gudgin, G. (1979). 'Regional Employment Change: A Subregional Explanation', *Progress in Planning*, 12, 155–219.

—— and —— (1982). *Unequal Growth: Urban and Regional Employment*. London: Heinemann.

Friend, J. K., Power, J. M., and Yewlett, C. J. L. (1974). *Public Planning: The Inter-Corporate Dimension*, London: Tavistock.

Gant, R., and Smith, J. (1983). 'Spatial Mobility Problems of the Elderly and Disabled in the Cotswolds', in Clark *et al.*

Giddens, A. (1985). *The Nation State and Violence*. Cambridge: Polity Press.

Gilder, I. (1984). 'State Planning and Local Needs', in Bradley and Lowe.

Gilg, A. (1978). *Countryside Planning*. London: Methuen.

—— (1984). 'Politics and the Countryside: The British example', in Clark *et al.*

—— (1985). *An Introduction to Rural Geography*. London: Edward Arnold.

Gloucestershire County Council (1976). *The Structure Plan for Gloucestershire: The Problems*. Gloucester: GCC.

—— (1977). *The Structure Plan for Gloucestershire: The Options—A Report to Policy and Resources Committee 7th December 1977*. Gloucester: GCC.

—— (1978). *The Structure Plan for Gloucestershire: Public Participation*. Gloucester: GCC.

—— (1979). *The Structure Plan for Gloucestershire: Submitted Written Statement*. Gloucester: GCC.

—— (1980). *Rural Community Services and Facilities: An Explicit Role for the County Council*. Gloucester: GCC.

—— (1981). *A Discussion of the Rural Settlement Policies of the Structure Plan*. Gloucester: GCC.

—— (1983). *Public Transport Plan*. Gloucester: GCC.

Glover, R. (1985). 'Local Decision-Making and Rural Public Transport', in P. J. Cloke (ed.), *Rural Accessibility and Mobility*. Lampeter: Centre for Rural Transport.

Glyn-Jones, A. (1979). *Rural Recovery: Has it Begun?* Exeter: Devon County Council.

Goldsmith, E., and Hildyard, N. (eds.) (1986). *Green Britain or Industrial Wasteland?* Cambridge: Polity Press.

Goldsmith, M. (ed.) (1986). *New Research in Central–Local Relations*. Farnborough, Hants: Gower.

Gordon, I. R. (1984). Review of Barrett and Fudge 1981, *Regional Studies*, 18, 267.

Gould, A., and Keeble, D. (1984). 'New Firms and Rural Industrialisation in East Anglia', *Regional Studies*, 18, 189–202.

Greenwood, R., and Stewart, J. (1986). 'The Institutional and Organizational Capabilities of Local Government', *Public Administration*, 64, 35–50.

Greenwood, R. K., Walsh, C. R., Hinings, C. R., and Ransom, S. (1980). *Patterns of Management in Local Government*. Oxford: Martin Robertson.

Gregory, D., and Urry, J. (eds.) (1985). *Social Relations and Spatial Structures*. London: Macmillan.

Groenendijk, J. (1984). 'A Key to Settlement Growth in Rural Areas: Local Administrators, their Scope and Size of their Territories', in Clark *et al.*

—— (1988). 'The Netherlands', in P. J. Cloke (ed.), *Policies and Plans for Rural People*. London: Unwin Hyman.

Groot, J. P. (1972). *Small Rural Communities in Dutch Society*. Wageningen, Netherlands: Veenman.

Gyford, J. (1984). *Local Politics in Britain*. 2nd edn., London: Croom Helm.

Ham, C., and Hill, M. (1984). *The Policy Process in the Modern Capitalist State*. Brighton: Wheatsheaf Press.

Hambleton, R. (1981). 'Policy Planning Systems and Implementation: Some Implications for Planning Theory', paper presented to the 'Planning Theory in the 1980s' Conference, Department of Town Planning, Oxford Polytechnic.

Hanrahan, P. J., and Cloke, P. J. (1983). 'Towards a Critical Appraisal of Rural Settlement Planning in England and Wales', *Sociologia Ruralis*, 23, 109–29.

Harper, S. (1987). 'The Rural–Urban Interface in England: A Framework of Analysis', *Transactions, IBG*, 12, 284–302.

—— (1988). 'Implications of Various Kinship Networks for the Rural Aged', paper presented at a joint meeting of the Rural Economy and Society Study Group and the British Society of Gerontology, London.

Harvey, D. (1989). *The Urban Experience*. Oxford: Blackwell.

Healey, P. (1979). 'On Implementation: Some Thoughts on the Issues Raised by Planners' Current Interest in Implementation', in C. Minay (ed.), *Implementation: Views from an Ivory Tower*. Department of Town Planning, Oxford Polytechnic.

—— (1982). 'Understanding Land Use Planning', in P. Healey,

G. McDougall, and M. Thomas (eds.), *Planning Theory: Prospects for the 1980s*. Oxford: Pergamon.

Healey, P. (1984). 'Emerging Directions for Research on Local Land Use Planning', paper presented to the Research in Local Land Use Planning Seminar, Oxford Polytechnic, May–June.

—— (1986). 'Emerging Directions for Research on Local Land Use Planning', *Environment and Planning B*, 13, 103–20.

—— McDougall, G., and Thomas, M. (eds.), (1982). *Planning Theory: Prospects for the 1980's*. Oxford: Pergamon Press.

McNamara, P., Elson, M., and Doak, A. (1988). *Land Use Planning And The Mediation of Urban Change*. Cambridge: Cambridge University Press.

Heller, T. (1979). 'Rural Health and Health Services', in Shaw.

Henney, A. (1984). *Inside Local Government: A Case for Radical Reform*, London: Sinclaire Brown.

Herington, J. (1984). *The Outer City*. London: Harper & Row.

—— and Evans, D. (1980). 'The Social Characteristics of Household Movement in "Key" and "Non-Key" Settlements', University of Loughborough, Department of Geography, Working Paper No. 4, Loughborough.

Hill, M. J. *et al.* (1979). 'Implementation and the Central–Local Relationship', in Social Science Research Council, *Central–Local Government Relationships*, Report of an SSRC Panel to the Research Initiatives Board. London: SSRC.

Hirsch, F. (1977). *The Social Limits to Growth*. London: Routledge & Kegan Paul.

Hirsch, J. (1981). 'The Apparatus of the State, and Reproduction of Capital, and Urban Conflicts', in M. Dear and A. Scott (eds.), *Urbanization and Urban Planning in Capitalist Society*. London: Methuen.

Hodge, G. (1985). 'The Roots of Canadian Planning', *Journal of the American Planning Association*, 51, 8–22.

—— (1988). 'Canada', in P. J. Cloke, (ed.), *Policies and Plans for Rural People*, London: Unwin Hyman.

Hoggart, K. (1981). 'Local Decision-Making Autonomy: A Review of Conceptual and Methodological Issues', Department of Geography, University of London, King's College, Occasional Paper No. 13.

—— (1984). 'Community Power and the Local State', in D. Herbert and R. Johnston (eds.), *Geography and the Urban Environment*, 6, 145–211. Chichester: Wiley.

—— (1988). 'Not a Definition of Rural', *Area*, 20/1, 35–40.

—— and Buller, H. (1987). *Rural Development: A Geographical Perspective*. London: Croom Helm.

Holland, S. (1975). *The Socialist Challenge*. London: Quarto Books.

Housebuilders' Federation (1988). *Affordable Homes in the Countryside: A New Approach by Private Housebuilders*. London: Housebuilders' Federation.

Hunter, F. (1953). *Community Power Structure*. Chapel Hill, NC: University of North Carolina Press.

Huron County Planning Board (1978). *Official Plan: County of Huron Planning Area*, Goderich, Ontario: HCPB.

—— (1984). *Information*. Goderich, Ontario: Department of Planning and Development, County of Huron.

Jenkins, W. I. (1978). 'Capitalism and Democracy: The Best Political Shell?', in Littlejohn G., Smart, B., Wakeford, J., and Yuval-Davies, N. (eds.), *Power and the State*. London: Croom Helm.

—— (1982). *The Capitalist State*. Oxford: Martin Robertson.

Johnson, J., and Price, C. (1987). 'Afforestation, Employment and Depopulation in the Snowdonia National Park', *Journal of Rural Studies*, 3/3, 195–205.

Johnston, R. J. (1982). *Geography and the State: An Essay in Political Geography*. London: Macmillan.

Jones, G., and Stewart, J. (1983). *The Case for Local Government*. London: Allen & Unwin.

Juhasz, J. (1988). 'Local Society: Satisfaction of the Inhabitants', paper presented at the 7th World Congress for Rural Sociology, Bologna.

Karpati, Z. (1986). 'Peripheral Settlement in Hungary', in Enyedi and Veldman.

Keeble, D. E. (1980). 'Industrial Decline, Regional Policy and the Urban–Rural Manufacturing Shift in the United Kingdom', *Environment and Planning A*, 12, 945–62.

Knowles, R. (ed.) (1985). *Implications of the 1985 Transport Bill*. Salford: Transport Geography Study Group.

Knox, P., and Cullen, J. (1981). 'Town Planning and the Internal Survival Mechanisms of Urbanised Capitalism', *Area*, 13, 183–8.

Lackō, L. (1986). 'The Place of Village Development in the Settlement Development Policy of Hungary', in Enyedi and Veldman.

Lapping, M. B. (1985). 'Perspectives in Canadian Planning', *Journal of the American Planning Association*, 51, 6–7.

—— and Fuller, A. M. (1985). 'Rural Develoment Policy in Canada: An Interpretation', *Community Development Journal*, 20, 114–19.

Larkin, A. (1978). 'Housing and the Poor', in Walker.

Lawless, P., and Brown, F. (1986). *Urban Growth And Change In Britain*. London: Harper & Row.

Leach, S. (1980). 'Organisational Interests and Inter-Organisational Behaviour in Town Planning', *Town Planning Review*, 51, 286–99.

—— and Moore, M. (1979). 'County/District Relations in Shire and

Metropolitan Counties in the Field of Town and Country Planning: A Comparison', *Policy and Politics*, 7, 165–79.

Lewis, J., and Flynn, R. (1978). *The Implementation of Urban and Regional Planning Policies*. Final report of a feasibility study for the Department of the Environment. London: DoE.

—— and —— (1979). 'The Implementation of Urban and Regional Planning Policies', *Policy and Politics*, 7, 123–42.

Little, J. (1984). 'Social Change in Rural Areas: A Planning Perspective', Unpublished Ph.D. thesis, University of Reading, Department of Geography.

—— (1986). 'Social Class and Planning Policy: A Study of Two Wiltshire Villages', in P. Lowe, T. Bradley, and S. Wright (eds.), *Deprivation and Welfare in Rural Areas*, Norwich: Geo Books.

—— (1987). 'Gentrification and the Influence of Local Level Planning', in Cloke 1987.

—— (1988). 'Women's Non-Agricultural Employment: Constraints and Opportunities within a Rural Development Area', paper presented at the 7th World Congress for Rural Sociology, Bologna.

Littlejohn, J. (1963). *Westrigg: The Sociology of a Cheviot Parish*. London: Routledge & Kegan Paul.

Lojkine J. (1977). 'Big Firm's Strategies, Urban Policy and Urban Social Movements', in M. Harloe (ed.), *Captive Cities*. Chichester: Wiley.

Lowe, P. (1977). 'Amenity and Equity: A Review of Local Environmental Pressure Groups in Britain', *Environment and Planning A*, 9, 39–58.

—— Cox, G., MacEwen, M., O'Riordan, T., and Winter, M. (1986). *Countryside Conflicts: The Politics of Farming, Forestry and Conservation*. London: Gower/Temple-Smith.

—— and Goyder, J. (1983). *Environmental Groups in British Politics*. London: Allen & Unwin.

Lukes, S. (1984). 'The Future of British Socialism', in B. Pimlott (ed.), *Fabian Essays in Socialist Thought*. London: Hutchinson.

McKee, W. A. (1984). 'Entrepreneurial Planning and Resource Availability', *Planner*, 70, 7–10.

McKinlay, P. (1987). *Corporatisation: The Solution for State Owned Enterprise?* Institute of Policy Studies, Victoria University of Wellington, NZ.

McLaughlin, B. (1983). 'The Rural Deprivation Debate: Retrospect and Prospect', paper presented at the Rural Economy and Society Study Group Conference, Keele University.

—— (1986). 'The Rhetoric and Reality of Rural Deprivation', *Journal of Rural Studies*, 2, 291–307.

—— (1987). 'Rural Policy into the 1990s: Self-Help or Self-Deception', *Journal of Rural Studies*, 3, 361–4.

McLennan, G. (1984). 'The Contours of British Politics: Representative Democracy and Social Class', in McLennan, *et al.*

—— Held, D., and Hall, S. (1984). *State and Society in Contemporary Britain: A Critical Introduction.* Cambridge: Polity Press.

MacPherson, C. B. (1977). *The Life and Times of Liberal Democracy.* Oxford: Oxford University Press.

Mandel, E. (1975). *Late Capitalism.* Trans. and rev. edn., London: New Left Books.

Mann, M. (1986). *The Sources of Social Power, vol. i: A History of Power from the Beginning to AD 1760.* Cambridge: Cambridge University Press.

Marsden, T., Munton, R., Whatmore, S., and Little, J. (1986). Towards a Political Economy of British Agriculture', *International Journal of Urban and Regional Research*, 10, 498–521.

Marsh, D. (ed.) (1983). *Pressure Politics: Interest Groups in Britain.* London: Junction Books.

Marshall, G., Newby, H., Rose, D., and Vogler, C. (1988). *Social Class in Modern Britain.* London: Hutchinson.

Massey, D. (1984). *Spatial Divisions of Labour: Social Structures and the Geography of Production.* London: Macmillan.

Mawson, J., and Miller, D. (1983). *Agencies in Regional and Local Government.* Centre for Urban and Regional Studies, University of Birmingham.

Miliband, R. (1969). *The State in Capitalist Society.* London: Weidenfeld & Nicolson.

—— (1973a). 'Poulantzas and the Capitalist State', *New Left Review*, 82, 83–92.

—— (1973b). *The State in Capitalist Society.* London: Quartet Books.

—— (1977). *Marxism and Politics.* Oxford: Oxford University Press.

Miller, C., and Miller, D. (1982). 'Local Authorities and the Local Economy', *Town and Country Planning*, 51, 153–5.

Moran, W. (1989). 'Sectoral and Statutory Planning for New Zealand', in P. J. Cloke (ed.), *Rural Land Use Planning in Developed Nations.* London: Unwin Hyman.

Mormont, M., (1985). 'The Emergence of Rural Struggles and their Ideological Effects', *International Journal of Urban and Regional Research*, 7/4, 559–75.

Moseley, M. J. (ed.) (1978). *Social Issues in Rural Norfolk.* Norwich: University of East Anglia.

—— (1979). *Accessibility: The Rural Challenge.* London: Methuen.

—— (1980a). 'Is Rural Deprivation Really Rural?', *Planner*, 66, 97.

—— (1980b). 'Rural Development and its Relevance to the Inner City Debate', Inner Cities Working Paper 9. London: Social Science Research Council.

Moseley, M. J. (1985). *The Waveney Project: The Role of the Catalyst in Rural Community Development*. Norwich: University of East Anglia.
—— and Packman, J. (1983). *Mobile Services in Rural Areas*. Norwich: University of East Anglia.

Murgatroyd, L., Savage, M., Shapiro, D., Urry, J., Walby, S., and Warde, A. (1985). *Localities, Class and Gender*. London: Pion.

Murie, A. (1980). 'The Housing Service', *Town Planning Review*, 51, 309–15.

Napier, T. L., and Maurer, R. C. (1978). 'Correlates of Commitment to Community Development Efforts', Department of Agricultural Economics and Rural Sociology, Ohio State University, Report ESS 555, Columbus, OH.

National Agricultural Centre Rural Trust (1988). *Village Homes for Village People*. London: NACRT.

Newby, H. (1977). *The Deferential Worker*. London: Allen Lane.
—— (1979). *Green and Pleasant Land? Social Change in Rural England*. Harmondsworth: Penguin.
—— (1980). 'Rural Sociology', *Current Sociology*, 28, 1.
—— (1981). 'Urbanism and the Rural Class Structure', in M. Harloe (ed.), *New Perspectives in Urban Change and Conflict*. London: Heinemann.
—— (1988). *The Countryside in Question*. London: Hutchinson.
—— Bell, C., Rose, D., and Saunders, P. (1978). *Property, Paternalism and Power*. London: Hutchinson.

Niskanen, W. (1973). *Bureaucracy: Servant or Master?* London: Institute for Economic Affairs.

Norfolk County Council (1980). *Council Structure Plan: Approved Written Statement*. Norwich: NCC.

Norwood, H. C. (1981). 'Regional Planning in New Zealand: The Political Dimension', *New Zealand Geographer*, 37, 79–82.

O'Connor, J. (1973). *The Fiscal Crisis of the State*. New York: St. Martin's Press.

Office of Population Censuses and Surveys (1981). 'County Changes in Population 1971–81', *Population Trends*, 29, 8–12.

Owen, D., Coombes, M., and Gillespie, A. (1986). 'The Urban–Rural Shift and Employment Change in Britain 1917–81', in M. Danson (ed.), *Restructuring the Regions?* Norwich: Geo Books.

Pacione, M. (1984). *Rural Geography*, London: Harper & Row.

Packman, J., and Wallace, D. (1982). 'Rural Services in Norfolk and Suffolk: The Management of Change', in M. J. Moseley (ed.), *Power, Planning and People in Rural East Anglia*. Norwich: Centre for East Anglian Studies.

Pahl, R. E. (1965). 'Urbs in Rure: The Metropolitan Fringe in Hertfordshire', London School of Economics Geographical Papers No. 2.

—— (1970). *Whose City?* 1st edn., London: Longman.

—— (1975). *Whose City?* 2nd edn., Harmondsworth: Penguin.

—— (1977). 'Collective Consumption and the State in Capitalist and State Socialist Societies', in Scase, R. (ed.) *Industrial Society: Class Cleavage and Control*. London: Tavistock.

—— (1982). 'Urban Managerialism Reconsidered', in C. Paris (ed.), *Critical Readings in Planning Theory*. Oxford: Pergamon. (Originally published as ch. 13 of *Whose City?*)

Parsons, D. J. (1977). 'Rural Gentrification and the Influence of Rural Settlement Planning Policies', University of Sussex Research Paper in Geography, Brighton.

Penfold, S. (1974). 'Housing Problems of Local People in Rural Pressure Areas', Department of Town and Regional Planning, University of Sheffield.

Perks, H. (1977). 'The Rural Dimension', in R. Darke and R. Walker, (eds.), *Local Government and the Public*, London. Leonard Hill.

Phillips, D., and Williams, A. (1982). *Rural Housing and the Public Sector*. Aldershot: Gower.

—— and —— (1983). 'Public Sector Housing in Rural Areas in England', in Clark *et al.*

—— and —— (1984). *Rural Britain: A Social Geography*. Oxford: Blackwell.

Picou, J. S., Weils, R. H., and Nyberg, K. L. (1978). 'Paradigms, Theories and Methods in Contemporary Rural Sociology', *Rural Sociology*, 43, 559–83.

Polgàr, E. (1988). 'The Influences of Modernization of the Agrarian Production in the Local Society', paper presented at the 7th World Congress for Rural Sociology, Bologna.

Polsby, N. W. (1963). *Community Power and Political Theory*. New Haven, Conn.: Yale University Press.

Porritt, J. (1984). *Seeing Green: The Politics of Ecology Explained*. Oxford: Blackwell.

Poulantzas, N. (1973*a*). 'The Problems of the Capitalist State', in J. Urry and J. Wakeford (eds.), *Power in Britain*. London: Heinemann.

—— (1973*b*). *Political Power and Social Classes*. London: New Left Books.

—— (1975). *Classes in Contemporary Capitalism*. London: New Left Books.

—— (1978). *State, Power, Socialism*. London: New Left Books.

Pressman, J., and Wildavsky, A. (1973). *Implementation*. Berkeley, Calif.: University of California Press.

Proudfoot, B. (1984. 'Rural Geography in Britain: Some Aspects of Rural Problems and Policies', in Clark *et al.*

Punter, J. V. (1982). 'English Landscape Tastes Revisited', paper presented to the Geography and Humanities Study Group, Conference of the Institute of British Geographers, Southampton.

Pye-Smith, C., and Rose, C. (1984). *Crisis and Conservation: Conflict in the British Countryside*, Harmondsworth: Penguin.

Rankin, D. G. (1979). 'Auckland Regional Authority 1963–1978', *New Zealand Geographer*, 35, 41–3.

Rawson, M., and Rogers, A. (1976). 'Rural Housing and Structure Plans', Countryside Planning Unit, Wye College, University of London.

Reade, E. (1987). *British Town and Country Planning*. Bletchley: Open University Press.

Redclift, M. (1985). 'Capitalism, Petty Commodity Production and the Farm Enterprise', paper presented at a Conference of the Rural Economy and Society Study Group, Oxford.

Rees, G. (1984). 'Rural Regions in National and International Economies', in Bradley and Lowe.

—— and Lambert, J. (1985). *Cities In Crisis: The Political Economy of Urban Development in Post-War Britain*. London: Edward Arnold.

Répássy, H. (1988). 'Roots of Female Employment in Agriculture: Feminisation?', paper presented at the 7th World Congress of Rural Sociology, Bologna.

Rex, J., and Moore, R. (1967). *Race, Community and Conflict*. Oxford: Oxford University Press.

Rhodes, G. (1986). 'Protecting Local Discretion: The Experience of Environmental Health and Trading Standards', in Goldsmith.

Rhodes, R. (1981). *Control and Power in Central–Local Government Relations*. London: Gower.

—— (1985). Inter-governmental Relations in the Post-war Period', *Local Government Studies*, 11, 35–57.

—— (1986). *The National World of Local Government*. London: Allen & Unwin.

—— (1988). *Beyond Westminster and Whitehall: The Sub-Central Government of Britain*. London: Allen & Unwin.

Richardson, J. J., and Jordan, A. G. (1979). *Governing Under Pressure*. Oxford: Martin Robertson.

Richmond, P. (1985). 'The State and Rural Housing Provision: Research at the Local Level', paper presented to the Rural Geography Study Group, Institute of British Geographers Annual Conference, Leeds.

Ridley, N. (1987). Address to the Royal Town Planning Institute Summer School, 1986, *The Planner*, 73/2, 39–41.

Robins, D. L. J. (1983). 'Rural Planning', in M. Pacione (ed.), *Progress in Rural Geography*. London: Croom Helm.

Rocke, T. (1985). 'Implementation of Rural Housing Policy', unpublished

Ph.D. thesis, Department of Geography, Saint David's University College, Lampeter.

Rogers, A. W. (1987). 'Voluntarism, Self-Help and Rural Community Development: Some Current Approaches', *Journal of Rural Studies*, 3, 353–60.

Rural Development Commission (1987). *Opportunity through Diversity*. Annual Report of the Rural Development Commission. London: HMSO.

Sandbach, F. (1980). *Environment, Ideology and Policy*. Oxford: Blackwell.

Saunders, P. (1979). *Urban Politics: A Sociological Interpretation*. London: Hutchinson.

—— (1981a). 'Community Power, Urban Managerialism and the Local State', in M. Harloe (ed.), *New Perspectives in Urban Change and Conflict*. London: Heinemann.

—— (1981a). *Social Theory and the Urban Question*. London: Hutchinson.

—— (1981c). 'Notes on the Specificity of the Local State', in M. Boddy and C. Fudge (eds.), *The Local State: Theory and Practice*, School for Advanced Urban Studies, University of Bristol.

—— (1982). 'Why Study Central–Local Relations?', *Local Government Studies*, 8, 55–6.

—— (1984a). *Urban Politics: A Sociological Interpretation*. 2nd edn., London: Hutchinson.

—— (1984b). 'Rethinking Local Politics', in Boddy and Fudge.

—— (1985). 'The Forgotten Dimension of Central–Local Relations: Theorising the "Regional State" ', *Government and Policy*, 3, 149–62.

—— (1986). 'Reflections on the Dual Politics Thesis: The Argument, its Origins and its Critics', in M. Goldsmith and S. Villadsen (eds.), *Urban Political Theory and the Management of Fiscal Stress*. Aldershot: Gower.

Schmitter, P., and Lehmbruch, G. (eds.) (1979). *Trends Towards Corporatist Intermediation*. London: Sage.

Shaw, J. M. (ed.) (1979). *Rural Deprivation and Planning*. Norwich: Geo Books.

Shropshire County Council (1983). *County Structure Plan: Approved Written Statement*. Shrewsbury: SCC.

Shucksmith, M. (1981). *No Homes for Locals?* London: Gower.

Smart, G. (1987). 'Co-ordination of Rural Policy-Making and Implementation', in Cloke 1987.

—— and Wright, S. (1983). *Decision Making for Rural Areas*. Bartlett School of Architecture and Planning, University College London.

282 *Bibliography*

Smit, B., Joseph, A., Alexander, S., and McIlravey, G. (1984). *Non-Farm Residential Development, Service Provision, Taxes and Policy: The Case of Puslinch Township*. Department of Geography, University of Guelph, Ontario, Occasional Paper No. 4.

Smith, A. G., Williams, G., and Houlder, M. (1985). 'Community Influence on Local Planning Policy', *Progress in Planning*, 25/1, 1–81.

Smith, T. (1979). *The Politics of the Corporate Economy*. Oxford: Martin Robertson.

Smith, T. B. (1973). 'The Policy Implementation Process', *Policy Sciences*, 4, 197–209.

SOLACE (1983). *Local Government: The Facts*. London: Society of Local Authority Chief Executives.

—— (1986). *Local Government: The Future*. Northampton: Society of Local Authority Chief Executives.

Standing Council for Rural Community Councils (1984). *New Directions for Rural Community Councils*. London: SCRCC.

Stebbing, S. (1984). 'Women's Roles and Rural Society', in Bradley and Lowe.

Stoker, G. (1988). *The Politics of Local Government*. London: Macmillan.

Strathern, M. (1981). *Kinship at the Core*. Cambridge: Cambridge University Press.

—— (1982). 'The Village as an Idea: Constructs of Villageness in Elmdon, Essex', in A. Cohen (ed.), *Belonging*. Manchester: Manchester University Press.

—— (1984). 'The Social Meaning of Localism', in Bradley and Lowe.

Taylor, P. J. (1985). *Political Geography: World Economy, Nation-State and Locality*. London: Longman.

Tewkesbury Borough Council (1984). *Rural Settlement Policy Statement*. Tewkesbury: TBC.

Thorburn, H. (1980). 'Ethnic Pluralism in Canada', in S. Erlich and G. Wootton (eds.), *Three Faces of Pluralism*. Farnborough: Gower.

Thrift, N. J. (1987a). 'Manufacturing Rural Geography?', *Journal of Rural Studies*, 3/1, 77–81.

—— (1987b). 'Introduction: The Geography of Twentieth Century Class Formation', in N. J. Thrift and P. Williams (eds.), *Class and Space*. London: Routledge & Kegan Paul.

—— and Willams, P. (1987). 'The Geography of Class Formation', in N. J. Thrift and P. Williams (eds.), *Class and Space*. London: Routledge and Kegal Paul.

Townsend, A. (1986). 'Spatial Aspects of the Growth of Part-Time Employment in Britain', *Regional Studies*, 20, 313–30.

Treasury (1978). *The Government's Expenditure Plans, 1978–9 to 1981–2*. Cmnd. 7049, London: HMSO.

Tricker, M. (1983). 'Rural Education Services: The Social Effects of Reorganisation', in Clark *et al.*

Urry, J. (1981*a*). *The Anatomy of Capitalist Society*. London: Macmillan.

—— (1981*b*). 'Localities, Regions and Social Class', *International Journal of Urban and Regional Research*, 5, 455–73.

—— (1984). 'Capitalist Restructuring, Recomposition and the Regions', in Bradley and Lowe.

Van Ginkel, H. (1986). 'Population Growth and Settlement Pattern in the Green Heart of the Randstad', in Enyedi and Veldman.

Van Meter, D. S., and Van Horn, C. E. (1975). 'The Policy Implementation Process: A Conceptual Framework', *Administration and Society*, 6, 445–88.

Vincent, A. (1987). *Theories of the State*. Oxford: Blackwell.

Walford, N. (1983). 'Population Structures in Rural Areas', paper presented to the Population Geography Study Group, Institute of British Geographers Annual Conference, Edinburgh.

Walker, A. (ed.) (1978). *Rural Poverty*. London: Child Poverty Action Group.

Warmsley, M. (1982). 'Non-participation in Planning: The Case of Mundford in Norfolk', in M. J. Moseley (ed.), *Power, Planning and People in Rural East Anglia*. Norwich: University of East Anglia.

Weiner, M. J. (1981). *English Culture and the Decline of the Industrial Spirit*. Cambridge: Cambridge University Press.

Wenger, C. (1988). 'Support Network Variation in Rural Communities', paper presented at a joint meeting of the Rural Economy and Society Study Group and the British Society of Gerontology, London.

West Coast United Council (1982). *West Coast Regional Planning Scheme: Approved Section 1*. Greymouth, NZ: WCUC.

Whatmore, S. (1987). 'Landownership Relations and the Development of Modern British Agriculture', in G. Cox, P. Lowe, and M. Winter (eds.), *Agriculture, People and Policies*. London: Allen & Unwin.

Widdecombe, D. (1986). *The Conduct of Local Authority Business*. Report of the Committee of Inquiry into the Conduct of Local Authority Business, Cmnd 9797, London: HMSO.

Williams, R. (1973). *The Country and the City*. London: Chatto & Windus.

Williams, W. M. (1963). *A West Country Village: Ashworthy*. London: Routledge & Kegal Paul.

Willis, R. (1988). 'New Zealand', in P. J. Cloke (ed.), *Policies and Plans for Rural People*. London: Unwin Hyman.

Winkler, J. (1976). 'Corporatism', *European Journal of Sociology*, 17, 100–36.

Witt, S. J. G. and Fleming, S. C. (1984). *Planning Councillors In An*

Area Of Growth: Little Power But All The Blame? Department of Geography, University of Reading, Geographical Paper No. 85.

Wolfe, A. (1977). *The Limits of Legitimacy: Political Contradictions of Contemporary Capitalism.* New York: Free Press.

Wright, E. O. (1985). *Classes.* London: Verso.

Wright, S. (1982). 'Parish to Whitehall: Administrative Structures and Perceptions of Community in Rural Areas', Gloucestershire Papers in Local and Rural Planning No. 16. Gloucester: Gloucester College of Art and Technology.

Young, D. (1987). 'The Heartland', *New Zealand Listener*, 13 June.

Young, K. (1986). 'What is Local Government For?' in M. Goldsmith (ed.), *Essays on the Future of Local Government.* Wakefield: West Yorkshire County Council.

Index